WALKING ON ARRAN

by Paddy Dillon

2 POLICE SQUARE, MILNTHORPE, CUMBRIA LA7 7PY
www.cicerone.co.uk

Third edition 2016
ISBN: 978185284 8255

First edition 2004
ISBN: 978185284 2697
Second edition 2011
ISBN: 1852844787
ISBN: 978185284 4783

Printed in China on behalf of Latitude Press Ltd
A catalogue record for this book is available from the British Library.

Updates to this Guide

While every effort is made by our authors to ensure the accuracy of guidebooks as they go to print, changes can occur during the lifetime of an edition. Any updates that we know of for this guide will be on the Cicerone website (www.cicerone.co.uk/825/updates), so please check before planning your trip. We also advise that you check information about such things as transport, accommodation and shops locally. Even rights of way can be altered over time. We are always grateful for information about any discrepancies between a guidebook and the facts on the ground, sent by email to info@cicerone.co.uk or by post to Cicerone, 2 Police Square, Milnthorpe LA7 7PY, United Kingdom.

Front cover: Looking from Beinn a' Chliabhain towards A'Chir, Caisteal Abhail and Cir Mhòr

CONTENTS

Map key 6
Overview map 7

INTRODUCTION 9
Getting to Arran 9
Getting around the island 10
Finding your bearings 13
A geology classroom 14
A turbulent history 16
Land ownership and access 19
Island animals 23
Island plants 24
Accommodation 25
Food and drink 27
Maps 28
The walks 29
Tourist information 30
Emergency services 30

THE WALKS 31
Walk 1 Goatfell and Brodick 32
Walk 2 Brodick Castle and Country Park 37
Walk 3 Brodick and the Clauchland Hills 42
Walk 4 Sithein and Glen Cloy 46
Walk 5 Lamlash and the Clauchland Hills 50
Walk 6 Sithein and The Ross 55
Walk 7 Lamlash to Brodick 59
Walk 8 Holy Isle from Lamlash 62
Walk 9 Tighvein and Monamore Glen 68
Walk 10 Glenashdale and Urie Loch 72
Walk 11 Glenashdale Falls and Giants' Graves 78
Walk 12 Lamlash and Kingscross 82
Walk 13 Eas Mòr and Loch Garbad 87
Walk 14 Lagg to Kildonan coastal walk 89
Walk 15 Kilmory forest circuit 94
Walk 16 Sliddery and Cnocan Donn 99
Walk 17 Tighvein and Glenscorrodale 104
Walk 18 The Ross and Cnoc a' Chapuill 109

Walk 19 Shiskine and Clauchan Glen 113
Walk 20 Balmichael and Ard Bheinn. 117
Walk 21 The String and Beinn Bhreac 122
Walk 22 Blackwaterfoot and King's Cave. 126
Walk 23 Machrie Moor Stone Circles 131
Walk 24 Dougarie and Beinn Nuis 134
Walk 25 Dougarie and Sail Chalmadale 141
Walk 26 Circuit of Glen Iorsa 145
Walk 27 Imachar and Mullach Buidhe 153
Walk 28 Pirnmill and Mullach Buidhe. 158
Walk 29 Coire-Fhionn Lochan 162
Walk 30 Catacol and Meall nan Damh 166
Walk 31 Catacol and Beinn Bhreac. 169
Walk 32 Catacol and Beinn Tarsuinn. 175
Walk 33 Lochranza and Meall Mòr 180
Walk 34 Gleann Easan Biorach. 185
Walk 35 Lochranza and the Cock of Arran 190
Walk 36 Lochranza and Sail an Im 194
Walk 37 Sannox and Fionn Bhealach 199
Walk 38 North Glen Sannox Horseshoe 204
Walk 39 Glen Sannox Horseshoe 210
Walk 40 Glen Sannox to Glen Rosa 218
Walk 41 Sannox, Goatfell and Corrie 223
Walk 42 Glen Rosa and Beinn Tarsuinn. 230
Walk 43 Western Glen Rosa 236
Walk 44 Eastern Glen Rosa 245

Appendix A Route summary table 250
Appendix B Arran Coastal Way 254
Appendix C Useful contacts. 259
Appendix D Gaelic/English glossary 263

Route symbols on OS map extracts
(for OS legend see printed OS maps)

route
alternative route
start/finish point
start point
finish point
alternative finish point
route direction

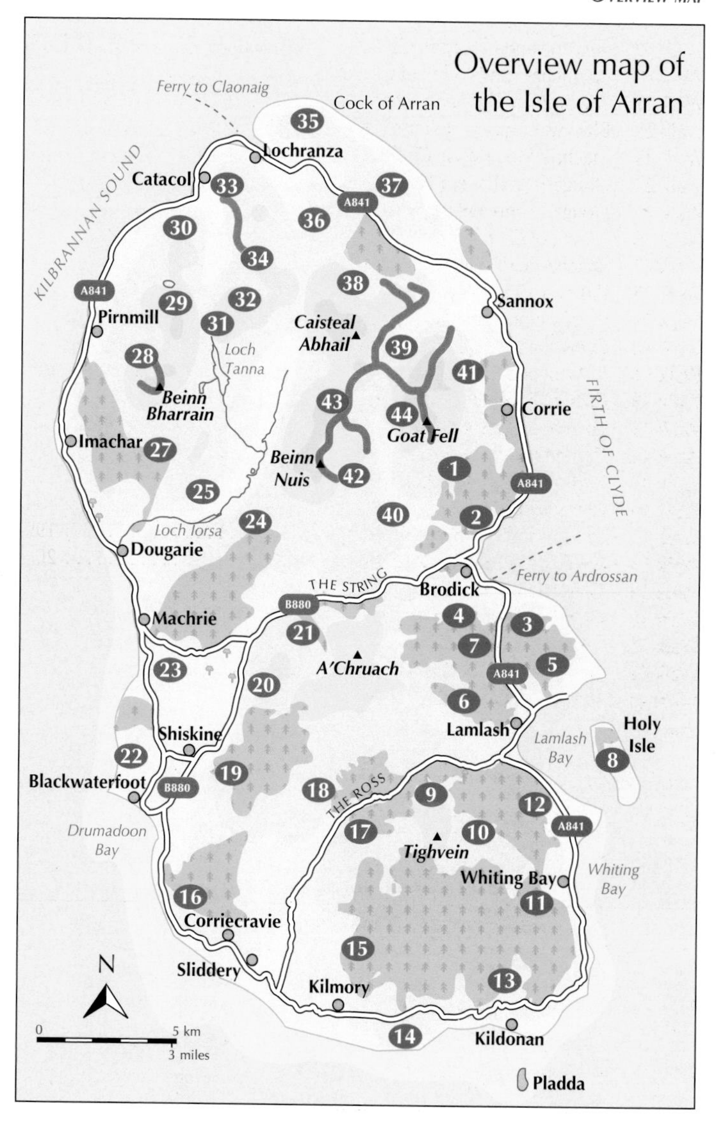

Overview map of the Isle of Arran
Ferry to Claonaig
Cock of Arran
Lochranza
Catacol
KILBRANNAN SOUND
A841
Pirnmill
Loch Tanna
Caisteal Abhail
Beinn Bharrain
Sannox
Corrie
FIRTH OF CLYDE
Goat Fell
Imachar
Beinn Nuis
Loch Iorsa
Dougarie
THE STRING
Brodick
Ferry to Ardrossan
B880
Machrie
A'Chruach
Shiskine
Lamlash
Lamlash Bay
Holy Isle
Blackwaterfoot
THE ROSS
Drumadoon Bay
Tighvein
Whiting Bay
Corriecravie
Sliddery
Kilmory
Kildonan
Pladda
N
0
5 km
3 miles

Craggy Cir Mhòr and Goatfell as seen from the 'Dress Circle' on Caisteal Abhail (Walk 39)

INTRODUCTION

The Isle of Arran rises proudly from the Firth of Clyde between Ayrshire and Kintyre. Its mountainous form dominates the open waters of the Clyde and its jagged peaks are a tempting challenge for walkers. We know that people first came to the island some 5500 years ago, although some periods of its history are only dimly recorded. Over the past hundred years or so, tourism has become an important industry here. Arran has much to offer the visitor and is often described as 'Scotland in miniature'. Roads are few, but opportunities to explore the island on foot are many and varied.

This guidebook offers a selection of 44 walks, along with a brief overview of the Arran Coastal Way. As many of the walks are inter-linked, there are opportunities to create longer treks traversing the length and breadth of the island.

GETTING TO ARRAN

Getting to Arran is easier than you might think. The island is close to Glasgow, which is a very important transport hub with busy road and rail services and nearby international airports. Onward connections from Glasgow to Arran are swift and frequent. See Appendix B for a list of useful transport contacts.

By air

Two airports are handy for Arran. Glasgow International Airport, www.glasgowairport.com, is served from around a hundred locations by over a dozen airlines, including budget and national carriers. Several British and European airports, as well as a few in the United States and Canada, serve Glasgow. Prestwick International Airport, www.glasgowprestwick.com, handles flights from around a dozen southern European airports, almost exclusively operated by Ryanair, www.ryanair.com.

By rail

Long-distance Virgin Trains start from London Euston, travelling via Birmingham to reach Glasgow Central; or from Kings Cross, travelling via York to reach Glasgow Central, www.virgintrains.co.uk. Transpennine Express trains, www.tpexpress.co.uk, operate from Manchester Airport to Glasgow Central. Caledonian Sleeper services allow passengers to travel overnight from London Euston to Glasgow Central, www.sleeper.scot. Once at Glasgow Central, simply change to ScotRail, www.scotrail.co.uk, to reach Ardrossan Harbour for the ferry to Arran. 'Rail & Sail' tickets are available through ScotRail, covering both the train and ferry journey.

By bus

National Express coaches, www.nationalexpress.com, run from many points around Britain, and combine with Scottish Citylink coaches, www.citylink.co.uk, to converge on Buchanan Street bus station in Glasgow. Stagecoach West Scotland X36 bus operates from Buchanan Street Bus Station to Ardrossan, and the same company also operates bus services around Arran, www.stagecoachbus.com.

By car

Driving from Glasgow, the following roads could be used to reach Ardrossan: the coastal A78 via Largs; the A737 via Beith; or the A736 via Irvine. Drivers from Northern Ireland who arrive at Stranraer simply follow the A77 and A78 main coastal road. Drivers from England should leave the M6 and follow the A75 and A76 for a scenic approach to Ardrossan through the Southern Uplands. Drivers coming from Western Scotland can avoid travelling through Glasgow by following the A83 road onto Kintyre, then use the summer ferry service from Claonaig to Lochranza.

By ferry

Caledonian MacBrayne, tel 0800 0665000, www.calmac.co.uk, operate between five and nine sailings per day between Ardrossan Harbour and Brodick throughout the summer, with a reduced service in winter. The typical crossing time is 55 minutes.

Keep an eye out for deer wherever you drive on Arran

There is also a summer ferry service between Claonaig on the Kintyre peninsula and Lochranza on Arran, with nine crossings each way per day, taking 30 minutes. Both ferries carry vehicles.

Following the introduction of the Road Equivalent Tariff (RET) for ferries throughout Scotland during 2014 and 2015, fares to Arran have been drastically reduced.

GETTING AROUND THE ISLAND

All public transport services on the Arran, including bus services and ferries, with some mainland connections, are contained in a single timetable booklet specially produced

Arran's excellent bus service can get you to the start of most walks

for use on the island. This can be obtained on the ferry, at the ferry terminals, or from the Brodick tourist information centre. Take note of the variations in services between schooldays and school holidays, as well as Saturdays and Sundays.

It is worth mentioning that this entire book was researched and updated exclusively using local bus services. There is no need to take a vehicle onto Arran, as almost every place that could be reached by car is also served by buses. Walking clubs from the mainland are regular weekend users of the buses. Appendix B includes a list of contacts that may be useful in planning journeys around the island.

By Stagecoach bus

Starting from the ferry terminal at Brodick, Stagecoach West Scotland buses, www.stagecoachbus.com, run around the island from early in the morning until late at night. Typically, buses start soon after 6am and run until 9pm, with some services running almost to 11.30pm on Fridays. There are slight seasonal variations, and Sunday services are less frequent than weekdays.

Several buses run between Brodick, Lamlash and Whiting Bay, which are the three largest villages on Arran. Buses also run back and forth along the B880 String road, between Brodick and Blackwaterfoot. A service running round the northern half of the island is complimented by another service running round the southern half of the island. Together, these buses cover a complete circuit around the coastal A841 road, linking all the villages.

Arran Day Rider tickets offer a day's unlimited travel around the island, while Arran Megarider tickets offer a week's unlimited travel. In the summer months, an open-top bus runs between Brodick and Whiting Bay, while a veteran coach service runs between Brodick and Brodick Castle. The only road without a bus service is the Ross, between Lamlash and Sliddery, although many years ago there were Post Bus services along it.

By car

While cars can be brought onto the Arran by ferry, it is an extra expense when the road use is so limited. So if you want to be 'green' it's easy enough to leave your car behind. Bus services on the island are perfectly adequate and reach the starting points of all the walking routes in this guidebook, with the exception of The Ross road and the short road into Glen Rosa.

Anyone taking a car to the island should bear in mind that roads are often narrow and winding. There are lots of walkers and cyclists about and sheep and deer frequently wander across the roads. A leaflet is available that encourages everyone to 'Share Arran's Roads Safely'.

By ferry
The only 'internal' ferry service is the one that serves Holy Isle from Lamlash. This ferry is subject to tides and the weather, and it is always best to check the schedule in advance (tel 01770 700463, 01770 600998, or mobile 07970 771960).

Traveline Scotland
Up-to-date information about all kinds of public transport can be obtained from Traveline Scotland, tel 0871 200223, www.travelinescotland.com. Services between Glasgow, Ayrshire and Arran can also be checked with Strathclyde Passenger Transport (SPT) www.spt.co.uk.

FINDING YOUR BEARINGS

Visitors arriving at the ferry terminal at Brodick are confronted by a sign offering only two directions: North and South. The A841 is the main road around the island and it links practically all the villages on the island. In a clockwise order these include: Brodick, Lamlash, Whiting Bay, Kildonan, Kilmory, Sliddery, Blackwaterfoot, Machrie, Pirnmill, Catacol, Lochranza, Sannox, Corrie and so back to Brodick.

Two roads run across the island: The String, or the B880, runs from Brodick to Blackwaterfoot via Shiskine, with a minor road spur to Machrie. The Ross is a minor road from Lamlash to Sliddery. All the roads around the island are equipped with distinctive red sandstone milestones.

Distinctive sandstone milestones stand alongside all the roads around the island

The road system is so simple that it is virtually impossible to get lost, and there are comprehensive bus services along most of them.

If it's your first visit, you might consider taking buses all the way round the island, taking note of where the villages are located, what they offer and where the access points are for most of the walking routes in this guidebook.

Throughout the summer, the last surviving Clyde paddle steamer, the Waverley, www.waverleyexcursions.co.uk, offers tours around the Clyde and its islands, including a circuit around the coast of Arran. Walkers who plan to complete the Arran

Coastal Way might enjoy a cruise around the island to have a look before they set off. (Cicerone publishes a guidebook to *The Ayrshire and Arran Coastal Paths.*)

A GEOLOGY CLASSROOM

The Isle of Arran is one of the most varied geological areas in the British Isles. Someone once noted that while some people write to *The Times* when they hear the first cuckoo of spring, others write to the *Arran Banner* newspaper when they hear the chipping of the first geologist of spring! The island is like a huge geological classroom and groups of students will often be seen out peering at the rocks.

James Hutton, the redoubtable scientist from Edinburgh, visited Arran in August 1787. He was the first person to identify an 'unconformity' – where rocks of widely differing ages rest together at different angles. In fact, an unconformity on the coast north of Lochranza is known to this day as Hutton's Unconformity (see Walk 35).

Hutton expounded his Theory of the Earth in which mountains were continually being uplifted and eroded, although few took the great man seriously. Geologists of Hutton's day were divided into the Vulcanists and Neptunists according to whether they believed rocks were formed by volcanic action or by deposition as sediments. Hutton's theory embraced both concepts and today he is widely regarded as the Father of Geology.

The study of the Isle of Arran's geology is very much a specialist subject, but there are a few notes worth bearing in mind. The oldest rocks occur on the northern half of the island. Cambrian strata, originally marine muds and sands, have been altered by tremendous heat and pressure into slates and sparkling schists, often streaked with veins of white quartz. In a semi-circle around this base rock are Devonian strata, composed originally of desert sand dunes, being revealed in an arc from Sannox to Dougarie.

A more disjointed arc of Carboniferous strata stretches from Lochranza to Sannox and from Corrie to The String road. These include limestones, sandstones and workable coal measures, all formed in shallow seas or on a swampy delta. Permian strata again indicate desert conditions with sand dunes, and these sandstones take up much of the central and southern parts of the island. Triassic strata stretch across the southernmost part of the island, from Blackwaterfoot to Kildonan, and are composed of muds and sands laid down in a lake or delta system.

Masses of molten rock were intruded into this basic layered rock succession under great heat and pressure, which had the effect of pushing existing layers into a dome, baking the surrounding strata and altering its mineral structures and appearance.

Igneous dykes often appear as linear walls of rock, especially along the south coast (Walk 14)

The granite peaks of northern Arran were formed from a massive intrusive 'boss' of granite. Around southern Arran, molten rock was squeezed into bedding planes and joints to create resistant sills and dykes. Some splendid igneous dykes stand out as obvious linear walls of rock, especially around the southern coast, where they are termed 'dyke swarms'.

On a geological timescale, the final act in the shaping of Arran occurred during the Ice Age. The island was prominent enough to support its own ice cap, grinding corries and 'U' shaped valleys quite independent of the massive Highland glaciers scouring out the troughs of the Clyde and Kilbrannan Sound. The power of the ice inexorably grinding into the rocky mountains was one thing, but the weight of the ice was also important. As the Ice Age drew to a close, melt-water raised the sea levels; but as the weight of the ice was lifted from the Earth's crust, there was a corresponding uplift of part of the Earth's surface. You can see this all around Arran, and the Scottish coast, where cobbly raised beaches, marooned sea stacks and marine caves some distance from the sea can be identified.

Walkers with a special interest in geology should use a dedicated field guide to the geology of the island, such as the classic *Macgregor's Excursion Guide to the Geology of Arran,* edited and revised by JG MacDonald and A Herriot, published by the Geological Society of Glasgow. Another interesting book presents a series of geological problem-solving excursions: *Exploring Geology on the Isle of Arran,* by CJ Nicholas, published by Cambridge University Press.

A TURBULENT HISTORY

The first hunter-gatherers approaching the Isle of Arran in simple canoes found a forested island with only the highest peaks protruding above the tree canopy. Evidence of this former forest can be seen in some peat bogs, where the trunks, branches and root systems of trees have been preserved.

Monumental standing stones were erected, such as this fine example on Machrie Moor (Walk 23)

Neolithic hunters and farmers left few discernible traces of their settlements, but they did leave massive chambered burial cairns, most notably around the southern half of the island.

Bronze Age communities left traces of hut circles, stone circles and smaller burial cairns. The best examples are found around Machrie Moor and Blackwaterfoot. The remains point to the development of settled, well-organised communities. The Iron Age is characterised by the construction of small, fortified hill forts, suggesting a measure of insecurity or strife, and again these are to be found mainly around the southern half of the island. The early language forms are unknown, with no written or spoken elements surviving. The Gaelic language of the later Celtic peoples, has survived in the Western Isles but it is not commonly spoken or written on Arran today.

St Ninian is credited with bringing Christianity into Scotland from his base at Whithorn. He and other missionaries sailed around the coastline, visiting small communities and hopping from island to island. Ninian is known to have visited Bute and Sanda, both near Arran, and he died in the year 424. The most notable saint on Arran was St Molaise, born in the year 566, who lived as a hermit in a cave on Holy Isle and later became the Abbot of Leithglinn in Ireland. He died in the year 639. King's Cave near Blackwaterfoot is thought to have been occupied by early missionaries on inter-island expeditions. The scattered island kingdom was known as Dalriada and was a great Gaelic stronghold.

Dukes of Hamilton, Brandon and Chatelherault once ruled the island

Viking raiding parties hit Iona in the year 759, and later harassed the Isle of Arran, surrounding islands and coastal areas. Later waves of settlers left traces of farmsteads and Norse placenames; including Goatfell. Arran became, along with neighbouring territories, very much a property of the Norsemen. The great Somerled, originally from Ireland and progenitor of the great clans MacDonald and Ranald, led a force against the Norse in 1156 and became ruler of old Dalriada, although the islands were still nominally under Norse sovereignty.

The emergence of Scotland as an independent state came a step closer following the defeat of the Norse at the Battle of Largs, on the mainland east of Arran, in 1263. When Norway sold the islands to Scotland in 1266, Alexander III granted the Isle of Arran to Walter Stewart. Much energy and strife accompanied Robert the Bruce's bitter campaign to secure the Scottish throne, culminating in the Battle of Bannockburn in 1314. For centuries Scottish history consisted largely of bitter border disputes with England. The islands, meanwhile, largely continued to exist as Gaelic strongholds with their own clearly defined culture and traditions.

Although little is known of Arran's history during certain periods, it is clear that many farmsteads were granted by Scottish kings, who claimed a rent on them. The few stout castles on the island were at some time controlled by the Stewarts before coming into the hands of the Hamiltons. The first Marquis of Hamilton was appointed to administer peace and justice on Arran in 1609, and the Hamilton family is strongly associated with the later development of the island. Successive generations held the title of Dukes of Hamilton, Brandon and Chatelherault, with Brodick Castle as their chief base.

The population of the island increased to the point where many

The Arran Clearances memorial and a white-washed row of estate cottages at Lamlash (Walk 6)

were living in poor 'clachans', or farming settlements, at a time of tremendous social changes. Much has been written about the Arran Clearances of the early 19th century, when people were displaced in favour of sheep, and the population was either re-settled in purpose-built cottages, or forced to emigrate to the New World, and in particular Canada. Immediately following the clearances, tourism began to develop and has continued apace, with walking and the enjoyment of the outdoors the principle draw. The Arran Heritage Museum near Brodick offers an insight into the last century of life on Arran with archive materials are available to researchers.

For further details of the Isle of Arran's history, read *Exploring Arran's Past*, by Horace Fairhurst, published by Kilbrannan Publishing.

LAND OWNERSHIP AND ACCESS

Much of the northern half of the Arran, including many high mountains and bleak, remote wilderness moorland areas, is surrounded by a tall deer fence. The Arran Deer Management Group includes a number of large landowners, including the Arran Estate, Dougarie Estate, National Trust for Scotland and Forestry Commission Scotland. Within the deer fence, red deer have free range, but are prevented from encroaching on neighbouring farms or forest properties, where they could cause great damage.

Deer stalking takes place from mid-August to mid-October, but never on Sundays, and walkers should be aware of this and take care. Call the Hillphone on 01770 302363 in advance of a visit. Deer culling aims to maintain a healthy deer population of around 600 stags, 700 hinds and 200 calves.

Much of the southern half of the island, and a forest at North Sannox, is owned by Forestry Commission Scotland, scotland.forestry.gov.uk. The Forestry Commission exists primarily to cultivate rotating stocks of timber. While the forests may seem dark and unattractive to many walkers, there is a policy of allowing a high level of access, except at times when harvesting operations constitute a hazard.

Not all the land owned by the Forestry Commission has been planted with trees. The Commission owns almost a fifth of the island, yet has only planted about half that area. Some very large areas that are unsuitable for planting, including wet moorland and steep hillsides, offer good walking and open views.

The National Trust for Scotland, www.nts.org.uk, owns Brodick Castle and its gardens, as well as a sizeable parcel of land which includes, and extends beyond, Glen Rosa, Goatfell and the surrounding mountains on the island. The land is managed both for conservation and recreation. Walkers are generally free to head in any direction they choose, and this tends to be the busiest mountain area on the island. The proximity of Brodick and the ferry ensures it will always be a popular area.

The coastal fringe of Arran is mostly occupied by small farms and villages. Access to farmland may be quite limited in some areas, and walkers should not cross fields and other enclosures by climbing over walls and fences. Use only bona fide paths and tracks through farmland, sticking to routes that are already in regular use, with stiles and gates. The Arran Coastal Way is an evolving route that is clearly signposted and waymarked where it passes through farmland.

There is very good access to the countryside on the island, but it is important that walkers and other visitors respect the rights of landowners and tenants for whom the land is their livelihood. The Arran Access Trust produces a leaflet outlining access opportunities around the island, and the majority of footpath signposts around the island are branded with the trust's logo, www.arran-access-trust.org.uk.

ARRAN DEER MANAGEMENT GROUP

The Arran Deer Management Group have placed notices at various access points around northern Arran and these read as follows:

'Walkers are welcome. The members of this Deer Management Group recognise the tradition of free access to the hill. The Deer Management Group is responsible for the management and conservation of the land, in particular the management of red deer. The main deer management aims are:

- to maintain a healthy red deer herd in balance with the natural habitat
- to maintain local employment and through this to support the rural community and local businesses
- to conserve the natural qualities of the land including its wildlife.

The National Trust for Scotland is also a member of this Deer Management Group. Its policies ensure that the public access is unaffected when culling/stalking takes place. Please help the privately owned stalking estates to achieve these aims, particularly during the main stag stalking season from mid-August to mid-October, by:

- avoiding areas where stalking is taking place
- seeking information in advance so that you can plan your visit to avoid disturbance to stalking
- following any local guidance on the day.

All members of this Deer Management Group will be pleased to recommend walking routes which will enable you to enjoy the area.

Red deer prefer forest cover but the deer here have adapted to moorland

Information on stalking in Arran is available through the Hillphone answering service, 01770 302363, whose message is updated daily. Thank you.'

A shortened version of the notice has also appeared in recent years, which reads:

'Walkers are welcome to enjoy freedom of access to these hills. This part of Arran has many red deer easily observed while walking.

To maintain a healthy deer population in balance with the natural habitat, control measures are carried out periodically. Mid-August to mid-October is a particularly sensitive time. For up-to-date information on stalking, please call the Hillphone Answer Service on: Brodick 01770 302363.'

SCOTTISH OUTDOOR ACCESS CODE

The *Land Reform (Scotland) Act 2003* established a statutory right of responsible access to land and inland waters for outdoor recreation. The *Scottish Outdoor Access Code* gives guidance on your responsibilities when exercising access rights. The act sets out where and when access rights apply. The code defines how access rights should be exercised. The *Scottish Outdoor Access Code* is available on leaflets that can be obtained from Scottish Natural Heritage, tourist information centres and local government offices, as well as on the website, www.outdooraccess-scotland.com.

Summary of the Outdoor Access Code

Three key principles for responsible access apply to both the public and land managers:

- Respect the interests of other people: be considerate, respect privacy and livelihoods, and the needs of those enjoying the outdoors.
- Care for the Environment: look after the places you visit and enjoy. Care for wildlife and historic sites.
- Take responsibility for your own actions: the outdoors cannot be made risk-free for people exercising access rights; land managers should act with care for people's safety.

The responsibility of recreational countryside users can be summarised as follows:

- Take responsibility for your own actions: the outdoors is a great place to enjoy, but it is also a working environment and has many natural hazards. Make sure you are aware of these and act safely, follow any reasonable advice and respect the needs of other people enjoying or working in the outdoors.
- Respect people's privacy and peace of mind: privacy is important for everyone. Avoid causing alarm to people, especially at night, by keeping a reasonable distance from houses and gardens, or by using paths or tracks.
- Help land managers and others to work safely and effectively: keep a safe distance from any work and watch for signs that tell you dangerous activities are being carried out, such as tree felling or crop spraying. Do not hinder land management operations and follow advice from land managers. Respect requests for reasonable limitations on when and where you can go.
- Care for your environment: follow any reasonable advice or information, take your litter home, treat places with care and leave them as you find them. Don't recklessly disturb or damage wildlife or historic places.
- Keep your dog under proper control: it is very important that it does not worry livestock or alarm others. Don't let it into fields with calves and lambs, and keep it on a short lead when in a field with other animals. Do not allow it to disturb nesting birds. Remove and carefully dispose of dog dirt.
- Take extra care if you are organising an event or running a business and ask the landowner's advice. Check the full version of the code for further details about your responsibilities.

ARRAN ACCESS TRUST

The Isle of Arran is a popular destination for walkers, but this can lead to problems of over-use on some paths, or problems with access in other places. The Arran Access Trust seeks to improve the provision of access around the island, repairing damaged and badly eroded paths, even into the highest mountains. The trust has great support on Arran and has acquired funding for its work, repairing and restoring several popular footpaths, as well as creating new paths to avoid busy roads. Trust members work with estate managers and farmers, installing gates and stiles at access points around the island. The trust welcomes a wider membership and volunteer workers, who are kept informed of the latest developments around the island. Look out for leaflets produced by the Arran Access Trust, or check their website, www.arran-access-trust.org.uk.

ISLAND ANIMALS

On the way over to the island keep a look out for occasional small whales or dolphins which might be seen from the ferry, and note that seals can be seen basking on rocky and bouldery parts of the shore all around the island. The South Arran Marine Protected Area and Lamlash Bay No Take Zone offer special protection to parts of the sea bed around the island. Further details can be checked with the Community Of Arran Seabed Trust (COAST), at www.arrancoast.com.

You can often spot seals hauled out on boulders, basking contentedly in the sun

There are no foxes or stoats on Arran. There are red squirrels, but no greys. Otters are under pressure from feral mink in the watercourses. Herds of red deer thrive on northern Arran and are selectively stalked and culled as they have no natural predators. Brown hares can often be seen around the southern half of the island.

Arran is home to plenty of reptiles, among them adders, lizards and slow worms, which can all be observed basking in the open on sunny days. There are plenty of frogs in wet places, as well as salmon and trout in the rivers. Dragonflies and butterflies fill the summer air, but the summer months also bring hordes of midges, best defeated by strong sun, steady rainfall, a stiff sea breeze, or copious applications of insect repellent!

A gull's nest found far from the coast on remote moorlands in the middle of the island

The Arran Natural History Society keeps track of the wildlife on the Isle of Arran, www.arranwildlife.co.uk.

Bird life is dominated by golden eagles, hawks and ravens in the mountain environment. Red grouse populate many heathery areas, particularly the southern moorlands. Black grouse have been introduced to the island. Owls include barn owl, tawny owl, long and short-eared owl. The varied coastal habitats support eider, shag, cormorants, mallard, shelduck, mergansers, redshank, ringed plover, turnstone, oystercatcher, wigeon, goldeneye and many types of gull. Gannets have a colony on Ailsa Craig and may be observed diving spectacularly for fish all around Arran, while fulmars nest on the cliffs. Herons are found along many watercourses, as well as beside the sea, and there are plenty of forest and meadow species to be spotted. Gulls are not confined to the coast, but may establish breeding colonies on remote moorlands in the centre of the island.

Keen ornithologists would find the *Arran Bird Atlas,* by Dr Jim Cassels, very useful and informative. An annual periodical is also available, called *The Arran Bird Report,* published by the Arran Natural History Society. See also the Arran Birding website, www.arranbirding.co.uk.

ISLAND PLANTS

The plant-life of Arran is another specialist study. The original canopy forest is now reduced to a few ancient stands of oak, ash, rowan or hazel. These areas will often be home to wood sorrel and bluebells. Notable species include the rare Arran whitebeams, protected from harm in Gleann Diomhan. Forest species include spruce, larch, pines and firs. There are some introduced species that have become nuisances, such as rhododendron and Himalayan balsam. There are also some small, specialised trees to be found in even the most barren mountain areas; generally dwarf willow and creeping juniper, barely lifting themselves above the grass and heather.

Leaves of the Arran Whitebeam – a rare hybrid of whitebeam and rowan trees

The range of habitat types gives a root-hold to some 900 species of flowering plants. A great variety of specialist plants are to be found on the raised beaches and sea cliffs, but there are far too many to list here. Lowland wetlands are often bright with wild iris; slopes may be dominated by invasive bracken; while moorland areas may be flushed purple with heather. Bilberry, bog myrtle and bog asphodel are common on the boggy uplands. The mountain environment supports plants such as alpine lady's mantle, alpine saw-wort, starry saxifrage, mossy saxifrage and mountain sorrel.

Some boggy areas feature insectivorous butterwort and sundew. Foxgloves, ragwort and rosebay willowherb are markers of disturbed ground, and hence tend to flourish alongside forest tracks and roads. Tucked away in many dark and damp crevices are an abundance of ferns, for which Arran is noted. Like the coastal plants, ferns are a specialist study. Plantlife, www.plantlife.org.uk, lists Arran among 150 Important Plant Areas (IPAs) in Britain.

ACCOMMODATION

There is a wide range of accommodation on Arran, but bear in mind that it becomes fully booked at peak periods. Less than 5000 people live on the island, but the figure can swell to almost 15,000 in the peak summer period! Either book a bed well in advance, or choose to walk off-season. At the budget level there are a mere handful of campsites around the island, notably: Glen Rosa, near Brodick; Cordon, near Lamlash;

Food and drink, including Arran specialities, can be found throughout the island

Kildonan, in the south-east of the island; Bridgend, near Shiskine; and Lochranza, in the north-west of the island. Wild camping is an option, but refer to the *Scottish Outdoor Access Code* and be scrupulous about making your camps low-key, removing all trace of your stay. There is only one youth hostel on Arran, at Lochranza, but there are well-equipped bunkhouses at Corrie, Kilmory and Lamlash.

The vast bulk of accommodation around the island is self-catering. This can be in the form of apartments, mobile homes, cottages or large houses. Generally, these places offer a full range of facilities, but you should check whether fuel or power is extra, and whether all linen is provided. Standards range from simple to luxurious and are priced accordingly. Self-catering accommodation can be in the villages, or situated in more remote areas.

There are B&Bs all the way around the island, notably in the villages, but also on some of the more remote farms. Small hotels are available at Brodick, Lamlash, Whiting Bay, Kildonan, Lagg, Blackwaterfoot, Catacol, Lochranza, Sannox and Corrie. The largest hotels on the island are near Brodick: the Auchrannie Spa Resort and the Auchrannie House Hotel, with their associated lodges and other facilities.

The tourist information centre at Brodick can offer help and advice about accommodation, and can handle bookings (tel 01770 303774). There is also an annual holiday and travel guide available that lists accommodation, which can be viewed at www.visitarran.com/arran-island-guide. Other useful accommodation websites include www.thearranteam.co.uk, www.stayarran.co.uk and arranaccommodationguide.com.

FOOD AND DRINK

Despite the fact that much of Arran is too bleak, boggy and mountainous to support agriculture, there are rich grasslands around the fringes of the island that support a thriving dairy industry. Here fields are largely given over to livestock. Heavy breeds of cattle include Angus and shorthorn. Hardy little blackface sheep manage on poorer upland grazing, although they will be brought into the richer pastures for lambing and fattening. The bleak and barren northern parts of the island support herds of red deer. The Arran Butcher shops sell beef, lamb, venison and fish. They have their own favourite ways of making pies, puddings and haggis, and also operate a mobile shop.

Milk produced on Arran is pasteurised, but not homogenised, so it still has a 'cream-line' and tends to be richer than mass-produced mainland milk. This milk is used for making a splendid range of cheeses, including the traditional Arran Dunlop, as well as Cheddar, blue, brie, smoked and many flavoured varieties. Cheese manufacture can be observed at Duchess Court, near Brodick and at the Torrylin Creamery at Kilmory. Arran milk is also used to create traditional ice-creams, which are available all around the island in the summer months.

While Arran no longer has a fishing industry, locally caught fish and seafood is available. Creelers smokehouse, at Duchess Court near Brodick, use local wood and shavings from old whisky barrels to give a distinctive taste to their salmon, kippers and duck. Wild salmon and trout frequent the rivers but there is also a salmon farm in Lamlash Bay. In the days when much of the island population lived in poor 'clachans', salmon and oysters were often regarded as poor man's food!

Arran was once famous for potatoes, and old 'lazy beds' or potato ridges can still be seen in depopulated parts of the island where it was once grown as a staple crop. Long after the Arran Clearances, in 1901, a Lamlash man called Donald McKelvie began to breed new varieties of potato, giving them names such as Arran Chief, Arran Cairn, Arran Pilot and Arran Victory. Although many of his varieties are no longer commonly available, a few are still grown on the island, notably at Kingscross near Whiting Bay.

Oats were once a staple crop on the island, contributing to the diet of man and beast, but land is seldom given over to growing cereal crops today. However, Wooleys Bakery at Brodick still produces millions of oatcakes, as well as other fare that serves the needs of islanders and visitors. Two baking ovens, over a century old, handle huge amounts of breads, cakes and biscuits. The bakery is also quite close to the Chocolate Shop, which makes and sells delicious chocolates.

Outside Lamlash, Arran Fine Foods once produced only a range of mustards, but has now expanded its range to include chutneys, relishes and fruit preserves. At Cladach, near Brodick, the Arran Brewery brews several styles of beer, while at Lochranza the Isle of Arran Distillery produces a range of single malt whiskies and liqueurs.

Visitors to the Arran could exist quite happily on locally produced island fare, all now promoted under the 'Taste of Arran' banner. For those who don't know where to start, entire hampers can be made up, either for use on the island, or dispatched off-island. Shops on Arran handle a lot of local produce, including the dedicated Taste of Arran shop at Brodick, the Village Shop at Whiting Bay, and the Co-op stores at Brodick and Lamlash. Island foodstuffs can be drooled over and ordered through www.taste-of-arran.co.uk.

A large Co-op supermarket is located at Brodick, with a smaller store nearby, and another at Lamlash. Groceries can also be bought at the Village Shop in Whiting Bay. Pubs, restaurants and cafés are dotted around the island, and many hotel bars and restaurant are open to non-residents. Some of the island's golf courses have tearooms attached, offering remarkably extensive menus with plenty of home-made fare.

Each of the walking routes in this guidebook indicates whether refreshments are available at the start or finish, and whether you would need to look elsewhere for food and drink. See also Appendix B for a list of producers on the island.

MAPS

The maps used throughout this guidebook are extracted from the Ordnance Survey 1:50,000 Landranger sheet 69, which is perfectly adequate for exploring the whole of the island. The spelling of place-names on OS maps occasionally differs from local spellings.

The Ordnance Survey 1:25,000 Explorer sheet 361 also covers the Isle of Arran, offering more detail, especially in complex areas such as forests and farmland, or on rocky ridges in the high mountains. The map is printed on both sides of the sheet, with a generous overlap between the northern and southern halves of the island.

Ordnance Survey maps can be obtained widely from bookshops, or ordered through the website www.ordnancesurvey.co.uk. Digital versions of OS maps are also available for use with GPS-enabled devices.

Harvey Maps produce the 1:25,000 Superwalker XT25 map of Arran. This is tough, light, waterproof and double-sided, with a generous overlap between the eastern and western halves of the island. Fine attention to detail on this map extends to showing the full extent of boggy ground around the island. (Harvey's first mapped the Isle of Arran in 1980 for the former Karrimor Mountain Marathon.) The map also contains information about Arran and lots of contact details for organisations and services on the island. See www.harveymaps.co.uk.

THE WALKS

The walks in this guidebook include a few easy, waymarked forest trails or low-level walks, as well as a dozen or so moderate glen or hill walks. The rest require more effort to complete, heading for the higher mountains and sometimes involving hands-on scrambling. Routes may run along roads or clear forest tracks, as well as following hill tracks or paths, but many routes also cross pathless slopes and traverse rocky mountain ridges.

The further off the beaten track the walker wanders, the more care needs to be exercised. Boulder-strewn slopes or tussocky moorlands are places where ankles are easily turned, so bear this in mind while making plans. Steep, rocky scrambles may require the use of hands, so cautious walkers can decide whether or not to proceed.

All 44 of the walks have been chosen to show off the rich variety of landscape types on Arran. They seek both popular and secluded spots, wander along the coast or aim for the heights, taking in wide-ranging views, or searching carefully for some hidden heritage detail.

Holy Isle looks like a mountain marooned at sea when viewed from the Clauchland Hills

Longer routes criss-crossing the island can be pieced together using portions of the route descriptions. Many of the walks in this guide overlap, or have sections in common, so it is easy to extend or shorten many of the routes.

The excellent bus services around Arran also means that there is often no need for walkers to return to their starting point. A few of the walks are linear, and there is plenty of scope for walkers to create longer linear walks simply by linking together adjoining route descriptions.

Only a brief outline of the Arran Coastal Way is given here but it is covered in detail elsewhere by *The Ayrshire and Arran Coastal Paths*, by Keith Fergus, published by Cicerone, and the website www.coastalway.co.uk.

TOURIST INFORMATION

The tourist information centre for Arran is located opposite the ferry terminal in Brodick. The office can handle requests about accommodation, attractions, public transport and other services. Beds can be booked, and it is possible to buy specific maps and field guides covering all aspects of the island. Contact: Tourist Information Centre, The Pier, Brodick, Isle of Arran KA27 8AU tel 01770 303774, www.visitarran.com, email info@visitarran.com.

EMERGENCY SERVICES

The Arran Mountain Rescue Team handles all requests for assistance on the mountains and moorlands around the island. The RNLI operates a lifeboat from Lamlash, and Arran is also covered by lifeboats operating from Campbeltown (to the west) and Largs (to the east) on the mainland. There is a hospital at Lamlash, with Health Centres at Brodick, Lamlash and Shiskine. Small surgeries with limited opening times are found at Whiting Bay, Kilmory, Lochranza and Corrie.

To call the Police, Ambulance, Fire Service, Mountain Rescue or Coastguard, dial 999 (or the European emergency number 112). Be ready to give full details about the nature of the emergency, and give the operator your telephone number so that they can stay in touch with you if they need further information, or to give you advice and instruction.

Non-urgent matters can be directed to the Police Station at Lamlash, 01770 302573, or to the Arran Medical Group at Lamlash, 01770 600516. Out of hours, contact NHS24 by dialling 111.

Goatfell can be seen, and climbed in a day, from the ferry terminal at Brodick

WALK 1

Goatfell and Brodick

Start/Finish	Ferry terminal, Brodick (NS 022 359)
Distance	16.5km (10½ miles)
Total ascent	850m (2790ft)
Time	5hrs
Terrain	Roads, forest tracks, rugged moorland and mountain paths. The upper parts are steep and stony.
Refreshments	Plenty of choice in Brodick. Pub and restaurant at Cladach.

Some walkers step off the Caledonian MacBrayne ferry at Brodick and head straight for Goatfell, hoping to climb to the summit and return in time to leave the island. It's a grand day out for those who have the energy to complete the ascent between ferries, and this route description is just for them. Others may enjoy Goatfell by a variety of routes and tackle the ascent with less urgency.

The route follows the roadside promenade through Brodick, switching to the Fisherman's Walk along the shore to Cladach, then climbs in earnest. The route is a combination of roads, tracks and a well-constructed mountain path. It is quite likely that many other walkers will be met on the way there and back, as this is the most popular way up and down Goatfell. The initial coastal walk could be omitted by catching a bus from the ferry terminal to Cladach, returning later, remembering to check up-to-date timetables.

Leave the ferry terminal and bus station, turning right to follow a promenade path beside the main coastal road through **Brodick**. On a clear day, Goatfell will already be in view. If food or drink is needed, there is a large Co-op supermarket, as well as other shops, pubs and cafés along the way. The promenade runs beside a pleasant green above a rocky shore, reaching a putting green and smaller Co-op store. Turn right to pass a car park and play park, picking up a coastal path signposted as the Fisherman's Walk.

The path crosses a footbridge over a river then soon crosses a longer footbridge over the broader Glenrosa Water. Turn right to return towards the coast and walk beside a golf course. Later, walk along a sandy, pebbly beach beside **Brodick Bay**, coming ashore to cross yet another footbridge to reach a car park and bus stop at **Cladach**. ▶

If using buses, start and finish here, saving a total of 5.5km (3½ miles).

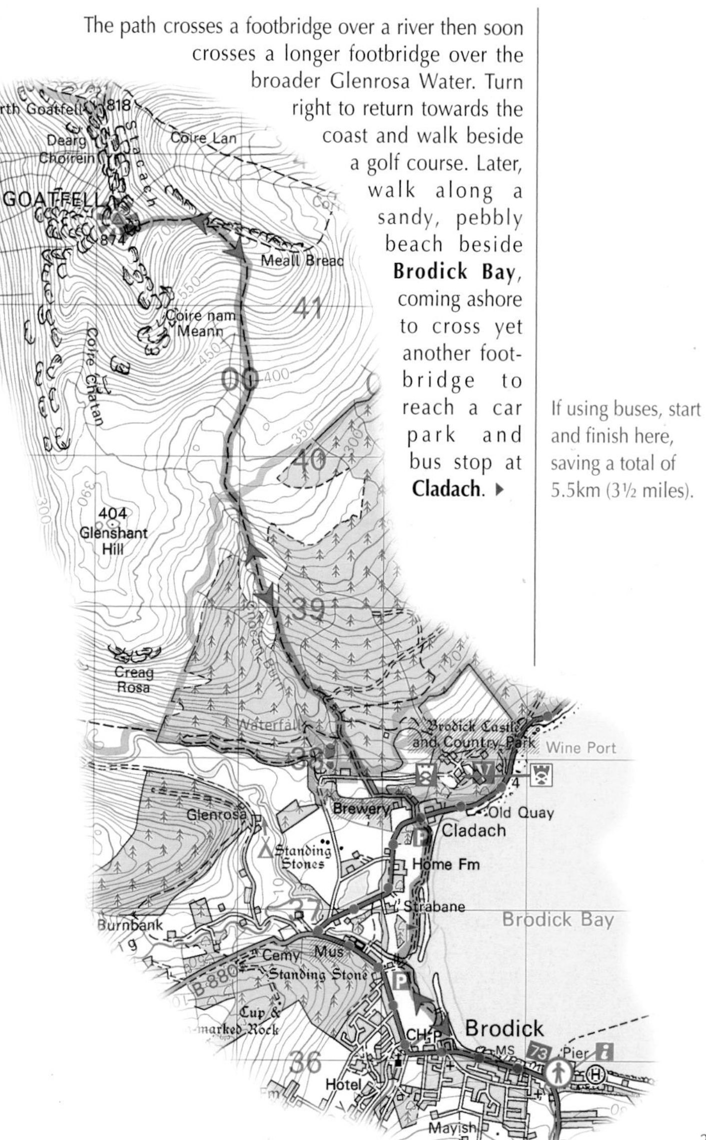

CLADACH

Cladach was once the main settlement on Brodick Bay, but it was gradually depopulated as Brodick developed. When Cladach was a larger huddle of buildings near Brodick Castle, it featured the Old Inn, the Village Inn, a woollen mill and a few houses. When the grounds surrounding Brodick Castle were redeveloped in 1853, the woollen mill moved to Millhouse and the tenants were re-housed at Douglas Place and Alma Terrace. A new school was built in 1854. Tourists had already started visiting the Isle of Arran, frequenting the Old Inn at Cladach, where goat's milk was a speciality. Tourism continued to develop and the new village of Brodick became equipped with a new and larger pier, a large hotel, shops and other businesses. Cladach has been redeveloped, retaining the appearance of a small village, with the Arran Brewery being a major attraction, along with The Wineport bar/bistro, Arran Active outdoor shop, gift shops, pottery and sawmill. There is also pedestrian access to Brodick Castle.

DUCHESS COURT

Duchess Court is a small retail development about 350m/yds from Cladach, in the direction of Brodick. It is based on Brodick Castle's original Home Farm and now features the Isle of Arran Cheese Shop, perfumed products at Arran Aromatics, Creelers seafood restaurant and the Smokehouse Shop.

Walk between the buildings at Cladach, passing the Arran Brewery, following a clear track gradually uphill as signposted 'Goatfell'. The well-wooded slopes are rich in rhododendrons and the track crosses a tarmac driveway that serves nearby **Brodick Castle**. Follow the track up into Forestry Commission property, passing a large sign confirming that this is the way to 'Goatfell'. As the track climbs, there are waymarked paths leading to left and right, but always stay on the clearest track. ◄ At a higher level, keep left up a clear path as marked 'Goatfell'.

Walk 2 is a short circular route that follows part of this track.

The path rises through an area where rhododendron scrub has been cut back, then climbs a slope of bracken and heather, bearing scattered stands of birch, where the forest is more distant. Small streams are crossed that flow

The steep-sided pyramidal peak of Cir Mhòr seen from the summit of Goatfell

into the nearby **Cnocan Burn**. The path remains quite clear as it climbs and the surroundings become more rugged. Cross a footbridge across a water channel cut across the hillside, quickly reaching a gate in a tall deer fence. Beyond the gate, the mountain is owned and managed by the National Trust for Scotland.

The path continues uphill at a gentler gradient for a while, and it was restored after suffering years of erosion. There are sections with pitched stone and gravel surfaces, with drains removing excess water, although in some places the path crosses bare granite bedrock. The surrounding moorland is mostly wet, grassy, heathery and boulder-strewn. The gradient gradually increases in **Coire**

nam Meann as the path climbs up onto the shoulder of **Meall Breac**. There is a level stance before the path swings more to the left and aims directly towards Goatfell. This is the toughest part of the ascent, as the path weaves steeply between boulders and granite outcrops.

The summit of **Goatfell** is reached quite suddenly and is composed of a bare table of granite bearing a few large boulders. There is a trig point at 874m (2867ft), with a view indicator provided by the Rotary Club of Kilwinning. This is the highest peak on Arran. ◄

Views are extensive and stretch far into mainland Scotland as well as embracing the Highlands, islands and Northern Ireland.

If a careful check has been made of progress so far, then walkers should be able to gauge whether they are able to catch their intended bus or ferry. The descent needs to be taken carefully at first, but it should take less time than the ascent. It is simply a matter of retracing steps back to **Cladach**, to catch a bus, or continue all the way to the ferry terminal in **Brodick**.

BRODICK

Brodick's main features and facilities can be spotted on the way back to the ferry terminal. In order of appearance they include: Brodick Pharmacy, Co-op store, a putting green, Shanghai Chinese take-away, Red Door gift shop, Bank of Scotland (with ATM), Inspirations of Arran gift shop and Wooleys of Arran bakery.

Several more businesses look across the main road towards the sea, including: Fiddlers Music Bar and Bistro, Invercloy Guest House, Hair and Beauty, Arran Estate Agents, The Byre at Brodick, Chocolate Shop, Hunters guest house, Arran-Asia Trading Company, Book and Card Centre, Royal Bank of Scotland (with ATM), Brodick Health Centre, Dunvegan Guest House and the Shorehouse Apartments. Next comes the Arran Active outdoor shop, a crazy golf course, Taste of Arran, Buntys furniture store and Little Rock Café. The former McLaran Hotel is due for redevelopment, then comes a large Co-op supermarket.

The Douglas is a hotel incorporating a bar and bistro, while buildings in the grounds feature an optician, Arran Team, Arran Banner newspaper and a domestic service centre. The Roman Catholic church is tucked away behind. Finally, in a group at the ferry terminal, are the bus station, a filling station, gift shops and the tourist information centre, tel 01770 303774.

WALK 2

Brodick Castle and Country Park

Start/Finish	Brodick Castle access road (NS 019 379)
Distance	5km (3 miles)
Total ascent	180m (590ft)
Time	1hr 30mins
Terrain	Clear, waymarked woodland paths and forest tracks.
Refreshments	Café inside Brodick Castle, as well as a bar/restaurant at Cladach.

The red sandstone towers and turrets of Brodick Castle are easily distinguished, poking above forests on the lower slopes of Goatfell. Castles have been built and rebuilt on this site for centuries, but the present one dates only from the 19th century and was the seat of the Dukes of Hamilton. Brodick Castle is the centrepiece of the National Trust for Scotland's holdings on Arran. It houses silverware and porcelain, paintings and sketches, with rooms full of fine furniture. Wrapped around Brodick Castle is a colourful woodland garden threaded by a variety of paths, lavishly planted with exotic trees and rhododendrons. A separate walled garden has a more regimented layout and features more flowers than trees.

The grounds around Brodick Castle were designated as a Country Park in 1980 and are managed by the National Trust for Scotland and North Ayrshire Council. There is a complex network of waymarked trails to explore, and this walk combines some of them into a circuit on the forested slopes above the castle. Free maps showing the full extent of the trails can be obtained in advance at the tourist information centre in Brodick, or on arrival at Brodick Castle. There are also map-boards around the Country Park.

There are several ways to reach the start of this walk. If driving a car, then use a car park close to the castle. Most buses run along the main road, so alight and follow the access road up to the castle. In summer, a few buses run up the access road to the castle car park. Anyone who wishes to walk from Brodick could follow Walk 1 to Cladach, then climb a flight of stone steps signposted

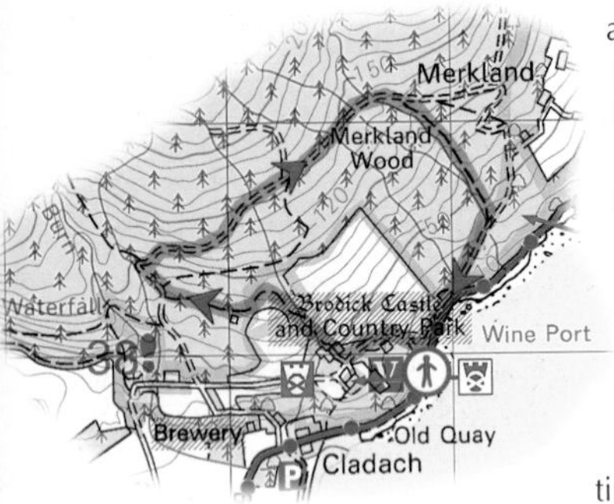

as a pedestrian route to the castle. This would effectively double the distance of the walk.

Assuming that a bus is used, start on the main road and follow the access road up to **Brodick Castle** car park. If the castle and walled garden are to be explored, then purchase a ticket from the Reception Centre. There is no charge to walk in the Country Park, in which case avoid the car park, continue along the access road and turn right at a junction as signposted 'Ranger Service'. A huddle of buildings is reached and one of them has a nature room equipped with an interesting display about local wildlife.

A path leaving the buildings is marked simply as 'trails', but later a bewildering number of named paths and tracks will be noticed, so take note of the route description. The path soon crosses a footbridge over a burn, and just to the left is a very short optional loop called Wilma's Walk. This simply runs down through the woods, crosses the burn and rises back to the buildings.

WILMA'S WALK

A small plaque explains: 'Wilma Forgie was Joint Representative at Brodick with her husband John from 1973 until her untimely death in 1983. She was greatly loved by staff and visitors alike and left her mark on Brodick in many ways; one of them was the inspiration for this short walk. It has now been named after her so that those who follow it will remember her.'

Follow the path up through an iron gate, turn right and continue across two more footbridges. Keep left at a big marker post and path junction. The path is enclosed by trees, which later part to reveal a view of Brodick Bay. The path runs down and up, with the walled Hamilton Cemetery lying to the left. A fine gateway allows access. Slabs mark the graves of the 11th Duke of Hamilton,

A remnant ancient woodland fills the Merkland Gorge in Brodick Country Park

Brandon and Chatelherault, as well as the 12th Duke and his wife. Continue along the path until a junction is reached with a clear forest track.

Turn right up the track, then keep left as indicated by a 'Goatfell' sign. At the next junction 'Goatfell' is marked to the left, so keep right and follow the track past a gate. ▸ The forest track rises gently, without decent views as it is flanked by tall trees. When a track junction is reached, keep right, in effect straight ahead. The track fords a stream and later ends in **Merkland Wood**, where a footbridge is crossed. Turn right down a path that runs roughly parallel to Merkland Burn. There are small waterfalls in a rocky gorge, although these are difficult to see.

Walk 1 can be used from this point to reach the summit of Goatfell.

MERKLAND WOOD

Plenty of rhododendron scrub has been cleared in Merkland Wood to help revive what is one of the few ancient woodland sites remaining on Arran. With light again able to reach the floor, birch, pine and oak have re-established themselves. Sycamore and Douglas Fir are being controlled in accordance with a management plan established by the National Trust for Scotland and the Arran Natural History Society.

Follow the path downhill alongside the gorge, eventually landing on a broad forest track. Turn right to cross a bridge over Merkland Burn and follow the track almost down to the main coastal road. Off to the left, close to the road, an optional short detour leads to the overgrown Heronry Pool near **Wine Port**.

WINE PORT

The rugged bay of Wine Port obtained its name after a French ship ran aground and its cargo of wine and silk was salvaged and taken up to Brodick Castle. The bay has a variety of wildlife habitats, and species that can be spotted include the red-throated diver, black-throated diver, great northern diver, pied wagtail, grey heron, oystercatcher, common sandpiper, red-breasted merganser, eider duck, shelduck and mallard. Grey and common seals can often be observed hauled out on boulders, basking in the sun.

Walkers with plenty of time to spare could explore Brodick Castle and a veritable maze of garden and woodland paths near the castle.

If not making the detour to the Heronry Pool, turn right along a track, then left along a woodland path running roughly parallel to the main road. The path quickly reaches the access road for Brodick Castle. If catching a bus, turn left for the main road, if one is due soon. Motorists should turn right and follow the access road back to the car park. ◂

BRODICK CASTLE

The foundations of Brodick Castle are lost in time. It was garrisoned against Alexander before the Isle of Arran was ceded to Scotland, and there are some rather shaky stories and legends concerning Robert the Bruce and the castle. More solid dates of 1351 and 1406

cover the destruction of the castle by English forces, while Scots themselves attacked the place in 1455. After a rather chequered and battered history, the original features are no longer present as the building has been rebuilt so many times, and the castle has been in the possession of many families. The most notable owners were the Hamiltons; Dukes of Hamilton, Brandon and Chatelherault. The Victorian part of Brodick Castle dates from 1844. In 1853 the castle grounds were redeveloped and tenants in the old village of Cladach were re-housed as Brodick began to develop. In order to pay death duties, Brodick Castle passed into the care of the National Trust for Scotland in 1957. Some 7000 acres of upland around Goatfell and Glen Rosa are also held by the Trust.

Brodick Castle is generally open daily from 11am to 3pm in April, 11am to 4pm from May to September, then 10am to 3pm in October. The shop and tearoom is generally open an hour earlier and later. The walled garden is open daily from 10am to 4.30pm from April to October, then 10am to 3.30pm on winter weekends. To confirm opening times tel 01770 302202. The Country Park is open all year round and rangers often lead informative guided walks, tel 01770 302462 for details.

A network of easy woodland trails can be explored in Brodick Country Park

WALK 3

Brodick and the Clauchland Hills

Start/Finish	Ferry terminal, Brodick (NS 022 359)
Distance	11km (7 miles), with a 1.5km (1 mile) optional extension
Total ascent	380m (1245ft)
Time	3hrs 30mins
Terrain	Roads, tracks and paths through pastoral and forested countryside.
Refreshments	Plenty of choice in Brodick.

The Clauchland Hills are a range of low, hummocky hills lying between Brodick and Lamlash. They are extensively forested, featuring a mosaic of mature, clear-felled and replanted areas. A strip of ground of varying width has been left unplanted along the crest of the hills, while the whole of Clauchlands Point remains as tree-free pasture. A stroll over the Clauchland Hills could be accomplished easily from Brodick in a morning or an afternoon. An extension can be made to include archaeological remains, and it is also possible to restructure the route and finish at Lamlash, with reference to Walk 5.

Leave the ferry terminal and bus station in **Brodick**, turning left to follow the main road uphill as signposted for Lamlash. The road climbs past a garden centre and Strathwhillan House, reaching a junction. Turn left and follow a road straight past several houses at **Strathwhillan**, almost reaching its end at Strathwhillan Farm. ◂

There might soon be a field path, avoiding the need for this initial road-walk.

Turn right to cross a stile and walk alongside a field. Turn left as marked through a gap in a hedge and walk alongside another field, turning right in a corner. Turn left across a footbridge and stile, walk across a field and cross another stile and footbridge. Cross the next field to cross a stile beside a gate, and follow the path as signposted through a small wood to reach a dirt road at **North Corriegills**.

The route so far has been part of the Arran Coastal Way, which continues straight ahead, but to continue

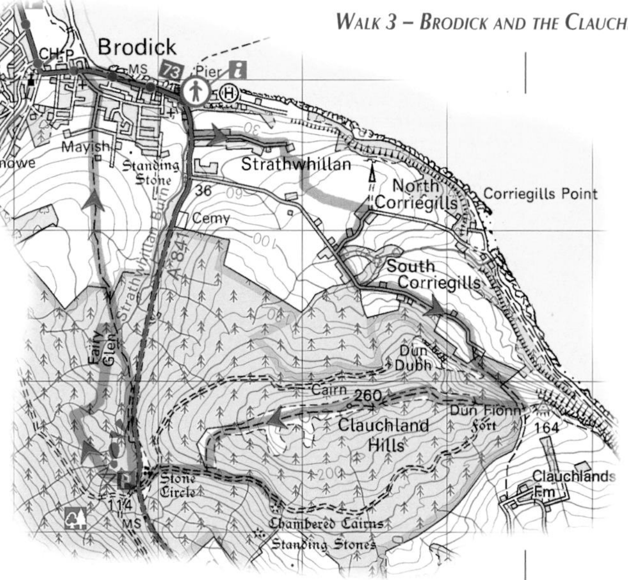

with this walk, turn right and follow the dirt road to a junction with a tarmac road, then turn left to cross Corriegills Bridge. Another dirt road rises, swings left and continues through **South Corriegills**. There are forested slopes above and a patchwork arrangement of fields

Goatfell can be seen from around Corriegills on the way to the Clauchland Hills

below. Walk to the last building on the road, where a gravel path is signposted on the right.

Follow the path uphill, crossing a little burn beside small water tanks. The path crosses a forested slope, then continues climbing with views only of the sea below and a rounded hill ahead, bearing the remains of the Iron Age hill fort of **Dun Fionn**. An information board is reached at a point where paths cross. Turn right and follow a winding path to a signpost near a turning space at the end of a forest track. Continue up the winding path, which runs through an unplanted strip flanked by forest. Another signpost is reached later, where the path continues through a much broader unplanted strip.

The path becomes something of a roller-coaster, rising more than it falls as it proceeds along the crest. There is a more significant gap to be crossed before the final pull up to the summit of the **Clauchland Hills**, where there is a sizable cairn at 260m (853ft), and a bench. A fine view extends across Brodick Bay to the highest mountains on Arran, and following extensive clear-felling, southwards over Lamlash Bay to Holy Isle.

The path leaves the cairn and runs along the broad crest, heading further westwards. Heathery, hummocky hills are crossed and the trend is gradually downhill. The path becomes a little steeper later, then runs close to the edge of the forest. There are areas of bracken among the heather, then the path swings left and there is a view across Lamlash Bay after passing a number of birch trees. The path finally drops to a forest track.

Extension to Dunan Mór and Dunan Beag (adds 1.5km (1 mile) and 30mins)

Turn left and follow the track gradually uphill through the forest. Eventually, a signpost on the right indicates a short path into a small clearing, where the **chambered cairns** of Dunan Mór and Dunan Beag, further downhill, can be inspected. Retrace steps afterwards to continue.

If the detour isn't followed, turn right and follow the forest track down to a junction, and keep left to pass a barrier gate and reach the main road linking Brodick and Lamlash at Cnoc na Dail, at 114m (374ft). A **stone circle** bearing this name lies off to the right just before reaching the main road, and can be visited by making a short detour.

CNOC NA DAIL

Cnoc na Dail means the 'hill of the meeting place', and is reputed to be the place where crofters would meet regularly in the past to discuss matters of common concern. The word 'dail' has been preserved in modern parlance and is the name given to the Irish Parliament. The Forestry Commission has acquired all the land around Cnoc na Dail, providing facilities such as car parking, picnic areas and waymarked trails.

Cross the main road and enter another forest. If in a hurry to return to Brodick, simply turn right as signposted and follow a path parallel to the main road, passing through a car park where there is a view indicator, then turn left to continue downhill, crossing two footbridges in the **Fairy Glen**. With more time to spare, however, it is worth following a more convoluted path, leaving the Cnoc na Dail car park, twisting and turning across a clear-felled and replanted forest slope, eventually joining the direct path further downhill as it leaves the Fairy Glen. There are other spur and loop paths that might also be followed if desired. ▶

The paths have been created by Roots of Arran Community Woodland volunteers.

Follow the main path onwards as it rises a little through a wooden area and an open area of heather, around 90m (295ft), crossing two gentle crests. Go through a gate and follow a track downhill, passing wooded areas and small fields. Walk straight through an intersection with another track at **Mayish** and follow a quiet road down past the Glenartney guest house. Turn left at a road junction to follow Alma Road down past the Brodick Bar and post office, to reach a junction with the main coastal road in **Brodick**. Simply turn right and follow the promenade running parallel to the road, passing through a pleasant coastal green to return to the bus station and ferry terminal. ▶

For a list of facilities along the road through Brodick, see Walk 1.

WALK 4

Sithein and Glen Cloy

Start/Finish	Cnoc na Dail, between Brodick and Lamlash (NS 018 333)
Alternative finish	Ferry terminal, Brodick (NS 022 359)
Distance	14km (8¾ miles)
Total ascent	610m (2000ft)
Time	4hrs 30mins
Terrain	Good forest paths and tracks on lower slopes, but also pathless upland moorland where good navigation is required.
Refreshments	None closer than Brodick and Lamlash.

Sithein, also known as Sheeans, or the Fairy Hills, display rounded humps rising above Glenrickard Forest. A rather fiddly forest path runs along a series of boggy forest rides, requiring careful route finding. There are no real paths over the exposed moorlands, apart from occasional vaguely trodden lines. The route over Sithein can be extended around the heads of Gleann Dubh and Glen Ormidale, before a steep descent into Glen Cloy. The whole walk is best attempted in clear weather as the open moorlands could be confusing in mist. A prominent forest path and track brings the circuit to a close. Alternatively, a slightly shorter and easier route leads through Glen Cloy to finish at Brodick.

Start at the Cnoc na Dail forest car park and picnic area, at the top of the main road between Brodick and Lamlash, at 114m (374ft). Walk past a barrier gate and turn right at a junction of forest tracks, as signposted for Glen Cloy. The track crosses two culverted streams. At the second of these, look carefully on the left to spot a vague path rising upstream. Although the path is vague at first, it becomes clearer later. The surface can be grassy, mossy or stony, and it crosses the rocky bed of another small burn, where a white-topped marker post stands. The path climbs alongside the burn and is muddy in places, crossing over a well-vegetated forest ride, where there is another marker post. Keep climbing to reach yet another marker post at an intersection of forest rides.

Turn right along a grassy, heathery and boggy forest ride, later passing two old marker posts at the edge of the forest. Ahead lies deep heather with barely any trodden paths, so head straight up the rugged moorland slope, passing a few widely spaced marker posts. A final short, steep climb leads to a trig point on top of **Sithein** at 373m (1224ft). There are views over Brodick Bay and Lamlash Bay, as well as the mountainous northern Arran and the rugged hump of Holy Isle.

To continue beyond Sithein, cross a small, heathery gap, then either climb a neighbouring summit bearing a cairn, or pass it on its left-hand side to reach a broader gap beyond. The line of an old fence is passed on the next ascent. The aim is to climb a rugged moorland slope dotted with a few trees,

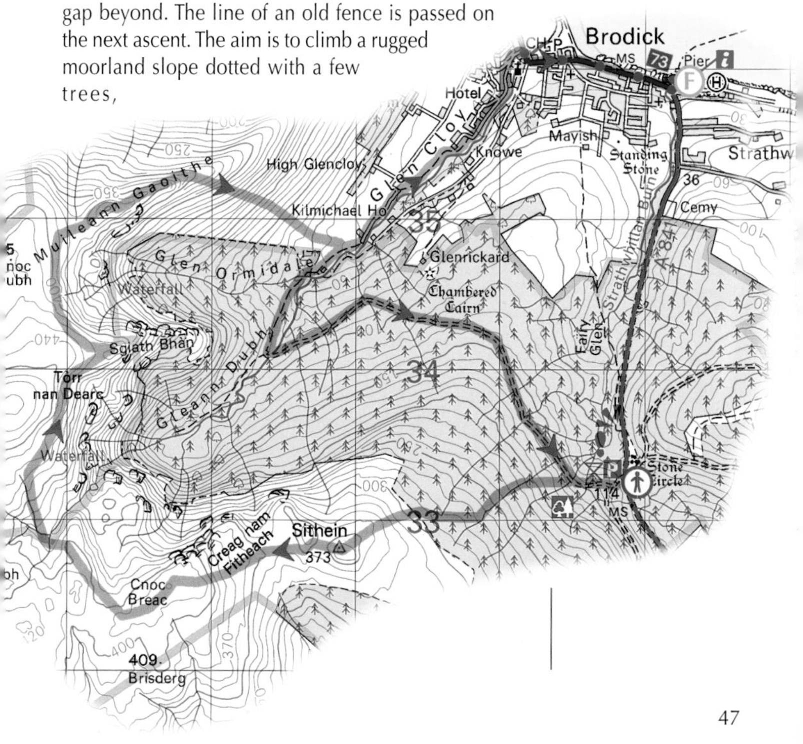

Westwards lie apparently endless moorlands where walking is difficult. However, it is possible to link with Walk 20 and Ard Bheinn.

while keeping well away from the awkward cliffs of **Creag nam Fitheach**. Continue over the broad, bleak, boggy top of **Cnoc Breac**, touching 420m (1380ft). ◂

The best strategy is to try contouring the moorland slopes, heading roughly northwest at approximately 400m (1310ft), then descending to cross a burn well below **Tir Dhubh**, around 370m (1215ft). There are opportunities to link occasional sheep paths, regaining height while gradually heading north. Later, swing right onto the heathery prow of **Sgiath Bhan**, where a small cairn stands at 427m (1405ft).

Double back a little and aim to contour around the moorland slopes at the head of **Glen Ormidale**, looking ahead to spot vague paths that can sometimes be linked to offer easier walking, while avoiding the top of **Cnoc Dubh**. Swing right to cross a broad moorland gap, then cross two little summits on **Muileann Gaoithe**. The first summit bears a small cairn at 401m (1316ft), and the second bears none. A clear path runs along a well-defined ridge, leading down to the corner of a fence. Turn right away from the fence to commence a rugged descent. A steep slope of heather and bracken gives way to a gentler slope of tussocky grass, but much of the way is awkward underfoot. Easier walking is found alongside a forest fence. Turn left to follow the fence away from the forest to find an old gateway where it is easiest to cross. At this point, a hedge runs between two fields, and there is a choice of routes: either return to Cnoc na Dail, or head for Brodick and save 1km (½ mile and 15mins).

To return to Cnoc na Dail turn right and walk across a field, finding a kissing gate leading into Glenrickard Forest. A notice points out that this is the way to Cnoc na Dail, and a footbridge crosses a stream at the foot of **Glen Ormidale**. Follow the undulating, winding path and it eventually joins a broad forest track at a concrete bridge spanning a stream in **Gleann Dubh**. ◂

Clear-felled slopes allow views up steep slopes to Sithean and Sgiath Bhan.

The forest track rises gently at first, then more steeply later, high above **Glenrickard**. At a higher level the gradient eases and there are good views of the highest peaks of

Boggy moors beyond Sithein contrast with the jagged peaks of northern Arran

Arran. The track finally returns to the car park and picnic area at Cnoc na Dail.

To finish in Brodick

Walk across the field towards a farmhouse, where a kissing gate gives access to a farm track. Follow this track alongside a river through **Glen Cloy**. Later, when the road suddenly turns left away from the river, continue straight ahead as signposted along a riverside path. Join another riverside track and pass an estate of bungalows. A tarmac road is joined which serves the Auchrannie Resort, its **hotel** and other extensive services. However, follow the Auchrannie Road straight ahead, passing an army cadet base and a few houses and small businesses, to reach a main road. Turn right to follow the road into **Brodick**, then follow the promenade running parallel to the road, passing through a pleasant coastal green to reach the bus station and ferry terminal. ▶

For a list of facilities along the road through Brodick, see Walk 1.

WALK 5

Lamlash and the Clauchland Hills

Start/Finish	Pier, Lamlash (NS 029 313)
Distance	10.5km (6½ miles), with a 1.5km (1 mile) optional extension
Total ascent	300m (985ft)
Time	3hrs 15mins
Terrain	Easy roads, tracks and paths through forest, over hills and along the coast.
Refreshments	Plenty of choice in Lamlash.

The low, hummocky Clauchland Hills lie between Brodick and Lamlash, and are largely covered in forest. However, a broad strip has been left unplanted along the crest of the hills, and there are open pastures around Clauchland Point. A circular walk based on Lamlash takes in the Clauchland Hills, Clauchlands Point and a stretch of coastline leading back to Lamlash. Holy Isle is seen at close quarters and appears like a mountain marooned at sea. A detour can be made to visit an archaeological site, and it is possible to restructure the route and finish at Brodick, with reference to Walk 3.

Start from the pier in **Lamlash** and follow the main road as if for Brodick. Turn left uphill from a road junction, then an old milestone might be noticed on the left just after passing mobile homes on Park Avenue. Lamlash Golf Club and its café lie to the right of the road at the top edge of the village. The pavement on the left-hand side of the road runs out shortly afterwards, but a fine path has been constructed between the road and an adjacent field. Look back to see Holy Isle completely filling Lamlash Bay.

Later, the path crosses a footbridge and passes alongside a clear-felled and replanted forest on the slopes of **Meall Buidhe**. Drift slightly away from the road and later reach a small car park and picnic area. Cross the road to continue along a broad forest track at Cnoc na Dail, at

114m (374ft). A **stone circle** bearing this name lies off to the left, and can be visited by making a short detour. Crofters once met there to discuss matters of common concern.

Pass a barrier gate and turn right at a track junction. Follow the forest track gently uphill until a path is signposted on the left. At this point, either turn left up the path, or keep straight ahead along the track for an optional extension.

Extension to Dunan Mór and Dunan Beag (adds 1.5km (1 mile) and 30mins)

Follow the forest track straight ahead and gradually uphill. Eventually, Turn left and follow the track gradually uphill through the forest. Eventually, a signpost on the right indicates a short path into a small clearing, where the **chambered cairns** of Dunan Mór and Dunan Beag, further downhill, can be inspected. Retrace steps afterwards to continue.

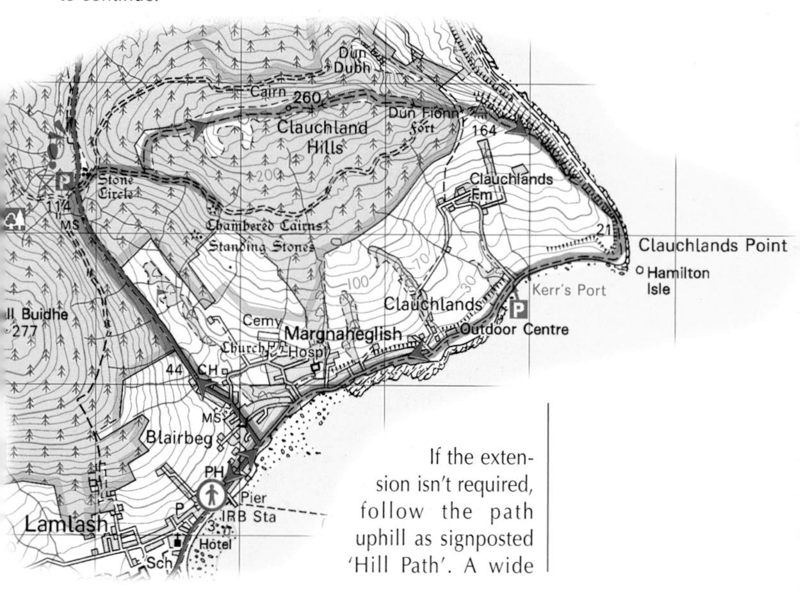

If the extension isn't required, follow the path uphill as signposted 'Hill Path'. A wide strip of land has been left unplanted, but at a higher level there are a number of birch trees as the path swings right. There are areas of bracken among the heather and the path runs closer to the forest before climbing more steeply. The continuation is along a gentler series of heathery, hummocky hills, reaching the summit of the **Clauchland Hills**, where there is a sizable cairn at 260m (853ft), and a bench. A fine view extends across Brodick Bay to the highest mountains on Arran, and following extensive clear-felling, southwards over Lamlash Bay to Holy Isle.

The path runs further along the crest, crossing a significant gap, becoming something of a roller-coaster, but descending more than it climbs. Walk straight past a signpost and keep to an unplanted strip flanked by forest. A winding path descends to another signpost near a turning space at the end of a forest track. Avoid this track, staying on the winding path to reach a point outside the forest where paths cross. An information board explains about the Iron Age hill fort of **Dun Fionn**, perched on a rounded hill straight ahead. Follow a grassy path onto the hill, reaching a trig point at 164m (538ft).

The grassy path runs beyond the hill, down a slope of bracken close to a cliff edge. Various devices have been employed to protect farm stock from the cliffs. The remains of an earthen embankment, a drystone wall and a number of fences have been constructed over time. Go through a gate into a field and walk to the end of **Clauchlands Point**. ◂

A rocky protuberance just offshore, Hamilton Isle, is often used as a perch by gulls, cormorants and shags.

A small quarry has been cut into the end of the point, and a clear track leads away from it. The track hugs the shore, following a scrub-covered raised beach, passing a couple of concrete lookout posts, eventually joining a minor road at a car park at **Kerr's Port**. The road also hugs the shore, passing the Arran Outdoor Centre near **Clauchlands**. Public footpath signposts offer other routes back uphill, otherwise keep following the coastal road past several houses. One bouldery stretch of shore is used by seals hauling out between tides.

Looking back towards the village of Lamlash, with Holy Isle rising from the bay

See Walk 6 for a list of facilities in the village.

Notable buildings are passed, starting with the Altachorvie Island Retreat. The former St George's United Free Church, which closed in 1947, has been converted into apartments. The Council Offices are passed before a road junction is reached. Keep straight ahead into **Lamlash** to finish back at the pier. ◂

LAMLASH

While Brodick may appear to be the capital of Arran to casual visitors, Lamlash is actually the administrative centre, containing the high school, hospital and police station for the island. The name Lamlash is derived from St Molaise (pronounced *M'lash*), who lived as a hermit on Holy Isle before becoming the Abbot of Leithglinn in Ireland. Holy Isle was previously known as Eilean Molaise. As the island offers good shelter to Lamlash Bay, the place has been used on occasions to shelter entire fleets of ships. King Haakon IV of Norway assembled his fleet in the bay before his disastrous performance at the Battle of Largs in 1263. During the Great War, parts of the North Atlantic and Home Fleets also anchored here.

Lamlash in its present form dates only from around 1830. Families had been cleared from old clachans and new buildings were constructed to house them. The parish church opened in 1886 and was funded by the 12th Duke of Hamilton. The hospital was constructed partly as a war memorial and opened in 1922. The high school was completed in 1939, but was immediately used as a wartime hospital and didn't take its first pupils until 1946.

Holy Isle is seen from the bouldery shore on the way back to the village of Lamlash

WALK 6

Sithein and The Ross

Start/Finish	Pier, Lamlash (NS 029 313)
Distance	12.5km (7¾ miles)
Total ascent	480m (1575ft)
Time	4hrs
Terrain	Roads, forest tracks and paths on lower slopes, but also pathless upland moorland where good navigation is required.
Refreshments	Plenty of choice in Lamlash.

Sithein, also known as Sheeans, or the Fairy Hills, display rounded humps rising above Glenrickard Forest. They are usually climbed from Cnoc na Dail, but this walk starts down in Lamlash. There is a trodden path through the forest above Cnoc na Dail, but the higher moorlands are exposed and bear only vague and intermittent paths, where walking is not particularly recommended in poor visibility. The ascent of Sithein can be extended across the moors, around the head of Glen Benlister, to The Ross. A steep and rugged descent finishes with a road-walk back into Lamlash.

Start from the pier in **Lamlash** and follow the main road as if for Brodick. Turn left uphill from a road junction, then an old milestone might be noticed on the left just after passing mobile homes on Park Avenue. Lamlash Golf Club and its café lie to the right of the road at the top edge of the village. The pavement on the left-hand side of the road runs out shortly afterwards, but a fine path has been constructed between the road and an adjacent field. Look back to see Holy Isle completely filling Lamlash Bay.

Later, the path crosses a footbridge and passes alongside a clear-felled and replanted forest on the slopes of **Meall Buidhe**. Drift slightly away from the road and later reach a small car park and picnic area at Cnoc na Dail, at 114m (374ft).

The trig point on the highest of the rounded hills at Sithein

Walk past a barrier gate and turn right at a junction of forest tracks, as signposted for Glen Cloy. The track crosses two culverted streams. At the second of these, look carefully on the left to spot a vague path rising upstream. Although the path is vague at first, it becomes clearer later. The surface can be grassy, mossy or stony, and it crosses the rocky bed of another small burn, where a white-topped marker post stands. The path climbs alongside the burn and is muddy in places, crossing over a well-vegetated forest ride, where there is another marker post. Keep climbing to reach yet another marker post at an intersection of forest rides.

Turn right along a grassy, heathery and boggy forest ride, later passing two old marker posts at the edge of the forest. Ahead lies deep heather with barely any trodden paths, so head straight up the rugged moorland slope, passing a few widely spaced marker posts. A final short, steep climb leads to a trig point on top of **Sithein** at 373m (1224ft). There are views over Brodick Bay and Lamlash Bay, as well as the mountainous northern Arran and the rugged hump of Holy Isle.

To continue beyond Sithein, cross a small, heathery gap, then either climb a neighbouring summit bearing a cairn, or pass it on its left-hand side to reach a broader gap beyond. The line of an old fence is passed on the next ascent. The aim is to drift left and keep high, contouring across a rugged moorland slope at around 350m (1150ft), while heading roughly southwards. By all means follow any vaguely trodden paths that might be encountered, but leave them the moment they head in the wrong direction. There are areas of tough heather, tussocky grass and boggy patches. Eventually, descend into a broad hollow in the moorland to cross a small burn, around 270m (885ft), before it breaks into a series of waterfalls at the head of **Benlister Glen**.

Once across the burn, climb straight up the heathery slope, still heading southwards, but then swing to the left to gain a broad crest of grass and heather, just short of 300m (985ft). Head eastwards, towards **The Ross**, which appears to stand directly in front of Holy Isle in the view ahead.

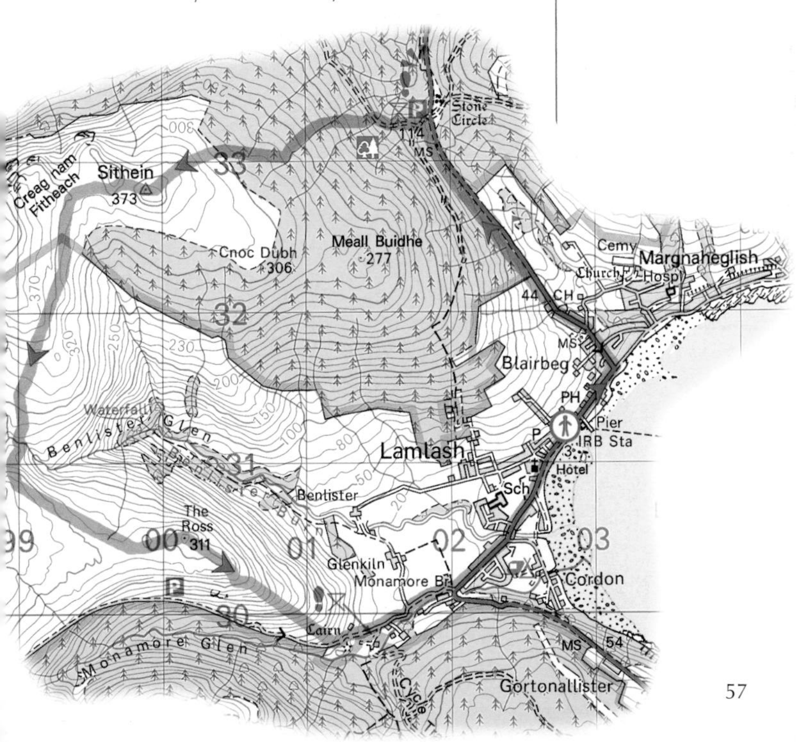

The broad crest is boggy in places, and there are some very vague paths. A short ascent on heather leads to a small summit cairn in a patch of short grass at 311m (1020ft). Enjoy the views one last time before the descent. ◀

Holy Isle fills Lamlash Bay, Tighvein sprawls to the south, the dome of Beinn Bhreac lies west, while the jagged peaks of northern Arran stretch from Beinn Nuis to Goatfell.

The descent starts along the heathery crest of The Ross, passing another small cairn. Continue downhill more steeply on heather and grass, reaching bracken on the lower slopes. A vaguely trodden path leads down to the road, but it is easily lost in the denser bracken towards the end. As there are also gorse bushes on the lower slopes, extra care is needed. Aim just to the right of a house seen at the foot of the slope. Once the road has been reached, turn left to follow it past the house and across a cattle grid, then pass the access road for the forest walks at Dyemill. Continue past the Arran Fine Foods factory to reach a junction at a bend on the main road.

Turn left along the main road, and if a bus comes along the road, by all means use it to return through **Lamlash**. If not, then walk along the road, later switching to a fine grassy strip between the road and the shore, to return to the pier.

LAMLASH

Practically all the shops and businesses in Lamlash are passed on the walk from the Arran Fine Foods factory to the pier. Facilities from south to north include: the fire station, Middleton Caravan and Camping Park, police station, Arran High School, a bakery/take-away, medical centre, coastguard and tennis court.

The long coastal green passes the parish church, Co-op store, Lamlash Bay Hotel, a shop called Ship House, with the Lamlash Garage behind. The post office is located at one end of a terrace of estate cottages, with a memorial to the Arran Clearances in front.

Next comes the Glenisle Hotel Bistro, Lilybank, Ivybank and Carraig Mhor B&Bs, Redhouse Pharmacy and the Made in Arran crafts and tearoom. Clustered around the pier are a car park, play area, Pierhead Tavern, Old Pier Café, toilets, Johnston's Marine Stores, Lifeboat Station, Arran Yacht Club, Holy Isle Ferry and Stonewater House B&B. Just beyond lie a couple of gift shops, the Lamlash Bowling Club and The Drift Inn.

WALK 7

Lamlash to Brodick

Start	Pier, Lamlash (NS 029 313)
Finish	Ferry terminal, Brodick (NS 022 359)
Distance	6.5km (4 miles)
Total ascent	200m (655ft)
Time	2hrs
Terrain	Roads and easy forest paths tracks.
Refreshments	Plenty of choice in Lamlash and Brodick.

One of the busiest roads on Arran is the one linking Brodick and Lamlash, crossing a forested gap in the Clauchland Hills at Cnoc na Dail. This was never a road that could be recommended for walking, but good paths have been created parallel to the road, and these can be linked with old and new paths running through the Fairy Glen. An easy and pleasant walk can be enjoyed from Lamlash to Brodick, or vice-versa, keeping safely away from the traffic. Clear-felling has opened up fine views of the northern mountains of Arran. Original woodland in the Fairy Glen has been spared the forester's axe, and a large area has become the Roots of Arran Community Woodland.

Start from the pier in **Lamlash** and follow the main road as if for Brodick. Turn left uphill from a road junction,

Cnoc na Dail is the highest part of the route between Lamlash and Brodick

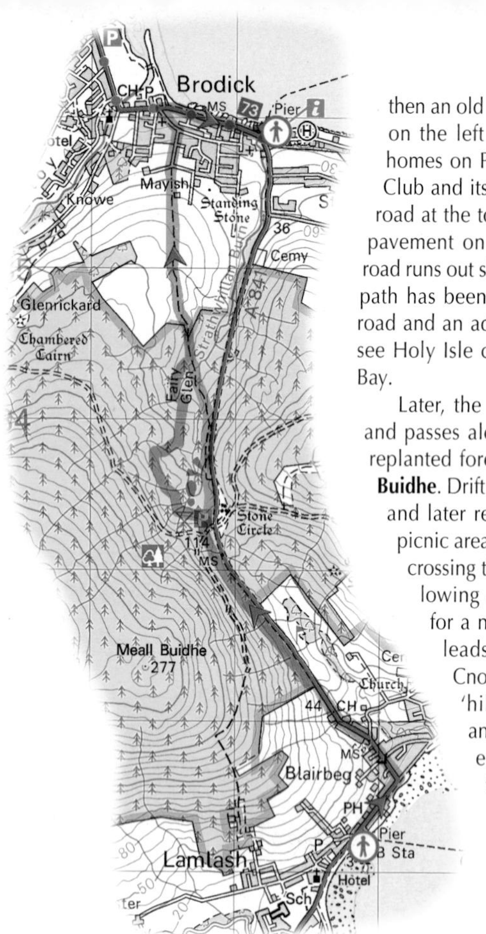

then an old milestone might be noticed on the left just after passing mobile homes on Park Avenue. Lamlash Golf Club and its café lie to the right of the road at the top edge of the village. The pavement on the left-hand side of the road runs out shortly afterwards, but a fine path has been constructed between the road and an adjacent field. Look back to see Holy Isle completely filling Lamlash Bay.

Later, the path crosses a footbridge and passes alongside a clear-felled and replanted forest on the slopes of **Meall Buidhe**. Drift slightly away from the road and later reach a small car park and picnic area at 114m (374ft). It is worth crossing the road, and instead of following a broad forest track, look for a narrow path nearby, which leads to a **stone circle** called Cnoc na Dail. The name means 'hill of the meeting place', and is reputedly where crofters would meet regularly in the past to discuss matters of common concern.

Come back across the road and continue the walk in one of two ways. If in a hurry to return to Brodick, simply turn right as signposted and follow a path parallel to the main road, passing through a car park where there is a view indicator, then turn left to continue downhill, crossing two footbridges in the **Fairy Glen**. With more time to spare, however, it is worth following a more convoluted path, leaving a nearby car park, twisting and turning across a clear-felled and replanted forest slope, eventually joining the direct path further downhill

Looking back along the woodland path to the forested gap at Cnoc na Dail

as it leaves the Fairy Glen. There are other spur and loop paths that might also be followed if desired. ▸

The paths have been created by Roots of Arran Community Woodland volunteers.

Follow the main path onwards as it rises a little through a wooden area and an open area of heather, around 90m (295ft), crossing two gentle crests. Go through a gate and follow a track downhill, passing wooded areas and small fields. Walk straight through an intersection with another track at **Mayish** and follow a quiet road down past the Glenartney guest house. Turn left at a road junction to follow Alma Road down past the Brodick Bar and post office, to reach a junction with the main coastal road in **Brodick**. Simply turn right and follow the promenade running parallel to the road, passing through a pleasant coastal green to return to the bus station and ferry terminal. ▸

For a list of facilities along the road through Brodick, see Walk 1.

WALK 8

Holy Isle from Lamlash

Start/Finish	North Jetty, Holy Isle (NS 053 309)
Distance	7km (4½ miles)
Total ascent	350m (1150ft)
Time	2hrs 30mins
Terrain	A rugged hill path, followed by a clear, level, easy coastal path.
Refreshments	Boathouse on Holy Isle. Plenty of choice in Lamlash.

Holy Isle is inhabited by a Buddhist community, who have designated it as a sacred space. Access to the island is actively encouraged, but visitors should respect the wishes of the community. Smoking, alcohol, drugs, pets and sound systems are not permitted, and there is no access to the eastern part of the island, which is maintained as a nature reserve and refuge for rare breeds, such as Soay sheep, Saanen goats and Eriskay ponies. Tens of thousands of trees have been planted, mostly in the north.

A ferry from Lamlash serves a jetty at the northern end of the island. Walkers usually climb along the crest of the island to the summit of Mullach Mòr, then descend southwards. They return northwards using a clear, level coastal path, brightened with interesting and intricate rock paintings, passing a cave inhabited for 20 years by St Molaise.

HOLY ISLE FERRY

The Holy Isle Ferry generally operates daily from May to September, running hourly between 10am and 5pm. However, the service is dependent on tidal and weather conditions, as well as public demand, and sailing times should be checked in advance. The crossing generally takes only 10 minutes. Spring and autumn services run at a reduced level, while winter services need to be arranged with the ferryman, tel 01770 600998, 01770 600463, mobile 07970 771960, or check at the ferry kiosk on the pier at Lamlash. Sailings around Holy Isle and fishing trips are also available if booked in advance.

View from Mullach Beag, across Lamlash Bay to Goatfell

The ferry departs from the pier at Lamlash, serving a floating jetty at the northern end of **Holy Isle**. An island resident usually meets the ferry and welcomes visitors ashore. If any specific information about the island and its community is required, this is a good time to ask. Information is also available at the nearby Boathouse, as well as basic refreshments. There is a map-board of the island, while eight white stupas lead the eye to a large building serving as the Centre for World Peace and Health.

Start walking by keeping well to the left of the centre, walking straight up a grassy slope, following a fence beside a young woodland plantation. A decorative plaque states 'to the top', unless you are coming the other way, in which case another one states 'to the ferry'. Cross a stile at a gap in a drystone wall and follow a winding path up a wooded slope. Cross a stile over a fence at a higher level to reach open slopes beyond.

Take care following the path uphill at first, but it becomes clearer later, with grass and bracken giving way to heather. The high mountains of northern Arran begin to rise above the low, forested rise of the Clauchland Hills. On a higher shoulder, Whiting Bay and the pyramidal island of Ailsa Craig appear in view. The path is narrow, but clearly trodden. It rises more steeply up a slope of heather, wrinkled boulders and outcrops of rock. The top of **Mullach Beag** bears a cairn at 246m (807ft) and offers fine views around both Lamlash and Whiting Bay, while ahead the taller Mullach Mòr beckons.

A short descent in two stages leads to a gap in the middle of the island. The path climbs steeply and hands might be needed in some places for balance, although there are plenty of good holds. An easier stretch of path continues to the highest point on the island, **Mullach Mòr**, where a trig point stands at 314m (1030ft). Prayer flags might be fluttering all around it. The summit ridge is fairly narrow and composed of grass, heather, bilberry and rocky outcrops. ◂

Views include Holy Isle, the forests and moors of southern Arran, the mountains of northern Arran, a good stretch of the Clyde and its hinterland, as well as the pyramidal island of Ailsa Craig.

The path runs roughly southwards, needing care as it descends more and more steeply on **Creag Liath** on worn, broken rock. On a gentler shoulder, beware of dark, deep, narrow fissures in the rock, staying strictly on the path as indicated by lengths of rope. Note a small house on the hillside to the right, which is inhabited by the Lama Yeshe Losal Rinpoche on his visits to the island. Smaller cabins are used for long-term retreats. The path descends one more rounded, heathery ridge, suddenly joining a clearer path in an area of bracken.

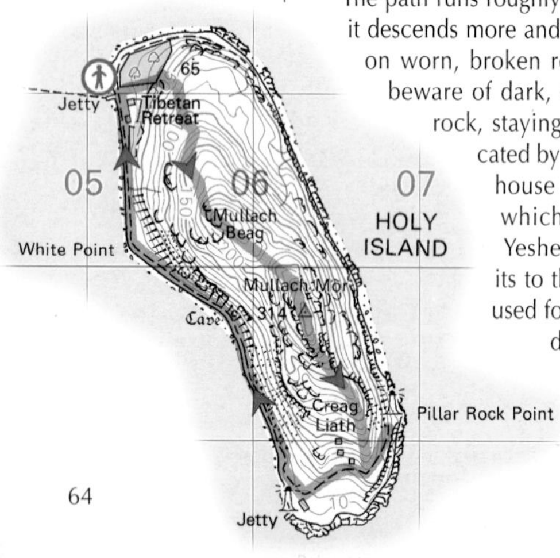

Prayer flags catch the breeze on the summit of Mullach Mòr

Turn left at this point to visit the square **Pillar Rock** lighthouse, although there is no further access, so steps have to be retraced. The path approaches another lighthouse and the former lighthouse keeper's cottages, but this is now a long-term women's retreat centre, with no access to visitors, and no disturbance should be caused. The buildings face Kingscross Point, across the narrowest strait between Holy Isle and the Isle of Arran.

Follow a grassy path as directed, through bracken, running roughly northwards from the lighthouse. The path is obvious, and it is accompanied by poles carrying electricity from one end of the island to the other. While following the path, keep an eye open to the right, to spot a number of splendid rock paintings. These were created by an artist called Dekyi Wangmo, working to a series of traditional Tibetan designs. The path becomes slightly more rugged as it turns around a bay fringed with a few trees. Steps on the right climb to a **cave** at the base of a cliff, once inhabited by St Molaise.

'Green Tara' is one of a series of Tibetan rock paintings on Holy Isle

ST MOLAISE

The most notable saint on Arran was St Molaise, who was born in the year 566. He lived as a hermit in this cave on Holy Isle for 20 years. His Judgement Seat and Healing Spring are nearby, and a ladle is provided for those who wish to taste the water. Molaise later became the Abbot of Leithglinn in Ireland and died in the year 639. Holy Isle was previously known as Eilean Molaise in his honour.

The path is smooth and level as it turns round the shingle of **White Point**. It is surfaced in short grass and runs through an area of bracken that has been planted with young trees. The Boathouse can be visited for basic refreshment or shelter while waiting for the ferry. Although the Centre for World Peace and Health isn't available for visiting, part of the adjacent Mandala Garden can be explored. Abundant information about the Holy Isle is available, and donations can be made to assist the work being carried out on the island.

HOLY ISLE PROJECT

Resdents of Holy Isle include Tibetan Buddhist monks, nuns and lay people, as well as people of other faiths and volunteers helping with conservation or construction work. As the island has been designated as a sacred space, residents observe five Golden Rules:

- to respect life and refrain from killing
- to respect other people's property and refrain from stealing
- to speak the truth and refrain from lying
- to encourage health and refrain from intoxicants
- to respect others and refrain from sexual activity that causes harm

The Centre for World Peace and Health is located at the northern end of the island. A variety of inter-faith and meditation courses are offered, along with accommodation and vegetarian meals. The nearby Boathouse offers basic refreshment, gifts and information. The Inner Light Retreat at the southern end of the island offers long-term retreats, traditionally lasting for three years and three months, and visitors should cause no disturbance nearby. A conservation project involves bracken control, tree planting and the development of a nature reserve on the eastern side of the island. Rare animal breeds, several species of birds and abundant wild flowers may also be spotted. For more information, tel 01770 601100, www.holyisland.org

WALK 9

Tighvein and Monamore Glen

Start/Finish	Dyemill car park, Monamore Glen (NS 015 297)
Distance	10km (6¼ miles)
Total ascent	490m (1605ft)
Time	3hrs
Terrain	Clear forest tracks and paths at first, followed by rugged, pathless moorlands, requiring careful navigation, finishing along a road.
Refreshments	None closer than Lamlash.

All walks on the flanks of Tighvein are rough and tough as there are very few trodden paths across the high moorlands. However, a waymarked forest trail runs from the Dyemill car park near Lamlash to the lonely moorland pool of Urie Loch. The loch is only a short walk from the summit of Tighvein, so the waymarked trail offers the easiest approach. Finding a way off the summit of Tighvein is reserved for those who can navigate competently across featureless moorlands, especially in mist. There is a route running roughly northwards across Cnoc Dubh and Garbh Bheinn that allows a descent to the head of Monamore Glen without grappling too much through forest plantations.

This walk starts at the Dyemill car park, off The Ross road. Whether arriving from Lamlash or Whiting Bay on the main coastal road, watch for a minor road signposted for 'Sliddery via Ross'. The turning looks like the entrance to the Arran Fine Foods factory, as the factory buildings occupy both sides of the road. The road later passes the Dyemill Lodges, then a turning on the left is signposted as a cycleway to Kilmory, and a forest road quickly reaches a grassy car park and picnic area at the foot of **Monamore Glen**. ◂

If arriving by bus from Lamlash or Whiting Bay, the Dyemill car park lies 1km (½ mile) from the main road.

Leave the car park and cross a bridge over Monamore Burn. The forest road is used as a **cycle trail**, so turn right along a path. A stout marker post indicates the

'Lagaville Walks' and 'Urie Loch'. Follow a path upstream and cross a footbridge over a smaller burn. Turn left and continue upstream, passing oak, birch and other trees, which contrast with the clear-felled and replanted forest alongside. Climb a few steps and reach a bench and path junction. A footbridge on the left overlooks a small waterfall in a rocky gorge. Don't cross the footbridge, which only offers a rapid return to the car park, but keep right to follow the other path, as marked for 'Urie Loch'.

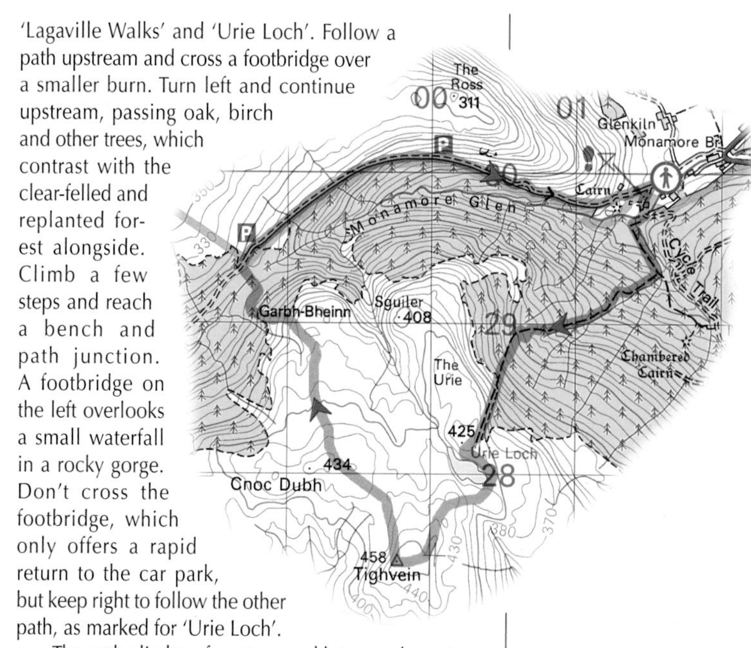

The path climbs a few steps and later reaches a junction where there is a marker post. The slope has been clear-felled and replanted, and the path pulls away from the burn for a while, then runs close to it briefly later. At a higher level, some parts can be quite wet and muddy underfoot, but one part is worn to its red sandstone bedrock. After climbing through denser forest, following a forest ride, there is a sudden view along another forest ride that reveals Holy Isle. Further uphill, a marker post is passed as the path leaves the forest, continuing along its upper edge below the rugged slopes of Creag na h-Ennie.

Continue walking over a crest on squelchy moorland near the 425m (1395ft) summit of **The Urie**. The path passes a couple of boulders and runs down to the boggy shore of **Urie Loch**. This is the end of the trodden path, and anyone whose navigation is not up to scratch should consider retracing steps to the Dyemill car park.

Those who can navigate confidently across bleak and pathless moorlands can continue onwards. Turn left to follow the shore, then climb roughly south-west, but feel free to change course slightly in order to maintain height and exploit the easiest terrain underfoot. The summit of **Tighvein** might not be seen until at close quarters, but it bears both a large cairn and white-painted trig point at 458m (1502ft). Views of the immediate surroundings embrace rugged, rolling moorlands, which can be explored further with reference to Walk 10 and Walk 17. Northwards, the higher mountains of Arran are well displayed.

Leave the summit of Tighvein by heading roughly northwards. There is only a short, steep slope before the gradient eases, then gradually swing roughly north-west towards the broad moorland rise of **Cnoc Dubh**, around 430m (1410ft). The heather moorland is broken by occasional grassy areas, with a few small boulders poking through, and there are many channels of squelchy sphagnum moss. Side-step the channels where possible, or take care crossing them, while forging roughly northwards. The only feature along the way is a stand of two or three

Dark and foreboding at times, sprawling moorlands surround Tighvein's summit

trees that have somehow 'escaped' from nearby forests. Swing north-west onto the broad top of **Garbh-Bheinn**, where the moorland slope overlooks forest plantations at the top of The Ross road.

Spend a few moments carefully studying the steep, heathery slope to spot a solitary marker post. Pass this and walk down a sudden short, steep slope to the edge of the forest. There is a gap between the trees where a trodden path can be followed, quickly leading to a broad, unplanted forest ride. Turn right to follow the ride, then left to follow another ride, bearing in mind that the ground is often wet and boggy. A plastic pipe is passed, and while there might be a problem with fallen trees, get past them and a marker post will be seen beyond. Simply step up onto The Ross road and turn right to follow it across a cattle grid.

There is a parking space and picnic bench beside the road – a useful place to clean off any debris that might have accumulated while walking across the moorland and through the forest. All that remains is a simple road-walk with fine views down through the **Monamore Glen**. Most of the forest on the right has been clear-felled. At the bottom of the road, turn right to return to the Dyemill car park, or if catching a bus, keep straight ahead to return to the main road beyond Arran Fine Foods.

ARRAN FINE FOODS

There was once a water-powered meal mill at the foot of Monamore Glen. It was closed in 1967 and as it was unsafe it was demolished. The Arran Fine Foods factory occupies the same site as the old mill, and originally manufactured a range of quality mustard products. The factory went on to produce a range of fine jams, chutneys and dressings. Products can be bought from the factory shop opposite. The enterprise is now part of Paterson's – a long-established family firm famous for its production of shortbread and 'Brontë' hospitality biscuits, www.paterson-arran.com

WALK 10

Glenashdale and Urie Loch

Start/Finish Shops, Whiting Bay (NS 045 261)
Distance 17km (10½ miles)
Total ascent 620m (2035ft)
Time 5hrs 30mins
Terrain Roads, forest tracks and paths on lower slopes, but also rugged upland moorland, pathless in places, where good navigation is required.
Refreshments Plenty of choice in Whiting Bay.

A popular short walk climbs through the well-wooded Glenashdale for a fine view of the Glenashdale Falls. There are extensive forests and bleak moorlands above, where more challenging walking is available. This route climbs easily through the forest, but becomes quite difficult on the higher moorlands, linking the lonely pools of Loch na Leirg and Urie Loch. Vague vehicle tracks cross the moors, but in poor visibility careful navigation is required. The descent uses a trodden path, linking with a lengthy forest track to return to Whiting Bay. In earlier editions of this book, this route was presented as two walks, sharing a common descent from Loch na Leirg to the main forest track, but that part is now in very poor condition and is very difficult to negotiate.

Start at a huddle of small shops in **Whiting Bay** and follow the coast road southwards, passing the Coffee Pot and crossing Ashdale Bridge. Turn right as signposted for Glenashdale Falls, following a track past a few houses. After the last house there is an information board, and shortly after that, a signposted path junction. ◄ Walk straight ahead as signposted for Glenashdale Falls.

The Giants' Graves, visited on Walk 11, lie uphill to the left.

The path runs parallel to **Glenashdale Burn**, fairly level at first, then climbing as it crosses a couple of little footbridges on the steep, well-wooded slopes. The woods are pleasantly mixed and mossy, then a few wooden steps are followed by a longer flight of wooden steps. A

remarkable wooden-decked, securely fenced viewpoint allows a splendid view of the **Glenashdale Falls**.

GLENASHDALE FALLS

Glenashdale was well wooded long before the Forestry Commission planted the higher slopes with conifers. The walk to Glenashdale Falls has always been a popular choice for a short, scenic stroll (see Walk 11). The best time to view the waterfalls is of course after a spell of wet weather. A short and a long fall plunge gracefully into a deep, wooded gorge.

Admire the waterfall, then cross another little footbridge, reach a path junction and turn left. The path quickly joins a broad forest track. Turn right and follow the track, which soon crosses a bridge over **Glenashdale Burn**. Follow the track up to a junction with another track, and turn left as signposted for Kilmory. ◀ Keep to the track as it climbs gradually higher, passing close to a huddle of wooden huts at Cloud Base – a remote outdoor site for groups of young people. The track rises gently around the slopes of **Cnoc Mor**, which are partly forested and partly clear-felled. When the track levels out, it passes above a small fenced-off **waterfall**.

The track is used as a forest cycleway from the Dyemill to Kilmory.

Leave the track and follow the burn called **Allt Dhepin** upstream. A substantial strip has been left unplanted, and while a path has been constructed, water and boggy ground are creeping onto it. On reaching the edge of the forest the path expires on rugged moorland. Turn right and head roughly north-east, away from the the forest, climbing a rugged heathery slope. Look out for a small cairn on a heathery rise, over 320m (1050ft), where there is a view of the lonely moorland pool of **Loch na Leirg**.

Loch na Leirg is a lonely pool on the slopes of Tighvein

Urie Loch occupies a moorland hollow on the sprawling slopes of Tighvein

There are two ways to link Loch na Leirg with the distant Urie Loch, and the general direction to walk is north-west. Either aim to stay high on a broad, rugged heather moorland crest, or keep just to the left of the crest, where there are at least a couple of old grooved lines that could be followed. Choose one or the other, or switch between them, in order to find the most acceptable walking surfaces on what is essentially awkward, rugged moorland dotted with hidden holes and boggy areas. A height of 410m (1345ft) is reached before there is a view of **Urie Loch** in a broad hollow, with the mountains of northern Arran seen far beyond. ▶

An ascent of nearby Tighvein could be contemplated, with reference to Walk 9.

Keep to the right-hand side of the loch, walking along the shore while watching for a boggy path rising on the right. This passes a couple of boulders and crosses a crest on squelchy moorland near the 425m (1395ft) summit of **The Urie**. The path descends across a slope beneath the rugged Creag na h'Ennie, reaching the edge of an extensive forest and passing a marker post. The path runs down an unplanted forest ride, losing views, apart from one sudden view along another forest ride that reveals Holy Isle.

Follow the path downhill, bearing in mind that some parts can be quite wet and muddy underfoot, but one part is worn to its red sandstone bedrock. The path runs close to a burn, then pulls away from it, then drifts back towards it, while descending a clear-felled and replanted slope. Go past a path junction where there's a marker post, then down a few steps, reaching another path junction and a bench. ◂

Follow the path downstream to reach the Dyemill car park, The Ross road, the main road near Lamlash and bus services.

Turn right to cross a footbridge that overlooks a small waterfall. Keep right to follow the path and soon cross another footbridge. A clear path climbs, later swinging right to pass around a small pond. Looking across a valley, a forest track is used as a **cycle trail**. Watch carefully on the clear-felled slope to spot a marker for 'Lagaville Village'.

LAGAVILLE

Lagaville was a poor clachan that was inhabited until the late 19th century. It was cleared, with a few of the inhabitants being re-housed in Lamlash, while others emigrated to Canada. Only a few low, mossy, tumbled walls remain, hidden deep in the undergrowth. A monument on a green at Lamlash commemorates the Arran Clearances.

Follow the path across a concrete footbridge and rise across the clear-felled slopes. A junction is reached

Three upright stones mark the chambered cairn of Meallach's Grave

where a short detour is recommended up to the right. A clear path climbs steeply for no more than 30m (100ft), reaching the **chambered cairn** of Meallach's Grave. Little remains of this ancient Clyde cairn, apart from three tall stones. Walk back downhill and follow the path to join a nearby forest road at **Lag an Daer**.

The forest road is broad and clear, offering easy walking as it rises, falls to cross a burn, then rises again to reach a quarry around 160m (525ft). At this point, a signpost points straight ahead for Whiting Bay, which is a long way to go, and left for 'Hawthorne', which is a quicker way to finish. So, turn left and walk down the narrow, stony track, which can be muddy in places. It suddenly bends left and lands on a tarmac road beside **Hawthorne Farm**. Turn right and the tarmac quickly gives way to a dirt road, passing a waterfall on the way to a farm at **Knockenkelly**. An odd-looking modern timber-clad building is passed at **North Kiscadale**, and once the dirt road descends steeply it becomes a tarmac road before landing beside the little shops back in **Whiting Bay**.

WHITING BAY

Whiting Bay is a long and straggly village with two distinct halves separated by a gap. Starting at the northern end of the village is the church of St Margaret of Scotland, Sandbraes Holiday Park and Sandbraes Park. Along the main road are the Whiting Bay Garage, Bay Stores, Trafalgar Restaurant, Arran Brewery Guest House, Burlington Guest House, Royal Arran Hotel, Whiting Bay Primary School and St Columba's Old Church.

After a gap comes the southern half of the village, featuring the MBS diesel pump/garden centre/home improvements, Coast café, Bay News and toilets. These are followed by the post office, chemist, Village Shop, village hall, putting green, Arran Art Gallery/County Carpets, Corriedoon Care Home, Eden Lodge Hotel, Bowling Club, Coffee Pot restaurant, Belford Mill and the access road for Viewbank Guest House and Whiting Bay Golf Course. At the southern end of the village is the Whiting Bay Surgery, Ashdale Bridge and a mobile home park.

WALK 11

Glenashdale Falls and Giants' Graves

Start/Finish	Coffee Pot, Whiting Bay (NS 046 256)
Distance	6km (3¾ miles)
Total ascent	250m (820ft)
Time	2hrs
Terrain	Easy roads, forest tracks and paths.
Refreshments	Plenty of choice in Whiting Bay.

A popular, short, circular walk runs around Glenashdale from Whiting Bay. The aim is to visit Glenashdale Falls, which is highly recommended after a spell of heavy rain, when the waterfalls are at their most powerful. There are two approaches to the falls, and the one used here climbs along a road and track. Walk 10 approaches the falls along a riverside path, which could be used instead. Either way, a broad forest track is used at a higher level to reach the Giants' Graves. This archaeological site was once hidden in dense forest but has been exposed by clear-felling and equipped with a zigzag path offering a fine descent.

Start by the Coffee Pot restaurant at the southern end of **Whiting Bay**, where a public footpath signpost points up a road, indicating the way to Glenashdale Falls and a golf course. The road climbs, turns right and left,

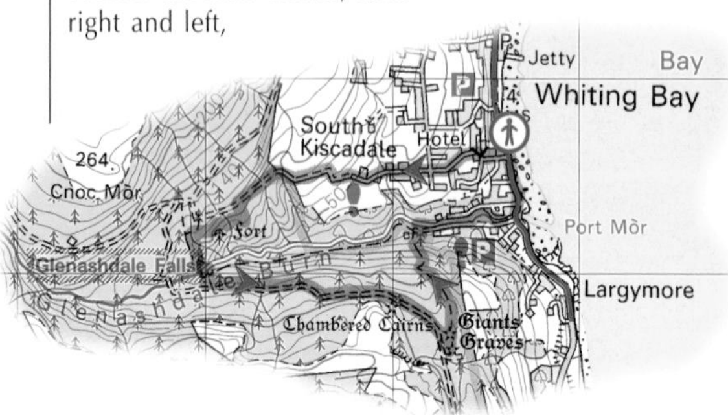

climbs further uphill and reaches a crossroads. Continue straight ahead and the road rises slightly, then descends to pass some cottages beside a burn, where a notice before a bench invites visitors to 'rest awhile'.

The road climbs further and becomes a track, which later runs through fields and enters a forest. The forest track rises gradually, then a path is signposted on the left. Follow the path downhill into the forest, and a spur leads straight ahead to a small viewpoint where there is a distant view of Glenashdale Falls. The surrounding woodlands are pleasantly mixed. Double back a short way and continue along the winding path, which soon reaches a clearing where there is an Iron Age **fort** and an information board.

The path continues winding through the forest, crossing a small burn, then descending to a picnic bench where a footbridge spans **Glenashdale Burn**. Cross the bridge and keep left, passing a path junction and a fenced viewpoint. Walk down the path a little further, reaching a remarkable wooden-decked, securely fenced viewpoint allowing a splendid view of the **Glenashdale Falls**.

GLENASHDALE FALLS

Glenashdale was well wooded long before the Forestry Commission planted the higher slopes with conifers. The walk to Glenashdale Falls has always been a popular choice for a short, scenic stroll. The best time to view the waterfalls is of course after a spell of wet weather. A short and a long fall plunge gracefully into a deep, wooded gorge.

Admire the waterfall, then double back up the path and turn left at the path junction. This quickly leads up to a signpost beside a broad forest track. Turn left as signposted for the Giants' Graves and simply follow the track as it rises across a clear-felled and replanted slope. Keep walking until a clear path heads off to the left, and keep left to reach some large stone-built structures known as the **Giants' Graves**.

Glenashdale Falls is best seen from a specially built viewing platform

GIANTS' GRAVES

The Giants' Graves stand high above Whiting Bay, and since the surrounding forest was clear-felled they have enjoyed a fine outlook. The remains are 'horned gallery graves', also known as 'Clyde' constructions. They are believed to have been used for the burial of people of close kinship in early Neolithic times, with the bodies being placed into stone chambers, which were then covered by large cairns. The 'horns' are the upright stones flanking the entrances to the graves, creating a semi-circular forecourt, which may have been a place where burial rituals were performed. There is an information board to study.

Pass the information board to start following a path gently downhill. As the slope steepens, the path zigzags back and forth. Many years ago, the path was more direct and featured over 300 steps! At the bottom of the slope, turn right at a path junction and pass an information board explaining about Glenashdale. Continue along a track, passing a few houses, then turn left along the main coastal road and cross Ashdale Bridge. The road quickly leads back to the Coffee Pot restaurant.

WHITING BAY

Human habitation dates back thousands of years around Whiting Bay. The Giants' Graves are early Neolithic and their construction suggests that there were communities in the area accustomed to working well together. At Kingscross there is a Viking burial mound. The area also has its share of stories concerning Robert the Bruce. He is said to have waited at Kingscross to see a signal lit on the Ayrshire coast, heralding his long and bitter campaign to gain the Scottish crown. Two large farmsteads called Knockenkelly and Auchencairn, above Whiting Bay, paid rent directly to the king for centuries. The main road around the bay dates only from 1843, and there was once a pier built out into the bay, later demolished, where tourists were brought in by boats and transferred to wagonettes. To this day the village has a range of accommodation. Facilities in the village, from north to south, are listed at the end of Walk 10.

WALK 12

Lamlash and Kingscross

Start/Finish	Lamlash Parish Church (NS 026 309)
Distance	13km (8 miles)
Total ascent	380m (1245ft)
Time	4hrs
Terrain	A rugged shore walk, impassable at high water, gives way to easier paths, forest tracks and roads. One path is often very muddy.
Refreshments	Plenty of choice in Lamlash and just off-route in Whiting Bay.

The sheltered waters of Lamlash Bay are well protected by the mountain-like mass of Holy Isle. Many visitors to Lamlash enjoy a stroll along the grassy ribbon that runs around the bay between the road and shore. Some must wonder if they could walk any further, but there is no coastal path to Kingscross, only a steep slope of tangled woodland. There are, however, patches of grass and shingle beaches along the shore that are rough underfoot, but if the tide is out for the duration of the walk, there is no problem covering the distance between Lamlash and Kingscross. This is all part of the Arran Coastal Way. Once Kingscross Point is reached walkers can come ashore, visit a Viking grave site, then make their way to Whiting Bay. From there a wet and muddy path climbs into extensive forest and a return is made to Lamlash on a broad and clear forest track.

Start at the parish church in **Lamlash** and walk south along the broad coastal green. When the green runs out, cross a minor road beside a tennis court and follow a gravel path flanked by hedges, signposted for Cordon and the Coastal Way. Cross a footbridge over Benlister Burn and note the view of Holy Isle seen beyond the river mouth. The path continues between masses of gorse bushes to reach another minor road. Turn left along the road and cross a bridge over Monamore Burn, passing houses in the little settlement of **Cordon**. ◂

A coastal path is planned beyond Cordon, but it wasn't in place at the time of writing, so watch for new waymarks

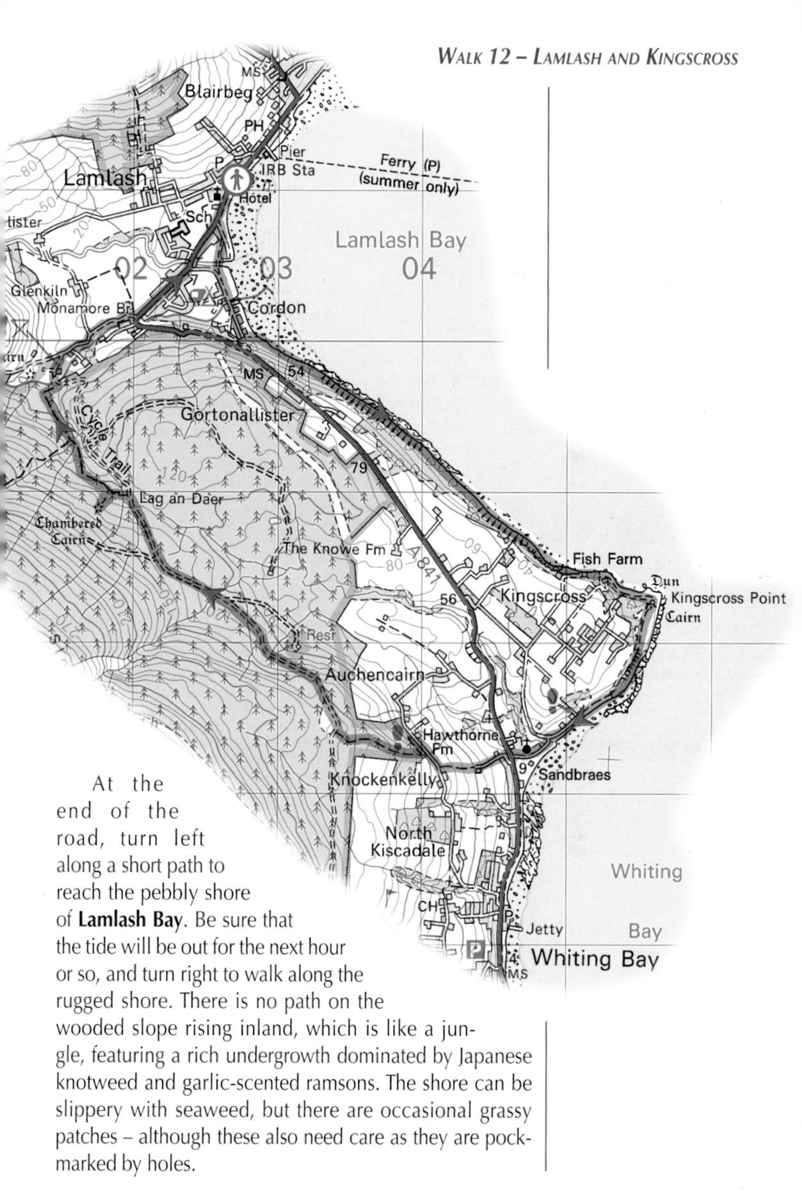

At the end of the road, turn left along a short path to reach the pebbly shore of **Lamlash Bay**. Be sure that the tide will be out for the next hour or so, and turn right to walk along the rugged shore. There is no path on the wooded slope rising inland, which is like a jungle, featuring a rich undergrowth dominated by Japanese knotweed and garlic-scented ramsons. The shore can be slippery with seaweed, but there are occasional grassy patches – although these also need care as they are pockmarked by holes.

The low, rocky shores of Lamlash Bay and the view north towards Goatfell

Step ashore briefly onto an access road running to a slipway that serves a **fish farm**. The beach can be followed onwards, but there is also a network of paths around the rocky **Kingscross Point**. Look for the remains of a Viking fort on the point.

KINGSCROSS POINT

Vikings were active around the Isle of Arran from about AD800, and eventually suffered defeat at the Battle of Largs in 1263. On that occasion, the Norse fleet was moored in Lamlash Bay ahead of the battle. Arran and many other islands held by the Norse were sold to Alexander III of Scotland in 1266. The remains of a Viking fort can be studied on Kingscross Point, and other Viking burial sites are known in the area.

Head inland from the point, rising gently through a mown grassy area, overlooking the waters of **Whiting Bay**. Further uphill, a path head left, back down to the shore. Walk along the pebbly beach, passing a huddle of buildings, and continue until it is possible to come ashore onto a track and minor road serving a row of houses.

Eventually, the road passes the church of St Margaret of Scotland and **Sandbraes Park** to reach the main road at the northern end of the village of **Whiting Bay**. At this point it is possible to follow the road into the village, or catch a bus back to Lamlash. ▸

For a list of facilities in Whiting Bay, see the end of Walk 10.

To continue this walk, cross the main road and follow the narrow road signposted uphill for Knockenkelly. The road becomes a track and the track becomes a path. Note that the path may be overgrown, and is prone to carrying water, so it can also be muddy underfoot. It joins a clear track near the farm of **Knockenkelly**. The farm lies to the left, but turn right to follow the track, passing a waterfall, to join a tarmac road at **Hawthorne Farm**. Turn sharp left up an old track signposted 'Forest Path'. This quickly swings right as it climbs, and the stony surface can be muddy in places. It joins a broad forest road beside a quarry, around 160m (525ft).

A signpost points back to Hawthorne, and left for Whiting Bay, but turn right to follow the forest road towards Lamlash, which isn't signposted. The forest road is broad and clear, offering easy walking as it descends to cross a burn, then rises and descends again to **Lag an Daer**. ▸

The forest road, which is also used as a cycle trail, can be followed onwards, directly to the Dyemill car park.

Turn left along a path signposted for Meallach's Grave. When a junction is reached, a short detour is recommended up to the right. A clear path climbs steeply for no more than 30m (100ft), reaching the **chambered cairn** of Meallach's Grave. Little remains of this ancient Clyde cairn, apart from three tall stones. Walk back downhill and follow the path onwards, later crossing a concrete footbridge. Watch carefully on the clear-felled slope to spot a marker for 'Lagaville Village'.

LAGAVILLE

Lagaville was a poor clachan that was inhabited until the late 19th century. It was cleared, with a few of the inhabitants being re-housed in Lamlash, while others emigrated to Canada. Only a few low, mossy, tumbled walls remain, hidden deep in the undergrowth. A monument on a green at Lamlash commemorates the Arran Clearances.

Follow the path downhill and around a small pond, then continue into a valley and cross a footbridge. The path quickly leads to another footbridge overlooking a waterfall, followed by a path junction and a bench. ◂ Turn right and follow the path downstream, passing oak, birch and other trees. Cross a footbridge and follow the path back to the forest road. Turn left to cross a bridge over Monamore Burn, then pass the Dyemill car park and picnic area at the foot of **Monamore Glen**.

The path climbing left is Walk 9 to Urie Loch.

Follow the forest road to The Ross road and turn right to pass the Dyemill Lodges. The road later passes the Arran Fine Foods factory to reach a bend on the main road. Turn left to follow the road back to **Lamlash**, and if a bus is due, feel free to catch it to shorten the journey back to the parish church. ◂

For a list of facilities in Lamlash, see the end of Walk 6, and for further information about the village, see the end of Walk 5.

The forest track from which you can visit Meallach's Grave

WALK 13

Eas Mòr and Loch Garbad

Start/Finish	Car park, Eas Mòr (NS 019 217)
Distance	5km (3 miles)
Total ascent	200m (655ft)
Time	1hr 30mins
Terrain	Easy forest paths throughout.
Refreshments	None closer than Kildonan.

This short and easy walk visits the splendid waterfall of Eas Mòr, which makes it an ideal walk after a prolonged spell of heavy rain. The path is a relatively new addition to the network on Arran, and surfaces are generally firm, dry and easy throughout. Although the full walk is short, it can be shortened further to a mere 1.5km (1 mile) if the intention is only to visit the waterfall. The full route follows a there-and-back path to Loch Garbad, which is frequented by fishermen. An interesting feature on the return is the 'Library' – an open shelter stocked with books and information.

Start at a car park at a road junction high above the village of Kildonan, where a decorative signboard reads 'Eas Mòr Waterfall'. ▸ An obvious track climbs from the car park, passing a map-board. At a higher level, simply keep right to follow a forest path flanked by a fence. Keep a lookout on the right to catch a couple of glimpses of **Eas Mòr** plunging over a rocky edge. The islands of Pladda and Ailsa Craig can also be seen out to sea.

Buses will stop at this junction if the driver is given due notice, because it's an awkward turn if other vehicles are also passing.

The waterfall is lost to view as the path makes its way a little further upstream, reaching a path junction. A left turn is signposted for Loch Garbad, and if this path is followed, then walkers will return to this junction later. The path is clear and obvious, heading upstream alongside the forest. It later enters the forest and bends

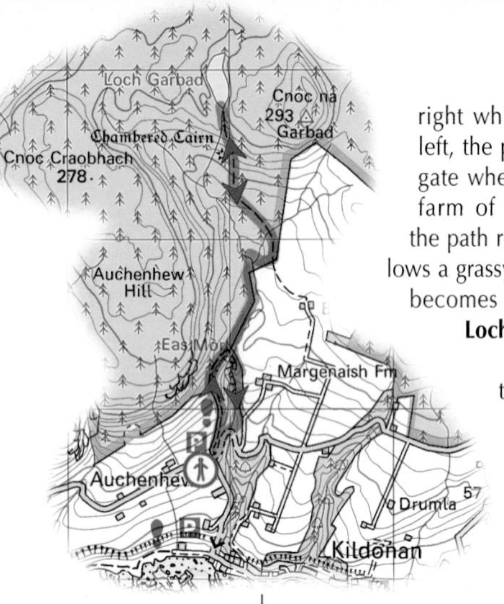

right while crossing the burn. Bending left, the path leaves the forest, passing a gate where there's access to the nearby farm of Ballymeanochglen. However, the path runs back into the forest and follows a grassy ride, which later broadens and becomes heathery, just before reaching **Loch Garbad**.

Retrace steps to the path junction near **Eas Mòr** and cross a footbridge. Another path junction is quickly reached, where a right turn runs up to a grass-roofed log cabin known as the 'Library'. Have a look inside, and take the opportunity to shelter for a while if it's raining.

THE LIBRARY

Many trees were damaged and felled after a storm in 1998. Some of them were used to build the 'Library'. A number of books are stored here, ranging from natural history to pure fantasy. Stacks of paper, pencils and crayons are available for anyone to write a comment or create a piece of artwork, leaving it for the pleasure of future visitors.

Return to the main path, which twists and turns as it descends, continuing as a track. When a junction is reached, turn right and descend to the burn, crossing it at a footbridge. Climb a wooded slope and follow the path back to the car park. Bear in mind that paths are also available across the road, descending further through the wooded valley to Kildonan.

WALK 14

Lagg to Kildonan coastal walk

Start	Lagg Hotel (NR 956 216)
Finish	Village hall, Kildonan (NR 022 210)
Distance	8.5km (5¼ miles)
Total ascent	200m (655ft)
Time	2hrs 30mins
Terrain	Rugged coastal walking. Some beach walks are boulder-strewn and some parts onshore are muddy or rugged.
Refreshments	Hotels with bar-restaurants at Lagg and Kildonan.

The southern shores of Arran offer a fine, rugged coastal walk, passing the Black Cave on Bennan Head. This linear route is part of the Arran Coastal Way and both ends of the walk have small parking spaces and bus services. It is necessary for the tide to be out to pass beneath Bennan Head, and to explore inside the Black Cave.

Start this coastal walk at **Lagg**, where the Lagg Hotel was founded in 1791. Follow the road across the river and turn right as signposted for Torrylin Cairn. A clear gravel track rises through woodland and runs along the edge of a valley. Keep right at a fork and continue along a path, which descends gently and swings left to reach a small gate. The gate gives access to a **chambered cairn**, the remains of which lie in a fenced enclosure.

TORRYLIN CAIRN

Much of the stonework from the 5300-year-old Torrylin Cairn has been plundered as building material, leaving only a fraction of the original burial chamber and cairn behind. Note how the chamber is aligned in the direction of distant Ailsa Craig. The structure is characteristic of the Clyde cairns found throughout this part of Scotland. The chamber was excavated in 1900, when it was discovered that only the innermost compartment was undisturbed. The remains of six adults, a child and an infant were identified, along with a small flint tool and a fragment of a pottery bowl. The Isle of Arran had been settled for at least 2700 years by the time the Torrylin Cairn was constructed. This and similar monuments indicate the development of small, dispersed agricultural settlements with a high degree of community involvement.

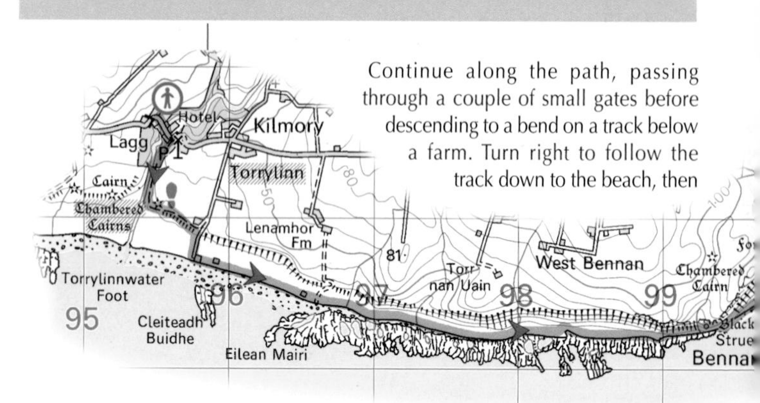

Continue along the path, passing through a couple of small gates before descending to a bend on a track below a farm. Turn right to follow the track down to the beach, then turn left to walk along the beach. Crunch along the pebbles and pass a small house. The only access to a series of fields along the coast is from the beach, so there may well be tractor wheel-marks to follow. The beach becomes boulder-strewn and many of the boulders are curiously pitted and banded, and have obviously come from a couple of outcrops projecting above the sand, but there are also other large boulders that have their origins from elsewhere on Arran.

Walk along the beach only until a waterfall is seen pouring through a rocky gorge. Come ashore at this point and go through a gate in a fence. A vague, grassy path can be followed onwards. There are a couple more gates in fences to be passed through, and above each fence is a small waterfall. A beach covered in huge, rounded boulders is passed and the ground gets rather wet and muddy in places. Some areas have abundant growths of wild iris and mint, but later there are patches of thorny scrub too.

A prominent igneous dyke is passed, as well as the ruins of a drystone wall. The ground gets rougher, wetter and muddier, with boulders poking through the ground beneath a blocky cliff and boulder-scree. There are also a couple more igneous dykes running out to sea. Another little waterfall is passed, which plunges into a small stand of trees. Immediately after fording the burn below the waterfall, a substantial upstanding outcrop is passed before the rugged point of **Bennan Head**.

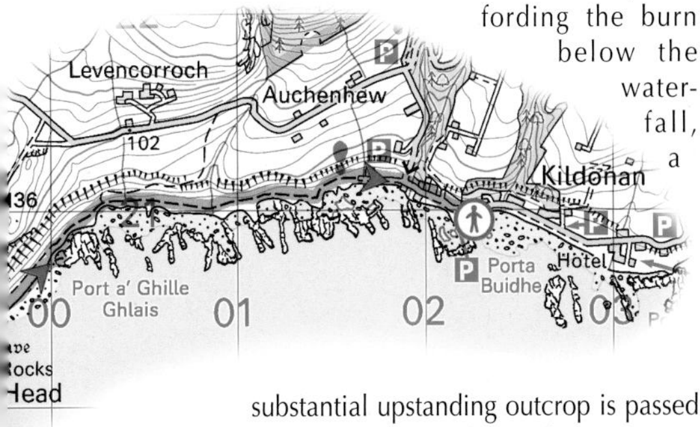

It's only possible to pass the foot of the point and explore Black Cave while the tide's out. Boulders are covered by the incoming tide, and the cliff above is covered in hoary lichen. Those who pass the point will find **Black Cave** is just round the corner and it is easily entered. If Bennan Head cannot be passed, double back along the coast, head inland to West Bennan, and either follow the road to Kildonan, or catch a bus.

BLACK CAVE

Before the Isle of Arran raised itself slightly from the sea after the Ice Age, as evidenced by encircling raised beaches, Black Cave must have been permanently full of sea water. Even now at high water the sea laps just inside the cave. A roof fall created an exit at the back of the cave, and a steep slope of collapsed boulder debris remains. Scrambling up through the cave to exit at the top is not recommended as it is very slippery.

Pick a way across boulders at low water to reach **Port a' Ghille Ghlais**, and continue walking along the coast, noting the large number of igneous dykes running across the bouldery beach and out to sea. A couple of slender waterfalls are spotted to the left, with a larger waterfall seen later. The path becomes progressively easier underfoot and passes a carved stone bench. Shortly afterwards, an information board explains about life on the shore, where seals are commonly seen hauled out on rocks and large boulders.

Follow the path onwards, reaching a gate that gives access to a track in front of a house. Another house,

A fine waterfall spills over the cliffs as the route approaches the village of Kildonan

set back from the track, is a B&B. The track leads to a bend on a minor road, where walking straight ahead leads all the way through the long and straggly village of **Kildonan**. ▸ The first bus stops and parking space are found at the village hall, near a prominent igneous dyke bears a war memorial plaque. The green island of Pladda and its lighthouse lie offshore, with the pyramidal rock of Ailsa Craig far beyond. To finish at the Kildonan Hotel or campsite, keep walking to the far end of the village.

Turn left up the road to link with Walk 13.

KILDONAN

Kildonan derives its name from St Donan, who arrived on the Isle of Arran with St Columba in the 6th century. Donan is buried in the area and the remains of an ancient chapel are still visible. The mouldering ruins of a castle can also be inspected, although little is known of its early history. It was a property of the Stewarts, but passed to the Hamiltons in the 17th century. The present village of Kildonan is a straggly affair, and of relatively recent origin, as previously the people in the area lived in simple clachans.

Looking back along the rugged coast from Kildonan to Bennan Head

WALK 15

Kilmory forest circuit

Start/Finish	Kilmory (NR 960 215)
Distance	13.5km (8½ miles), with 10km (6¼ miles) of optional extensions
Total ascent	260m (855ft), or 530m (1740ft)
Time	4hrs to 7hrs
Terrain	Mostly easy roads, forest tracks and paths.
Refreshments	Hotel with a bar-restaurant at Lagg.

Much of southern Arran is under forest cover and the walking tends to be rather similar in many places. However, an interesting forest circuit is available north of Kilmory, where farm tracks link with a series of forest tracks. There are options to make diversions in search of archaeological sites hidden deep in the forest. The walk starts and finishes in the village of Kilmory, near the Torrylin Creamery. At the end of the walk, another short optional circuit visits the Torrylin Cairn. The main circuit is fairly easy, but bear in mind that anyone walking all the optional extensions will almost double the distance.

Start at a staggered crossroads beside a bus shelter in the village of **Kilmory**. Follow a minor road marked for the Kilmory Workshop and Kilmory Parish Church. The road quickly runs down to a junction beside the church, where walkers keep left, or straight ahead. Follow the road across the **Kilmory Water**, then walk uphill and keep right. The road is partly concrete and flanked by hedges as it approaches the Kilmory Workshop, where woodwork and pottery is made, at **Cloined**.

A track proceeds beyond the workshop, descending gently and flanked by beech hedges, covered in grass for the most part. The track reaches a forest that is mostly clear-felled and replanted, rising to a gravel turning area. Join a firm forest track and follow it straight ahead. The track climbs to 180m (590ft) on the shoulder of **Meall Buidhe**, and later descends a little to pass the isolated farmstead of **Aucheleffen**. This is no more than a house, outbuildings, small fields and a little water-wheel. Keep following the forest track straight ahead until a junction is reached. Either keep straight ahead again, or turn left for an optional there-and-back extension.

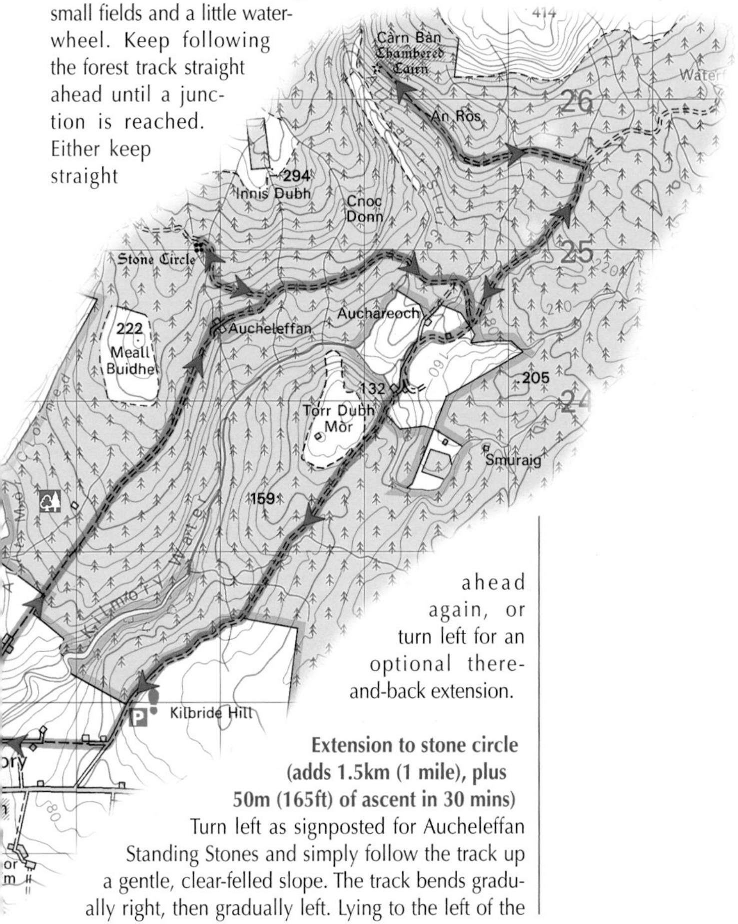

Extension to stone circle (adds 1.5km (1 mile), plus 50m (165ft) of ascent in 30 mins)

Turn left as signposted for Aucheleffan Standing Stones and simply follow the track up a gentle, clear-felled slope. The track bends gradually right, then gradually left. Lying to the left of the track, four blocky stones constitute a **stone circle**, or more correctly a stone square. This feature used to be hidden among the trees, but following clear-felling, there is now a view all the way to the sea. Retrace steps to the junction to continue.

The forest track continues across the lower slopes of **Cnoc Donn**. Keep right at a junction and descend slightly to cross a burn called **Allt an t-Sluice**. Continue to the next junction of tracks, around 170m (560ft), where there's a signboard and another optional there-and-back extension. Note that a cycleway also passes, linking Kilmory with Whiting Bay and Lamlash.

Extension to Càrn Bàn (adds 6km (3¾ miles), plus 130m (425ft) of ascent in 2hrs)

Turn left as signposted for Càrn Bàn, Whiting Bay and Lamlash. Further up the track, at almost 250m (820ft), turn left again as signposted for Càrn Bàn. Follow the track across extensively clear-felled slopes until a turning space is reached at **An Ros.** At this point, continue along a path that rises across the slope, until **Càrn Bàn** is noticed on the left, in a grassy clearing.

Explore, then retrace steps all the way back to the lowest junction.

From the junction around 170m (560ft), follow the forest track onwards, passing the access track for the remote

CÀRN BÀN

This dilapidated Neolithic chambered tomb was used for communal burial about 5300 years ago. A Mesolithic hunting camp has also been discovered nearby, taking signs of human activity on the Isle of Arran back 8000 years. The main burial chamber was excavated in 1902 and found to be divided into four compartments. Small fragments of bone and two stone tools were retrieved. A possible second burial chamber at the lower end of the cairn has not been excavated. The existence of a burial cairn of these proportions, and their obvious frequent use, indicates that the inhabitants of Arran at the time were living in fairly well-structured communities with a great sense of purpose.

The remote farmstead of Auchareoch lies deep inside the forest

farmstead of **Auchareoch**. The track soon passes another farm, where it crosses a burn. After quickly climbing onto the shoulder of **Tor Dubh Mòr**, the track runs gradually downhill through clear-felled and replanted forest. There is a gradual rise as the track crosses the heather moorland slope of **Kilbride Hill**. Pass a small parking space and map-board on leaving the forest, then descend further.

Turn right at a junction and follow a farm track that is firm and dry for a short distance. Its continuation straight ahead and downhill is wet and muddy, and is a sort of trough between hedges. Another firm and dry track continues straight ahead past a farmhouse, then a more rugged track continues. This soon joins a tarmac road to pass Kilmory Parish Church. When a road junction is reached beside the churchyard, simply turn left to return to the main road and bus shelter in **Kilmory**. A short detour left along the main road leads to the **Torrylinn Creamery**.

TORRYLINN CREAMERY

The Torrylinn Creamery, or Arran Creamery, stands beside the main road in Kilmory and is open to visitors Monday to Saturday. Three Arran dairy farms supply milk to the creamery, where traditional Arran Dunlop cheeses are made and matured. The process can be observed from a viewing gallery, and products can be tasted and bought at the adjoining cheese shop. When the creamery opened in 1946 the entire Royal Family paid a visit. Tel 01770 870240, www.realarrancheese.com

It is also worth adding a final optional extension.

Extension to Torrylin Cairn (2km (1½-mile) circuit, plus 50m (165ft) of ascent in 46mins)
Follow the main road from **Kilmory**, down past the primary school and public hall, towards **Lagg**. Turn left as signposted for Torrylin Cairn. A clear gravel track rises through woodland and runs along the edge of a valley. Keep right at a fork and continue along a path, which descends gently and swings left to reach a small gate. The gate gives access to a **chambered cairn**, the remains of which lie in a fenced enclosure.

TORRYLIN CAIRN

Much of the stonework from the 5300-year-old Torrylin Cairn has been plundered as building material, leaving only a fraction of the original burial chamber and cairn behind. Note how the chamber is aligned in the direction of distant Ailsa Craig. The structure is characteristic of the Clyde cairns found throughout this part of Scotland. The chamber was excavated in 1900, when it was discovered that only the innermost compartment was undisturbed. The remains of six adults, a child and an infant were identified, along with a small flint tool and a fragment of a pottery bowl. The Isle of Arran had been settled for at least 2700 years by the time the Torrylin Cairn was constructed. This and similar monuments indicate the development of small, dispersed agricultural settlements with a high degree of community involvement.

Continue along the path, passing through a couple of small gates before descending to a bend on a track below a farm. Turn left to follow the track uphill, returning directly to the main road and bus shelter in **Kilmory**.

WALK 16

Sliddery and Cnocan Donn

Start/Finish	Sliddery (NR 931 229)
Distance	13.5km (8½ miles)
Total ascent	360m (1180ft)
Time	4hrs 30mins
Terrain	Roads, tracks and some good paths, but also a rugged moorland walk and a bouldery coastal walk.
Refreshments	None closer than Blackwaterfoot.

Cnocan Donn is a hill between Sliddery and Blackwaterfoot, which is half rugged moorland and half forested. It provides exceptional views in fine weather for such a lowly height. Walkers who cross the hill can descend to Kilpatrick, then either catch a bus or pick a way back around Brown Head to return to Sliddery. The return route uses a patchy, rugged coastal path. There are features of interest at either end, such as the Preaching Cave near Kilpatrick and Torr a' Chaisteal Dun near Corriecravie.

Sliddery is a small settlement on a slight bend in the main coastal road between Blackwaterfoot and Kilmory. There is a crossroads on the bend, with a track running downhill from Sliddery Supplies and a minor road running uphill. Start by following the minor road up past a few houses and farms. The road rises, falls and rises gently, then turns left to reach a farm where OS maps mark a **quarry**. Turn right along a clear track running towards another farm called Corriecravie Moor. However, walk only as far as a rise on the track, where there is a gate on the left. This gives access to a rugged moorland walk alongside Kilpatrick Forest.

Walk uphill alongside the forest fence, or some distance away from it, to make use of vague paths on the rugged moorland slope. There is tussocky grass, a little bog, an abundance of heather and bracken on the slope, as well as a scattering of boulders. A short detour away from the forest fence can include the undistinguished top of **Cnoc Reamhar** at 225m (738ft). Walk back to the forest fence and follow it across a squelchy gap and over a heathery rise. There is another descent to another rather wet gap, where fences meet in a swamp. Straight ahead, the heathery slope of **Cnocan Donn** is crowned by a trig point at 219m (719ft). From this lowly eminence, there is quite an extensive view. The highest peaks of northern Arran stretch from the Pirnmill Hills to those around Glen Rosa, crowned by Goatfell. The lower hills and moorlands of southern Arran stretch from Ard Bheinn to Tighvein. Ailsa Craig and the coast of Ayr and Galloway can be seen, along with Antrim, Kintyre and Jura.

Head back towards the forest fence and walk downhill. There is an easy, bulldozed strip beside the forest fence, leading down to where a forest track meets the main coastal road. Turn right along the road, cutting across the slopes of **Suidhe Phadruig**, as if walking to Blackwaterfoot. The road bends suddenly

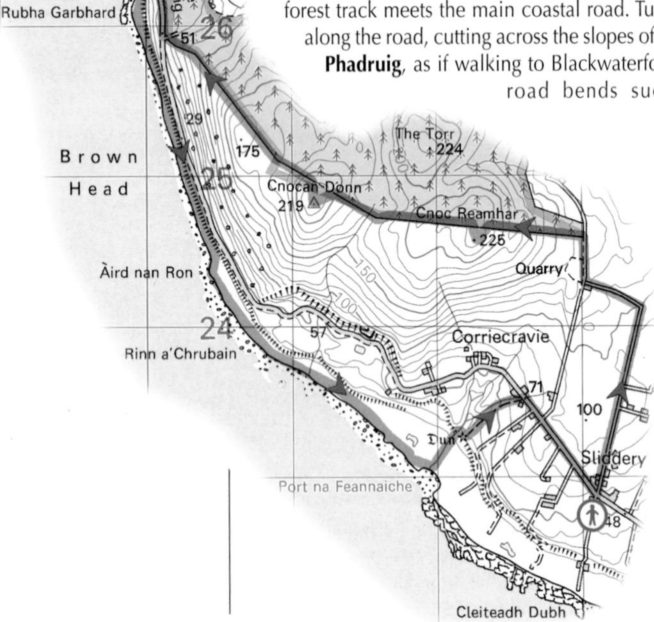

to the right and drops down to the tiny settlement of **Kilpatrick**.

Good grazing for livestock is available in the gentle pastures around Kilpatrick

Turn left as signposted through a gate, and follow a grassy track flanked by gorse bushes to the shore at **Kilpatrick Point**. Turn left to walk along a grassy strip beside a bouldery beach at the foot of a low cliff line. There are a couple of caves in the low cliff line, including the Preaching Cave.

PREACHING CAVE

The Preaching Cave is a fairly spacious, smoke-blackened cave cut into the low cliff-line below Kilpatrick. It is said to have been used for church services and there are also stories of it being used as a schoolroom at a time when the area was very poor.

A good grassy path can be followed for a while past **Rubha Garbhad**, but it gets more and more overgrown later with grass, heather, bracken, brambles and even honeysuckle and clumps of thrift. Transfer to the bouldery beach to continue, taking care while hopping from

A rugged walk along a raised beach leads from Kilpatrick back towards Sliddery

boulder to boulder. Looking uphill and along the cliff, the main road is out of sight, although it runs very close and traffic may be heard. Looking ahead, only one corner of the road can be seen, while down on the shore around that point, at **Àird nan Ron** the walking becomes easier again. Watch for a path leading up to the road, if an exit is needed.

It is possible to walk along a narrow, grassy path again, although it can feel lumpy underfoot in places, as the raised beach isn't far beneath the grass. There is a view of Ailsa Craig ahead, while seals might be hauled out, basking on large boulders. Some wet and muddy parts of the path are flanked by wild iris. Drift inland from the shore along a broader, cobbly path, but not the nearby tractor track, along the foot of a slope of bracken overlooked by a house. Later, don't follow a path inland towards a pool, but keep seawards of a field.

When the little bay of **Port na Feannaiche** is reached, head inland alongside a small burn, to the far side of a field. Rising ahead is the prominent knoll of Torr a' Chaisteal, which has a grassy track slicing across its face. Follow the track uphill and have a look at an information board explaining about this ancient **dun**.

The distinctive Torr a' Chaisteal Dun is passed near the end of the walk

TORR A' CHAISTEAL DUN

The natural grassy knoll of Torr a' Chaisteal bears the remains of a thick-walled dun which was built around 1800 years ago. The dun was a defended farmstead, situated next to an area of good agricultural land, yet close to the resources offered by the sea. The interior was partially excavated in the 19th century, revealing human bones, a stone quern, pieces of haematite iron ore and midden material.

The grassy track quickly becomes vague, but head straight inland alongside fields overlooking a valley full of hawthorns and other trees. When a cottage is reached at **Corriecravie**, cross a stile to reach the main road. To complete the circuit, turn right to follow the road over a rise, then descend to **Sliddery**. However, bear in mind that buses can be caught at either Corriecravie or Sliddery.

WALK 17

Tighvein and Glenscorrodale

Start/Finish	Allt Mòr, The Ross, Glenscorrodale (NR 976 298)
Distance	12.5km (7¾ miles)
Total ascent	460m (1510ft)
Time	4hrs
Terrain	After an easy road-walk, a potentially awkward river crossing, followed by rugged, pathless heather moorlands and bog.
Refreshments	None closer than Lamlash and Lagg.

Tighvein appears unapproachable, and maps suggest that it is flanked on all sides by pathless, featureless moorlands, which is mostly true. It also appears to be surrounded by forestry plantations, yet it is possible to side-step them, or at least limit contact with them. While paths may be few, the summit can be approached from any direction simply by climbing uphill until there is nothing left to climb. The approach on this route is simplified by following a fence across the moors. This is a remote part of Arran, far removed from public transport, where the only habitation is a Buddhist retreat centre at Glenscorrodale.

Parking along **The Ross** road is very limited, and it's important not to park in designated passing places. There's a small parking space at a picnic table where the road makes a tight bend as it crosses a burn called **Allt Mòr**, around 200m (655ft) in the middle of a forest at the head of Sliddery Water. Starting here, simply follow the minor road downhill. Overlook a derelict building, follow the road out of the forest and later pass the **Retreat Centre** at Glenscorrodale.

GLENSCORRODALE

Glenscorrodale was a remote 'steading' or small farm, with a few outbuildings. It was once the home of one of Scotland's former First Ministers, Jack McConnell, now Baron McConnell of Glenscorrodale. The Buddhist community from Holy Isle acquired the site and demolished the old farmhouse, erecting a new building and refurbishing the old outbuildings. The site has been renamed as Samye Dechen Shing, or 'valley of the pervading bliss', and operates as a men's retreat centre, complementing the women's retreat centre around the old lighthouse on Holy Isle. Thousands of trees have been planted in what was formerly a rather bare, sheep-grazed part of the glen.

Follow the road for another 1.5km (1 mile) to find a track descending on the left. This leads to a ford on **Sliddery Water**, where wet feet are to be expected. ▸ Climb from the river and gradually swing left. However, keep watching to the right to spot tumbled ruins on the other side of a shallow valley. This was once a small clachan known as Gargadale, which may be explored, but afterwards it is important to

Do not attempt to cross if the river is in spate after heavy rain. The nearest bridge is another 2km (1¼ miles) further downstream.

The broad moorland slopes surrounding Tighvein as seen across Glenscorrodale

locate a rectangular stone-walled sheepfold further up the valley.

GARGADALE

Gargadale's gaunt ruins are all that survive of a small clachan tucked away in a fold in the hillside. There is rather more shape and form to these ruins than there is to many other deserted villages around Arran, as more stone seems to have been used in its construction, rather than 'blacksod' constructions of peat. Unfortunately, unlike some of the other settlements, little is known about the fate of the tenants who were cleared from the land, although it has been suggested that they may have gone to Canada and settled at Cahleur Bay near Prince Edward Island.

Leave the sheepfold by heading roughly north-east up a rugged moorland slope towards **Cnocan na Caillich**. The gradient eases on the way, but the heather slopes are awkward underfoot, and although occasional sheep paths might be encountered, these often lead quickly off-route. The aim is to reach the corner of a forest plantation around 350m (1150ft). From that point, follow a fence that runs almost in a straight line across the heather moorland. The fence rises from the forest, passes a gateway at a junction with another fence and undulates to an altitude of 400m (1310ft) above **Cnoc Lean na Meine**.

Descend past another stand of forest and cross little burns in the small valley of **Coire Leathaid**. The fence is marked by decaying posts and broken wires, so take care not to trip on any lengths that are tangled in the grass and heather. A narrow ditch also accompanies the line of the old fence on the final climb to **Tighvein**. The summit bears both a large cairn and white-painted trig point at 458m (1502ft). ◄

Views of the immediate surroundings embrace rugged, rolling moorlands, which can be explored further with reference to Walk 9 and Walk 10. Northwards, the higher mountains of Arran are well displayed.

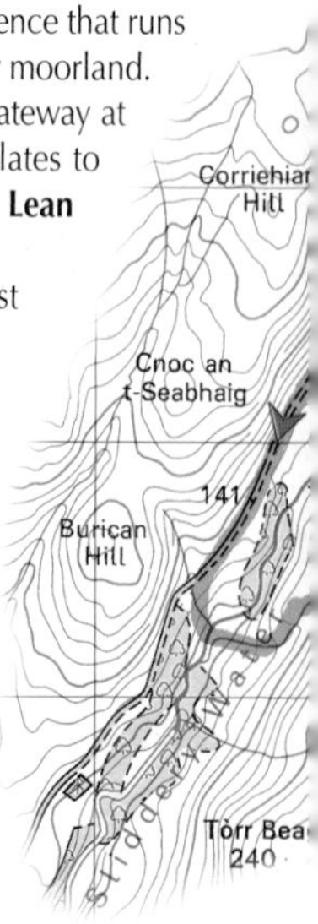

Leave the summit of Tighvein by heading roughly northwards. There is only a short, steep slope before the gradient eases, then gradually swing roughly north-west towards the broad moorland rise of **Cnoc Dubh**, around 430m (1410ft). The heather moorland is broken by occasional grassy areas, with a few small boulders poking through, and there are many channels of squelchy sphagnum moss. Side-step the channels where possible, or take care crossing them, while forging roughly northwards. The only feature along the way is a stand of two or three trees that have somehow 'escaped' from nearby forests. Swing north-west onto the broad top of **Garbh-Bheinn**, where the moorland slope overlooks forest plantations at the top of The Ross road.

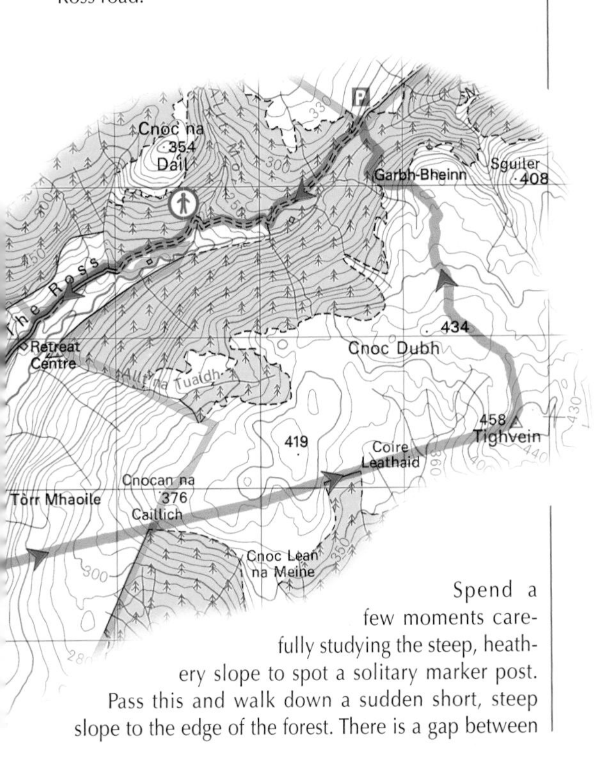

Spend a few moments carefully studying the steep, heathery slope to spot a solitary marker post. Pass this and walk down a sudden short, steep slope to the edge of the forest. There is a gap between

The trig point on Tighvein, looking towards Goatfell and northern Arran

the trees where a trodden path can be followed, quickly leading to a broad, unplanted forest ride. Turn right to follow the ride, then left to follow another ride, bearing in mind that the ground is often wet and boggy. A plastic pipe is passed, and while there might be a problem with fallen trees, get past them and a marker post will be seen beyond.

Simply step up onto The Ross road and turn left to follow it straight back into the forest. The road twists and turns, leading back to the little parking space beside the **Allt Mòr**.

WALK 18

The Ross and Cnoc a' Chapuill

Start/Finish	Allt Mòr, The Ross, Glenscorrodale (NR 976 298)
Distance	16km (10 miles)
Total ascent	400m (1310ft)
Time	5hrs
Terrain	A road-walk and a long, vague track are followed by extensive and pathless rugged moorlands.
Refreshments	None closer than Lamlash and Lagg.

The Ross road threads through Glenscorrodale, where the upper part of the dale is well forested, but plenty of land remains open along the length of the dale and on the higher moors. This walk takes a look at the un-forested moorlands to the north of Glenscorrodale, crossing the broad and pathless slopes of Cnoc a' Chapuill. The Ross road is used at the beginning and end of the walk, while an old track is used to access the higher moorlands. The highest parts of the route are really only for competent navigators – especially in poor visibility – although a couple of fences later form useful guides.

Parking along **The Ross** road is very limited, and it's important not to park in designated passing places. There's a small parking space at a picnic table where the road makes a tight bend as it crosses a burn called **Allt Mòr**, around 200m (655ft) in the middle of a forest at the head of Sliddery Water. Starting here, simply follow the minor road downhill. Overlook a derelict building, follow the road out of the forest and later pass the **Retreat Centre** at Glenscorrodale. ▶

See the beginning of Walk 17 for information about the centre.

Walk away from Glenscorrodale by following the road down through the glen. The road is unfenced and traverses some rugged slopes overlooking **Sliddery Water**. Later, fences are noticed off to the right on the slopes of **Burican Hill**, enclosing three large fields.

Continue walking along the road, overlooking Sliddery Water. Follow the road until it passes through

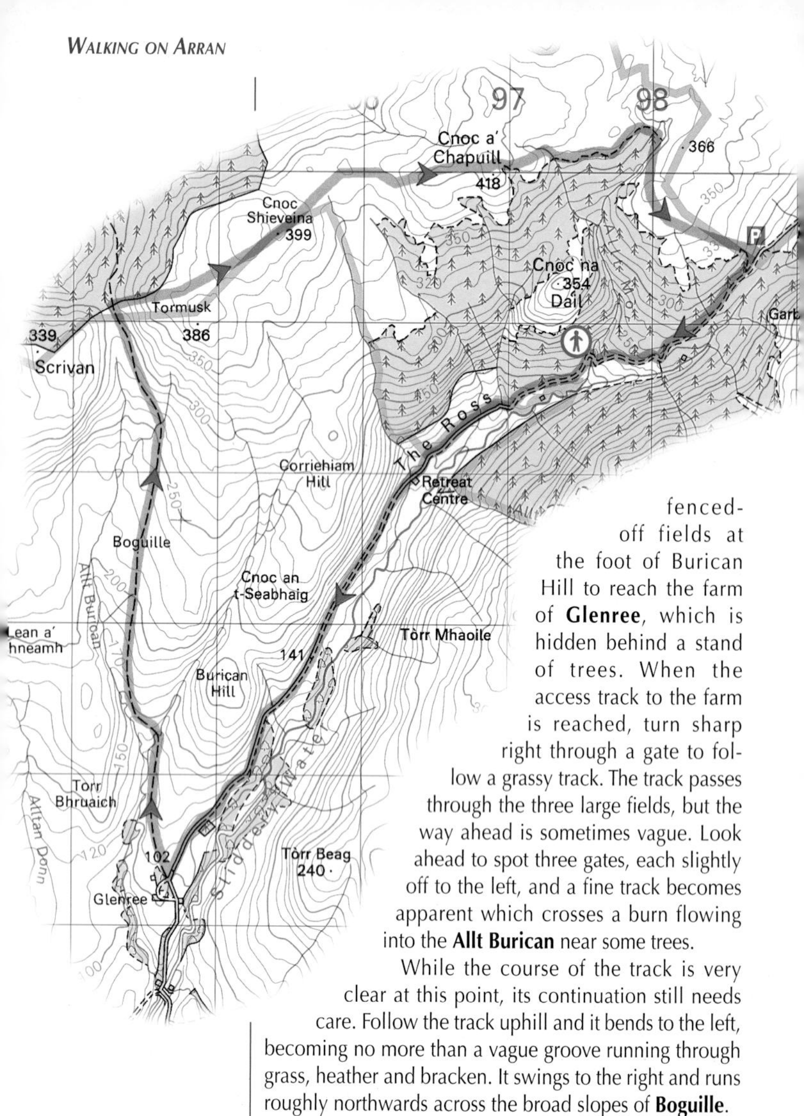

fenced-off fields at the foot of Burican Hill to reach the farm of **Glenree**, which is hidden behind a stand of trees. When the access track to the farm is reached, turn sharp right through a gate to follow a grassy track. The track passes through the three large fields, but the way ahead is sometimes vague. Look ahead to spot three gates, each slightly off to the left, and a fine track becomes apparent which crosses a burn flowing into the **Allt Burican** near some trees.

While the course of the track is very clear at this point, its continuation still needs care. Follow the track uphill and it bends to the left, becoming no more than a vague groove running through grass, heather and bracken. It swings to the right and runs roughly northwards across the broad slopes of **Boguille**.

The track rises very gently across the moorland slope and is fairly clear at times. Quad bikes have been ridden

A lonely moorland pool on Cnoc a' Chapuill and a distant glimpse of Goatfell

alongside and a few walkers have trodden a narrow path. Only one small burn of any note is crossed, where a small willow tree grows and the track swings to the left. Eventually, a gap in the broad moorland is reached, where the spiky profile of a forest can be seen, even from a distance. A gate gives access to the forest, but don't use it. ◂

Walk 19, from Shiskine, comes through the gate and climbs nearby Scrivan.

Turn right and walk up the heathery slope alongside the forest fence. It is best to walk some distance from the fence to avoid rutted ground and cross an area of more uniform heather on **Tormusk**. Drift further and further away from the fence to gain height, crossing more hummocky and awkward ground on **Cnoc Shieveina**. There are channels of squelchy sphagnum moss to be crossed, and no trodden paths anywhere. Look out for a small cairn at 399m (1309ft), overlooking a broad moorland gap. Descend to cross the gap, which proves to be quite richly vegetated. A fence also needs to be crossed, then any route can be chosen up the broad, heathery slopes beyond.

Clear weather is a distinct advantage on the pathless moorland. There is nothing to mark the 418m (1371ft) summit of **Cnoc a' Chapuill** and the moorland slopes spread in all directions. ◂ Walk very roughly eastwards along the hummocky moorland crest. Keep well above the forested slopes, cross a fence and turn right to follow it. The fence runs alongside the forest for a short while, then it turns right and zigzags on the moorland slope.

There are distant views of the jagged peaks of northern Arran, while across Glenscorrodale lies Tighvein and more extensive moorlands.

Decide whether to follow the fence, or to stay fairly close to the edge of the forest, trying to choose which course offers the best walking conditions. There is a climb onto a moorland hump, where the fence swings left and descends across the moorland towards another part of the forest. Continue down towards **The Ross** road, where there is a small parking area and picnic table. Turn right to follow the road across a cattle grid and enter the forest. The road twists and turns, leading back to the little parking space beside the **Allt Mòr**.

WALK 19

Shiskine and Clauchan Glen

Start/Finish	Shiskine (NR 913 300)
Distance	10.5km (6½ miles)
Total ascent	360m (1180ft)
Time	3hrs 30mins
Terrain	Mostly good tracks and paths through farmland and forest, but also some rugged moorland walking at a higher level.
Refreshments	None closer than the Balmichael Centre or Blackwaterfoot.

A varied circular walk from the village of Shiskine includes many clear paths and tracks. The route runs up through Clauchan Glen, climbs through forest, then takes in fine heather moorland and a scenic loch, before descending through forest and running down through farmland. The walk starts and finishes on The String road, which was surveyed and designed by Thomas Telford, linking Blackwaterfoot and Brodick. A campsite is available near Shiskine, but there are no other services of note.

Parking is limited in **Shiskine**, but there are regular bus services. Walk out of the village by road in the direction of Brodick. As soon as the road crosses a bridge, turn right along a track that serves the Bridgend Campsite. The track quickly reaches the ruins of Clachan Church and its old **burial ground**.

CLACHAN CHURCH

Clachan Glen might have been a place of worship for thousands of years, and it is possible that two chapels were built in the glen in the past few hundred years. The current ruins incorporate stone from earlier structures, and it was abandoned by 1898, as a new church had been built at the other end of the village. The decay was arrested in 2010, when the ruins were consolidated and information boards were placed inside.

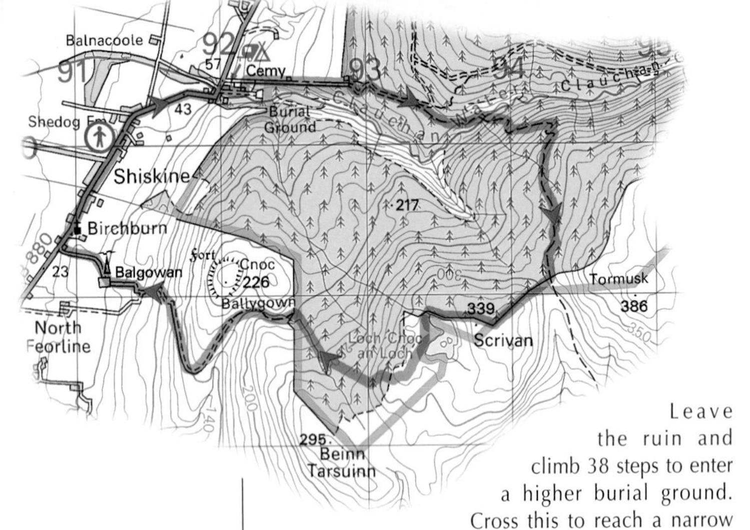

Leave the ruin and climb 38 steps to enter a higher burial ground. Cross this to reach a narrow road and turn right to follow it. The road has a line of leaning beech trees to the left, and the tarmac later gives way to a gravel road. Follow the road up to a house called Sron na Carraige. Pass a barrier gate and continue up a slope of clear-felled and replanted forest. The track bends as it climbs, then after a straight stretch, watch for a path heading off to the right.

The path drops gradually to reach a bouldery ford on the **Clauchan Water** deep in the **Clauchan Glen**. A grassy path zigzags up from the ford, with heathery banks alongside, occasional clearings and occasional peeps through the trees back into the glen. There is a broad slope of heather at a higher level, where a marker post stands on a bend. There is an awkward stretch that can be muddy, with fallen trees to negotiate, then a small burn is crossed. There is a slight descent before a gentle ascent to a gate at the edge of the forest. ◂

Walk 18, from Glenree, climbs nearby Tormusk.

Don't go through the gate, but turn right to walk between the forest and a fence. A track made by quad bikes climbs uphill on the slopes of **Scrivan**. Anyone crossing the fence and climbing to the 339m (1112ft) summit can enjoy views stretching beyond Ard Bheinn, taking in some of the larger hills to the north. The forest fence turns right where there is a large area of squelchy sphagnum moss, then leads down towards **Loch Cnoc an Loch**, which features two little islands. Walk between the shore of the loch and the edge of the forest, following the wheel marks left by quad bikes on the rugged moorland, swinging left until all the way past the loch. Watch carefully to follow the wheel marks gently downhill, passing from the moorland onto a forest ride.

Follow the track down along the forest ride, then turn left to contour across the forested slope on a broader heathery ride. A right turn leads down along another heathery ride, with another slight right bend taking the

The Pirnmill Hills are in view during the descent to Ballygown and Shiskine

track downstream beside a little burn. Go through a gate in the forest fence, from where the track proceeds more clearly through a small valley, crossing the burn a couple of times. The hill to the right is **Cnoc Ballygown**, whose summit is encircled by a vague ditch that archaeologists have determined is an unfinished hill fort.

Follow the track through the valley as heather and bracken give way to more grassy ground. The track passes through a gate and continues down to another gate, swinging sharply right. As the track cuts down across the slope, it is often flanked by dense gorse bushes, and views extend across Blackwaterfoot and Machrie to the higher hills. Go through yet another beside a line of beech trees and turn left. The track bends right and left on the way down to the farm of **Ballygown**, passing through two more gates to reach the farmyard.

Keep right of the farm buildings and follow the access track down to the road. Turn right to follow the road back towards **Shiskine**. The Parish Church, or 'Red Kirk', is built of red sandstone that contrasts markedly with the green fields. Shiskine Primary School is also passed on the way back to the bus stops.

SHISKINE

The name Shiskine refers to marshy ground, yet there is plenty of good farmland in the area. A story relates that St Molaise brought Christianity to Shiskine and that his remains were interred in Clauchan Glen, although history says he became the Abbot of Leithglinn in Ireland. A pilgrim path once ran from Shiskine, up through Clauchan Glen, over to Lamlash and so by ferry to Holy Isle. Up until the 1930s Shiskine was an industrious village, with a number of shops and businesses, but now it is quiet, with only a nearby campsite and self-catering properties. There are regular bus services through the village.

WALK 20

Balmichael and Ard Bheinn

Start/Finish	Balmichael Centre (NR 924 315)
Distance	13km (8 miles)
Total ascent	650m (2130ft)
Time	4hrs
Terrain	Easy forest track and path at the start, followed by rugged and sometimes pathless moorland needing careful navigation. The route finishes with a long road.
Refreshments	Café at the Balmichael Centre.

Beinn Bhreac and Ard Bheinn are rough and largely pathless hills rising east of The String road above Balmichael. Access is most easily gained using a forest track in Clauchan Glen, but after that the walking is rough and tough. There are few trodden paths and in poor visibility accurate navigation is essential. In order to make a complete circular walk, a stretch of The String road, surveyed and designed by Thomas Telford, is followed back to Balmichael. The Balmichael Centre can be explored at the start or finish of the walk.

There is hardly any room to park along The String road. The car park at the Balmichael Centre is for patrons only, but permission could be sought there, and it might be granted on a quiet day. Anyone arriving by bus will have no parking problems, and could also omit the entire road-walk.

CLACHAN CHURCH

Clachan Glen might have been a place of worship for thousands of years, and it is possible that two chapels were built in the glen in the past few hundred years. The current ruins incorporate stone from earlier structures, and it was abandoned by 1898, as a new church had been built at the other end of the village. The decay was arrested in 2010, when the ruins were consolidated and information boards were placed inside.

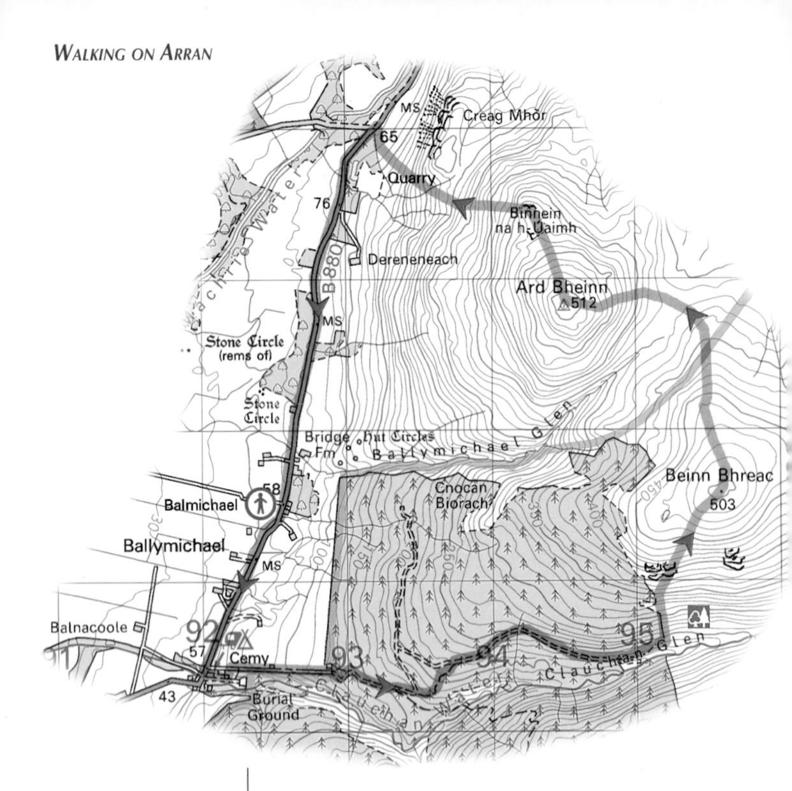

Follow the road away from **Balmichael** as if heading for the nearby village of Shiskine. Either turn left up a narrow tarmac road when the Bridgend campsite is seen, or walk a little further and turn left just as a bridge is reached. The latter turning quickly reaches the ruins of Clachan Church and its old **burial ground**.

Leave the ruin and climb 38 steps to enter a higher burial ground. Cross this to reach a narrow road and turn right to follow it. The road has a line of leaning beech trees to the left, and the tarmac later gives way to a gravel road. Follow the road up to a house called Sron na Carraige. Pass a barrier gate and continue up a slope of clear-felled and replanted forest. The track bends as it climbs, then after a straight stretch, Walk 19 follows a path on the right, but keep straight ahead until the track bends left.

Leave the bend and follow an older, grassy track as it winds uphill past a small quarry. The old track cuts out a loop on the main forest track, rejoining it at a higher level. Turn right to continue ascending gently, reaching the top of the track beside another small quarry, around 250m (820ft).

The track begins to descend gently into **Clauchan Glen**. Don't go all the way down to the river, as the vegetation cover is too dense and awkward. Look instead for a gravel ramp rising to the left, giving access to a rugged forest ride. Forge a way along the ride to reach the edge of the forest, then turn left to walk uphill alongside the forest. The vegetation cover on the lower slopes of Beinn Bhreac is remarkably varied, comprising bracken, grass, heather and a host of flowering plants. This makes the ascent interesting, but also difficult, and it is best to walk some distance from the edge of the forest.

Start drifting right, away from the forest, to climb straight up the open slope. There is tough heather cover, broken by a few rashes of boulders. At a higher level the gradient eases and there is mixed grass and heather cover. Go through a small gate in a fence and walk along a broad shoulder, looking left to spot a pool. Make the final ascent to the broad summit of **Beinn Bhreac**, where there is a cairn at 503m (1650ft) situated amid low heathery peat hags. ▸

Views northwards stretch from Ard Bheinn and the Pirnmill Hills to Beinn Nuis, Glen Rosa and Goatfell. In a southerly arc are Holy Isle, Tighvein, Ailsa Craig, Antrim and Kintyre, with Jura beyond.

Descend very roughly northwards from the broad summit, but try and pick up the course of quad bike wheel marks while weaving down a gentle slope of heather, grass and low peat hags. The ground becomes steeper and the wheel marks pass just to the right of a broad gap. A few boulders and rock outcrops are passed then the broad gap, around 370m (1215ft), is squelchy with sphagnum moss. Once across the gap, climb fairly steeply and drift a little more to the left, still following the wheel marks. The ground becomes predominantly heathery and there are some boulders and rocky outcrops to pass. The summit of **Ard Bheinn** bears a trig point at

A distinctive red sandstone pillar box at a road junction at the foot of Ard Bheinn

512m (1670ft) inside a circular stone shelter. There is also a cairn nearby.

Descend very roughly northwards from the top of Ard Bheinn, but drift slightly to the left. The aim is to pick up and follow a broad, hummocky ridge, which ends in a dome bearing a cairn at **Binnein na h-Uaimh**. The underlying rock is a bouldery conglomerate. Head west to start the descent, but gradually swing right until heading more to the north-west further downhill. It is important to look carefully down the slope to avoid the steepest ground and rocky outcrops. It is possible to pick a way down steep heathery ground, drifting to the right to enter a little valley well below the hump of **Creag Mhòr**. The upper part of the valley is a bit wet and bears bog myrtle.

The final part of the descent is quite short, but it is very tough underfoot and needs special care. Stay well away from the Dereneneach Stone **Quarry** and the forest that lies to the right of it. Heather gives way to areas of bracken and boulders, which has to be taken slowly and carefully. At a lower level lies an ankle-wrenching slope of tussocky grass and more bracken. Aim to reach The String road to the right of the forest. Cross a fence to reach a road junction, where there is also a fine red sandstone pillar box.

Turn left along The String road, as signposted for Blackwaterfoot. Forest lies to the left of the road and fields to the right. Pass the access roads for the quarry and the farm at **Dereneneach**. The road is then often flanked on both sides by fields. After passing **Bridge Farm**, which lies to the left of the road, the Balmichael Centre lies to the right of the road.

BALMICHAEL CENTRE

Based on a former farm complex, the Balmichael Centre includes a number of attractions, mostly aimed at families, around a fine courtyard. The Old Mill Coffee House serves refreshments, and there are small shops and toilets. There is a huge inflatable pillow for children to bounce on, a play park, a 'climby jumpy thingy', pedal karts, a synthetic skating rink, golf driving range, small movie theatre, a 'zorse' and a donkey, as well as ducks to feed. Tel 01770 465072, www.balmichael.com

WALK 21

The String and Beinn Bhreac

Start/Finish	Glenloig, The String road (NR 946 351)
Distance	12km (7½ miles)
Total ascent	680m (2230ft)
Time	4hrs
Terrain	A forest path and rugged, largely pathless moorlands needing careful navigation in poor visibility.
Refreshments	None closer than the Balmichael Centre.

Wild, empty moorlands and hills extend far south of The String road. Farmland and forestry makes access difficult in places, but this particular walk uses a rugged forest path through Glen Craigag to reach A' Chruach. Most of the whole walk is over rough, tough, pathless hill and moorland slopes, finishing with a road-walk at the end. Parking is very limited beside The String road, but there are regular bus services between Brodick and Blackwaterfoot. The route takes in three summits – A' Chruach, Beinn Bhreac and Ard Bheinn – which are arranged in a circuit around the head of Glen Craigag.

A small car park lies across the road from the former farmstead of **Glenloig**. This is the last habitation seen when travelling up The String road towards Brodick, or the first one seen on the way down the road. A small notice about Glenloig stands beside the car park, and an old milestone stands beside the road. Although a path leaves the car park, it goes nowhere and shouldn't be used. Instead, leave the car park by turning right along the road, then turn right again where an old gate is tangled among bracken. A tiny yellow disc states 'walkers welcome here', and a grassy path leads into the forest.

The whole of the eastern side of **Glen Craigag** has been forested, but there is a single grassy ride through it that has been left unplanted. While this ride bears a trodden path, it is also covered in bracken, tussocky grass and

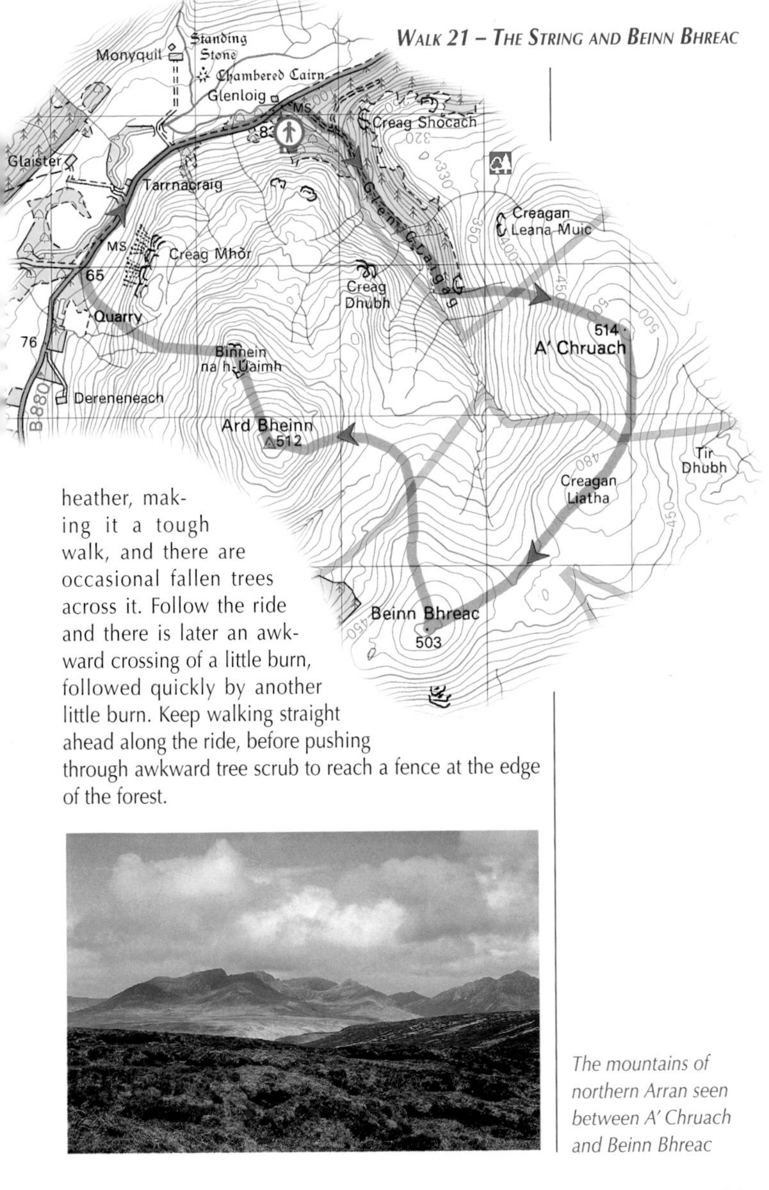

heather, making it a tough walk, and there are occasional fallen trees across it. Follow the ride and there is later an awkward crossing of a little burn, followed quickly by another little burn. Keep walking straight ahead along the ride, before pushing through awkward tree scrub to reach a fence at the edge of the forest.

The mountains of northern Arran seen between A' Chruach and Beinn Bhreac

Turn left to follow the fence steeply uphill on a difficult slope of deep heather. Cross the fence at some convenient point and gradually drift away from it across rugged, pathless moorlands. The gradient eases as height is gained, and the heather is less of a drag on the feet. Aim for the summit of **A' Chruach**, where a small cairn stands on a broad grass and heather rise at 514m (1686ft). ◄

Views stretch from the high peaks of northern Arran to the extensive moorlands of southern Arran, taking in the Ayr and Galloway coasts, Antrim and Kintyre. Islands in view include Cumbrae, Holy Isle, Ailsa Craig and Jura.

Head southwards in the direction of Ailsa Craig, along the broad moorland crest. There is a trace of a path, but not much, and not enough to follow confidently in poor visibility. After crossing the next broad moorland gap, drift to the right to cross the broad, bleak moorland summit of **Creagan Liatha** at 490m (1610ft), where there are plenty of peat hags. The next gap on the moorland crest is very broad and gentle, but it is also very boggy and covered in grass, sphagnum moss and peat hags. It is best avoided altogether by keeping to the slope just north of it. Firmer ground is reached for the ascent of **Beinn Bhreac**. There is a stony cairn on top at 503m (1650ft), situated amid low heathery peat hags.

Descend very roughly northwards from the broad summit, but try and pick up the course of quad bike wheel marks while weaving down a gentle slope of heather, grass and low peat hags. The ground becomes steeper and the wheel marks pass just to the right of a broad gap. A few boulders and rock outcrops are passed, then the broad gap, around 370m (1215ft), is squelchy with sphagnum moss. Once across the gap, climb fairly steeply and drift a little more to the left, still following the wheel marks. The ground becomes predominantly heathery and there are some boulders and rocky outcrops to pass. The summit of **Ard Bheinn** bears a trig point at 512m (1670ft) inside a circular stone shelter. There is also a cairn nearby.

Descend very roughly northwards from the top of Ard Bheinn, but drift slightly to the left. The aim is to pick up and follow a broad, hummocky ridge, which ends in a dome bearing a cairn at **Binnein na h-Uaimh**. The underlying rock is a bouldery conglomerate. Head west to start the descent, but gradually swing right until heading more to the north-west further downhill. It is important to look carefully down the slope to avoid the steepest ground and rocky outcrops. It is possible to pick a way down steep heathery ground, drifting to the right to enter a little valley well below the hump of **Creag Mhòr**. The upper part of the valley is a bit wet and bears bog myrtle.

The final part of the descent is quite short, but it is very tough underfoot and needs special care. Stay well away from the Dereneneach Stone **Quarry** and the forest that lies to the right of it. Heather gives way to areas of bracken and boulders, which has to be taken slowly and carefully. At a lower level lies an ankle-wrenching slope of tussocky grass and more bracken. Aim to reach The String road to the right of the forest. Cross a fence to reach a road junction, where there is also a fine red sandstone pillar box.

Turn right along The String road as signposted for Brodick. Simply follow the road, passing the farm access tracks for Glaister and Monyquil. The road finally crosses Glenloig Bridge to finish back at the little car park at **Glenloig**.

THE STRING

The String road, or B880, slices Arran in half. To the north are high, jagged, rocky mountain peaks, surrounded by a tall deer fence. To the south are lower hills, extensive rugged moorlands and forests. The String road was surveyed by Thomas Telford in 1817, although traces of earlier paths and tracks can still be distinguished, following parallel courses on the slopes to either side of the road.

WALK 22

Blackwaterfoot and King's Cave

Start/Finish	Harbour, Blackwaterfoot (NR 895 281)
Distance	10km (6¼ miles)
Total ascent	200m (655ft)
Time	3hrs
Terrain	Easy roads, tracks and paths.
Refreshments	Hotel bar and restaurants at Blackwaterfoot, as well as a café on the golf course.

One of the most popular easy walks on Arran visits the King's Cave. Two paths allow easy approaches: one from Blackwaterfoot and the other from Machrie Moor. These can be combined into a circular walk, ending with a road-walk, but the road is also served by buses. Many years ago, a gate was installed at the mouth of the King's Cave, protecting the interior from vandalism and misuse. In recent years the gate has been left open, but this is only likely to continue if visitors respect the place.

Start from the car park and bus stop between the Kinloch Hotel and tiny harbour at **Blackwaterfoot**. Follow the main road across a bridge, looking upstream to see a little waterfall. Continue along the main coastal road, then turn left along a minor road signposted for a golf course. This road ends at a private car park for the Shiskine Golf and Tennis Club, where a public footpath sign indicates the way to the King's Cave.

Follow a broad coastal track beside the golf course, noting a couple of rocky dykes standing above the level of the sandy beach. Low sand dunes are covered in spiky marram grass. The track turns inland and reaches the piers of a gateway in a fence. Don't pass through, as this leads off-route to the farm of **Drumadoon**. Instead, turn left as signposted for the King's Cave, and continue until a sign indicates a right turn up to another gate, with a stile alongside. A path runs through two fields before a gate reveals a path zig-zagging down onto a raised beach.

Note the columnar cliffs facing the sea at **The Doon**, draped in ivy and covered in plants and flowers safe from grazing sheep. The top of the hill bears traces of an Iron Age hill fort. Keep right to follow grassy path on cobbles past an old sea stack now marooned on the raised beach. The rock is exotically encrusted with lichens. The route proceeds easily on short grass, then climbs as a narrow, rocky path to avoid a bouldery beach walk. ▸

A series of caves are encountered; at least fifteen distinct examples. The first cave is small and choked with brambles. The second is larger, while the third and fourth are separated only by a pillar of rock. There is plenty of headroom for those who want to walk from one to the other. The fifth cave is narrower and is like a passageway leading through to the entrance to the **King's Cave**, which is itself the sixth in the series.

The seventh cave is a narrow slit, found just beyond the entrance to the King's Cave, which can be walked through. The eighth cave is choked with scrub and the ninth is just beyond a short drystone wall. The 10th cave is a step up above the raised beach, while the 11th is quite low-cut. The 12th is almost obscured by boulders

Avoid a path heading inland before reaching the King's Cave.

The columnar cliffs of The Doon are seen on the way to the King's Cave

and it is possible to crawl beneath a low arch to reach the 13th. Only consider crawling if you are wearing old clothes, as the floor of the cave is quite mucky. The 14th cave is wet and muddy, while the 15th has a pool of water inside.

KING'S CAVE

History and mystery surround the caves between Blackwaterfoot and Machrie. There are some interesting carvings from the early Christian and Pictish periods, and the caves are thought to have been used by early Christian voyagers and missionaries to the islands. Some legends state that Robert the Bruce hid in the King's Cave (hence the name) and had his renowned encounter with the spider, or waited for a signal beacon to be lit, but there is no evidence to support either tale. In fact, it was called Fingal's Cave a couple of hundred years ago. However, it is quite possible that Bruce used the cave briefly while fleeing to Rathlin Island off the Antrim coast of Northern Ireland. A torch is useful for exploring deep inside the cave.

The path climbs uphill immediately beside the 15th cave, rising from a pebbly beach and later running through a rocky cutting. A clear, broad path rises parallel to the edge of a forest on the slopes of **Torr Righ Beag**. It runs along the edge of a heathery brow overlooking the sea and the distant hills of Kintyre. The path climbs over a rise offering views over the gentle farming landscape of Machrie. It then runs gently downhill, then climbs a little inside the forest before passing a **hut circle** to reach a car park. ▸

An information board offers notes about the King's Cave and a circular walking route.

Maps show paths on nearby Machrie Moor, and the Machrie Moor Stone Circles look deceptively close, but there is no easy way to link everything in a circular walk. The moor is rough and boggy and the few paths that cross it are overgrown and difficult to follow.

MACHRIE MOOR

The farming landscape of Machrie Moor has a very long history. Hut circles are dotted all over the slopes of Torr Righ Mòr, while a series of famous stone circles, standing stones and burial cairns are located nearby. The hut circles date from the late Neolithic to early Bronze Age. The stone circles on Machrie Moor are reckoned to be around 4000 years old. The existence of these remains and monuments indicates that a series of settled, agricultural communities lived in this area, which might have been the most fertile and productive area on Arran. Walk 23 visits the Machrie Moor Stone Circles.

To return to Blackwaterfoot, the main road is the only option. Leave the car park and turn right to follow it. The road is often flanked by shrubs and scrub, and a small sign later announces the scattered settlement of **Torbeg**. Shiskine Free Church of Scotland church stands to the right, while to the left at a road junction is a memorial to a former minister, the Rev Archibald Nichol. The main road continues straight onwards, rising and passing farms, houses and the Shiskine Hall. Later, the road runs gradually downhill, returning to the coast on the way into **Blackwaterfoot**.

The tiny harbour at Blackwaterfoot, where the walk starts and finishes

BLACKWATERFOOT

Originally Blackwaterfoot was a small, close-knit community with a few houses positioned around the tiny harbour. There was a massive burial cairn above the village, but this was gradually reduced and plundered for building material. In 1900 a bronze dagger with gold decoration was retrieved from the centre of the cairn.

Facilities on the north side of the village include: the golf course and its café, the Harbour Shop and Arran Butcher. On the south side of the harbour are toilets, a car park and the Best Western Kinloch Hotel, with a bakery behind it. Uphill are the Brae Salon, post office and grocery (with ATM). The Blackwaterfoot Lodge incorporates the Black Grouse bar and restaurant, facing a garage. On the way out of the village, the Cairnhouse Riding Centre is passed.

WALK 23

Machrie Moor Stone Circles

Start/Finish	Near Machrie Water (NR 895 330)
Distance	4.5km (2¾ miles)
Total ascent	40m (130ft)
Time	1hr 30mins
Terrain	A good track ending on moorland that can be wet underfoot.
Refreshments	Machrie Bay tearoom off-route.

One of the easiest and most interesting walks on Arran is the one to the Machrie Moor Stone Circles. This could be accomplished in almost any weather, but in fine weather there is a chance to experience the refreshing spaciousness of the site. A number of stone circles and standing stones can be inspected from a gravel track and moorland path. All around are ranged some of the highest and most rugged mountains on the island, which make a superb backdrop for photographers wanting to capture the spirit of the place. The only drawback is that the area can be busy with other visitors, so walking there in the quiet times of the year can be a good idea.

This short, easy walk starts beside the main road near a bridge spanning Machrie Water. A sign beside the road reads 'Machrie Moor Stone Circles 1 mile', and there is a small car park available. Leave the car park and follow a clear and obvious track across fields. The track rises gently and bends right and left. At a gate

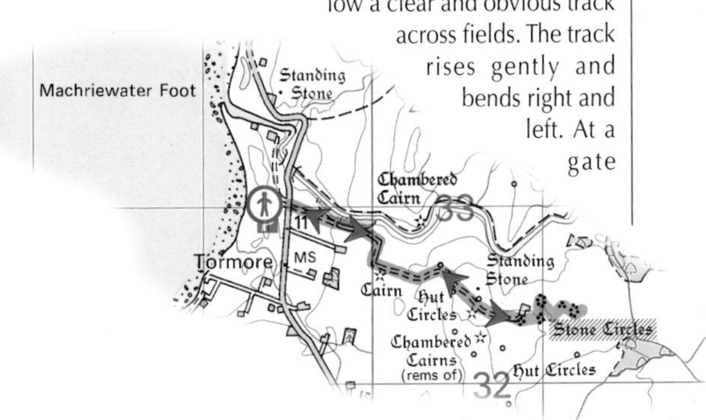

One of the prominent standing stones seen on the spacious Machrie Moor

and stile, the Moss Farm Road Stone Circle stands in a fenced enclosure and can be inspected.

The track continues over a gentle moorland rise, and there are small **standing stones** to right and left. Shortly afterwards, pass through a gateway to find a stone circle to the right, near the derelict buildings of Moss Farm. Cross a nearby stile and study information boards relating to Machrie Moor.

There is a small stone circle to the right of the information boards, and a narrow moorland path leads to three tall standing stones. Beyond these are two more **stone circles**. Retracing steps a little, but branching off to the right, is a tall, solitary standing stone. All around this moorland setting are ranged the peaks of Beinn Bharrain, Sail Chalmadale, Beinn Nuis, Goatfell and Ard Bheinn. When all the stone circles and standing stones have been thoroughly investigated, simply retrace steps from Moss Farm, back along the gravel track to return to the small car park beside the main road. Anyone who arrived by bus, who might have time to spare before the next one arrives, could head for the nearby golf course and tearoom at Machrie Bay Hall.

MACHRIE MOOR STONE CIRCLES

Machrie Moor is a well-preserved Neolithic and Bronze Age ritual landscape. The Moss Farm Road Stone Circle is unusual as it may actually be a kerbed cairn, or the cairn was constructed before the stone circle. Apart from stone circles and standing stones, the area around Machrie Moor is dotted with numerous hut circles, indicating that people lived in a settled, agricultural community. There must have been a high degree of community involvement for them to have raised so many fine structures and monuments, and this must have been one of the most fertile parts of the Isle of Arran to sustain such a population.

WALK 24

Dougarie and Beinn Nuis

Start/Finish	Dougarie (NR 882 370)
Distance	23km (14¼ miles) or 16km (10 miles)
Total ascent	900m (2950ft) or 400m (1310ft)
Time	7hrs 30mins or 5hrs
Terrain	Tracks on lower slopes, but mostly pathless moorlands and mountain, boggy and bouldery in many places. Road-walking at the end.
Refreshments	Machrie Bay tearoom and Café Thyme at Auchencar are both off-route.

Beinn Nuis is almost always climbed from Glen Rosa, so all its trodden paths are on that side. Its rugged form dominates Glen Iorsa, but few walkers climb from that direction and there are very few trodden paths. The route described here uses the access track leading to Loch Iorsa, climbs a desolate slope and reaches Beinn Nuis by way of a fine, bouldery ridge. There's an opportunity to walk round the bouldery bowl of Coire Nuis, then head back across empty moorlands to Loch Nuis. While steps could be retraced through Glen Iorsa, another ending is possible, following a forest fence across boggy moorland slopes to descend to Machrie. A short road-walk leads from Machrie to Dougarie. A shorter alternative route simply omits Beinn Nuis. Note that when Iorsa Water is in spate it is difficult to complete this walk, but Walk 25 could be attempted instead.

There are small spaces to park cars at Dougarie, some distance either side of the bridge spanning Iorsa Water at its confluence with the sea. The whitewashed **Dougarie Lodge**, which is seen briefly near the bridge, is private. A nearby farm access road for **High Dougarie**, however, is signposted as 'footpath to Loch Iorsa'. The tarmac quickly gives way to a concrete track that soon bends left. Another sign on the bend indicates the footpath climbing straight up a flight of broken stone steps.

Dougarie Lodge and distant Beinn Bharrain are seen from the coastal road

Cross a stile over a wall, then the path follows the wall through a field, crossing a stile over a fence. Continue through a small wood, leaving it later to follow a track towards a rugged slope. Watch carefully for the line of the path, negotiating boggy patches and looking for occasional marker posts. The path reaches a bend on a track where a sign points back, reading 'footpath to main road'. Cross either a concrete ford or a footbridge over the Allt na h' Airighe and keep walking along the track parallel to the broad and bouldery Iorsa Water, which is the biggest river on the island.

The river cuts through masses of glacial rubble, whose ill-bedded layers can be seen alongside the track. Go through a gate in a tall deer fence and cross a concrete ford across a river draining Glen Scaftigill. When the river is in spate, wet feet are guaranteed at this point. A footbridge was once available upstream, but was swept away many years ago. The track continues across a slope of tussocky grass, heather and bog myrtle to reach the foot of **Loch Iorsa**, where there is a tiny boathouse.

A grassy, wet and boggy track pushes further up into Glen Iorsa, running alongside the shore of the loch, then continuing beside Iorsa Water. Bog myrtle grows amid the grass and heather. Watch carefully to spot shoals of reddish gravel where the river channel is braided and there is a chance of fording the river without getting wet feet. However, in times of spate after heavy rain, it may be impos-

sible to continue further, in which case walkers might prefer to switch to Walk 25 over Sail Chalmadale instead.

If the river can be safely forded, then head straight uphill alongside a burn called Allt Airidh Mhuirich, which is full of delightful waterfalls. Avoid areas of bracken at the foot of the burn, and walk through tussocky grass, heather and bog myrtle at a higher level. There are even a few trees tucked into a little gorge drained by the burn. Views open up both ways along the bleak and barren length of the glen, then the gradient eases and **Loch Nuis** is suddenly reached. ▸

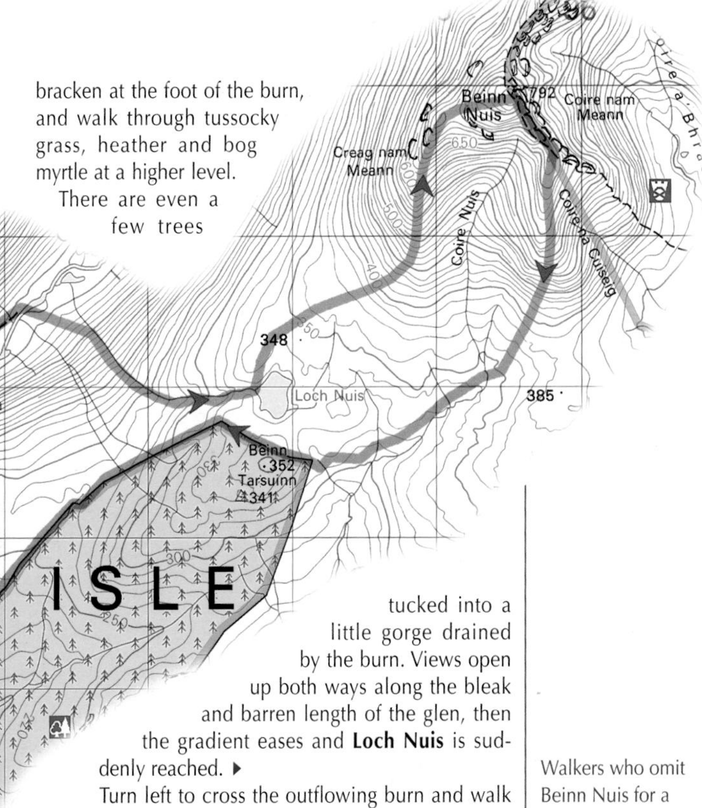

Turn left to cross the outflowing burn and walk away from the loch, heading roughly north-east across a huge, boggy, grass and heather moorland. Keep well to the left of **Coire Nuis** to climb up a boulder-strewn ridge. The ground steepens and the rounded ridge features views extending from Kintyre and Antrim to Holy Isle and the Ayrshire coast. The climb up the ridge proves relatively easy after the tussocky moorland. The ground becomes predominantly bouldery, then rather gritty, before a fine, blocky ridge of granite develops, with good views across Glen Iorsa to the Pirnmill Hills. Cross a little gap, then climb up a steep slope of short heather and boulders. After passing a wrinkly little granite tor a gentler, grassier, less bouldery slope leads

Walkers who omit Beinn Nuis for a shorter walk should turn right and walk away from the loch, picking up the route description at a forest fence.

to the top of **Beinn Nuis**. The bouldery summit bears a little cairn at 792m (2598ft) and features dramatic views around Glen Rosa.

Turn right to follow a path away from the summit cairn, running down a steep, rocky slope beside a precipitous cliff. When a gentle gap is reached, the path heads off towards Glen Rosa, but this route turns right to cross a gentle rise of short grass, heather, low outcrops and boulders above **Coire na Cuiseag**. The end of this little crest steepens abruptly and falls southwards towards a broad, boggy moorland. In clear weather, the lonely moorland pool of Loch Nuis will be in view. All sorts of vague paths cross the moorlands below, but none of them are really useful. Head roughly south-west and aim to reach the course of the Garbh Allt, crossing the burn to continue roughly parallel downstream. Loch Nuis will have passed from sight, but aim instead for the corner of a forest seen ahead on a moorland rise. The grass and heather is tussocky in places and makes for a rough passage.

The forest fence is the key to the long descent from the moors. Turn right to follow the fence uphill across a rise of moorland on **Beinn Tarsuinn**. Loch Nuis comes into view again, with Beinn Nuis framed beyond it. The fence runs downhill a short way, then turns left around a corner. Continue following the fence downhill, then cross a fairly level area with many boggy patches. There is a rise and fall as the hump of **Beinn Chaorach** is passed. The fence descends to cross the **Auchencar Burn**, rises a little, then descends again. Bracken patches impede progress near the hump of **Cnoc a' Choire Mhòir**.

Look out for a track just to the right of the forest fence. Follow it and use a ladder stile to cross a tall deer fence. The grassy track can be traced across fields, crossing the gentle slopes of **Cnocan Cuallaich** and continuing down towards a huddle of farm buildings at **Auchagallon**. Go through a gate and keep right of all the buildings to pick up their access road further downhill. A bend on the track turns round a small enclosure where the **Auchagallon Cairn** is located.

AUCHAGALLON CAIRN

Although often referred to as a stone circle, the site at Auchagallon is actually a kerbed cairn. The remaining upright slabs lie inwards around an ancient grassy cairn, probably dating back 4000 years. Excavations carried out in the 19th century revealed a cist burial in the middle of the cairn. Kerbed cairns are thought to have been constructed as burial places for important people, creating a site which would impress visitors and remind them of the importance of the person within. The nearby Moss Farm Road Stone Circle on Machrie Moor, passed on Walk 23, may be of the same type of construction.

Continue down to a minor road and turn right. ▸ When the main coast road is reached, turn right again. Simply walk along the road all the way from the Machrie Garage back towards Dougarie. A scrub-covered sandstone cliff along the way features a handful of caves and a small burial ground, followed by the **Old Schoolhouse**, which is a fine red sandstone building flanked by trees. A signposted turning further along the road offers an optional short detour up to **Auchencar** and the Old Byre Showroom.

Alternatively, visit the nearby tearoom at Machrie Bay Hall on the coast road, which is a good place to catch a bus.

AUCHENCAR STANDING STONE

Situated in a large field off the access road for Auchencar, the 'Druid Stone' is the tallest standing stone on Arran. The stone itself is a blade of rock, which looks tall and broad from one side, yet tall and narrow from the other. Its isolation in a large field removed from habitation, yet within view of the mountains, adds to its impressiveness. The broken remains of a similar stone lie embedded in the grass alongside.

OLD BYRE SHOWROOM

The Old Byre Showroom is signposted from the main road, and in this remote setting it is an unlikely place to go shopping for sheepskins, leather goods, woollens and other items of clothing – some with designer labels. A pottery and the Café Thyme are also available.

The 'Druid Stone' near Auchencar

Simply continue walking along the main coastal road, or walk along a pleasant grassy strip beside the road, finally finishing back at **Dougarie**.

WALK 25

Dougarie and Sail Chalmadale

Start/Finish	Dougarie (NR 882 370)
Distance	16.5 km (10¼ miles)
Total ascent	555m (1820ft)
Time	5hrs
Terrain	Tracks on lower slopes, but also pathless uplands that are boggy in places.
Refreshments	None closer than the Machrie Bay tearoom.

When the high mountains around Glen Iorsa are shrouded in cloud, it is often the case that Sail Chalmadale might be clear. A combination of its lower height and its proximity to loftier neighbours gives it some measure of protection from inclement weather, but a traverse would require careful navigation in poor visibility. The access track from Dougarie to Loch Iorsa is an obvious way to reach Sail Chalmadale, and the mountain can be climbed gradually in a sort of spiral route from the glen. A descent can be made back towards the main track in the glen, retracing steps to the main road at Dougarie.

There are small spaces to park cars at Dougarie, some distance either side of the bridge spanning Iorsa Water at its confluence with the sea. The whitewashed **Dougarie Lodge**, which is seen briefly near the bridge, is private. A nearby farm access road for **High Dougarie**, however, is signposted as 'footpath to Loch Iorsa'. The tarmac quickly gives way to a concrete track that soon bends left. Another sign on the bend indicates the footpath climbing straight up a flight of broken stone steps.

Cross a stile over a wall, then the path follows the wall beside fields, crossing a stile over a fence. Continue through a small wood, leaving it later to follow a track towards a rugged slope. Watch carefully for the line of the path, negotiating boggy patches and looking for occasional marker posts. The path reaches a bend on a track where a sign points back, reading 'footpath to main road'. Cross either a concrete ford or a footbridge over the Allt na h' Airighe and keep walking along the track parallel to the broad and bouldery Iorsa Water, which is the biggest river on the island.

The river cuts through masses of glacial rubble, whose ill-bedded layers can be seen alongside the track. Go through a gate in a tall deer fence and cross a concrete ford across a river draining **Glen Scaftigill**. When the river is in spate, wet feet are guaranteed at this point. A footbridge was once available upstream, but was swept away many years ago. The track continues across a slope of tussocky grass, heather and bog myrtle to reach the foot of **Loch Iorsa**, where there is a tiny boathouse.

A grassy, wet and boggy track pushes further up into **Glen Iorsa**, running alongside the shore of the loch, then continuing beside **Iorsa Water**. Bog myrtle grows amid the grass and heather. The track has been blazed by quad bikes being ridden into the glen and avoids the broad and boggy floor of the glen, sticking instead to the lower slopes of Sail Chalmadale. Follow the track as far as the **Allt Tigh an Shiorraim** and cross the boulder-strewn burn. Turn left to follow it upstream, but also keep well to the right of it for easier walking.

A small boathouse stands beside Loch Iorsa deep within the remote Glen Iorsa

Aim to walk along the top of a high bank overlooking the boulder-strewn watercourse. A vague path can be traced through the grass and heather, weaving past scattered boulders. At a higher level all traces of the path are lost, but it is still a good idea to keep to a rugged moorland shelf above the burn. Later, choose any point at which to ford the burn, even to the extent of going all the way up to **Loch Tanna** to enjoy a close-up view of Arran's largest lake. The higher the burn is forded, the less climbing there is on the slope opposite.

Walk roughly southwards towards a broad and rugged crest. This is boulder-strewn, with grass and heather, as well as exposed gritty soil in places. Walk along the crest, passing well to the left side of the little **Lochan nan Cnamh**. Walk up a slope of rocky ribs and low boulders, crossing the rugged, domed

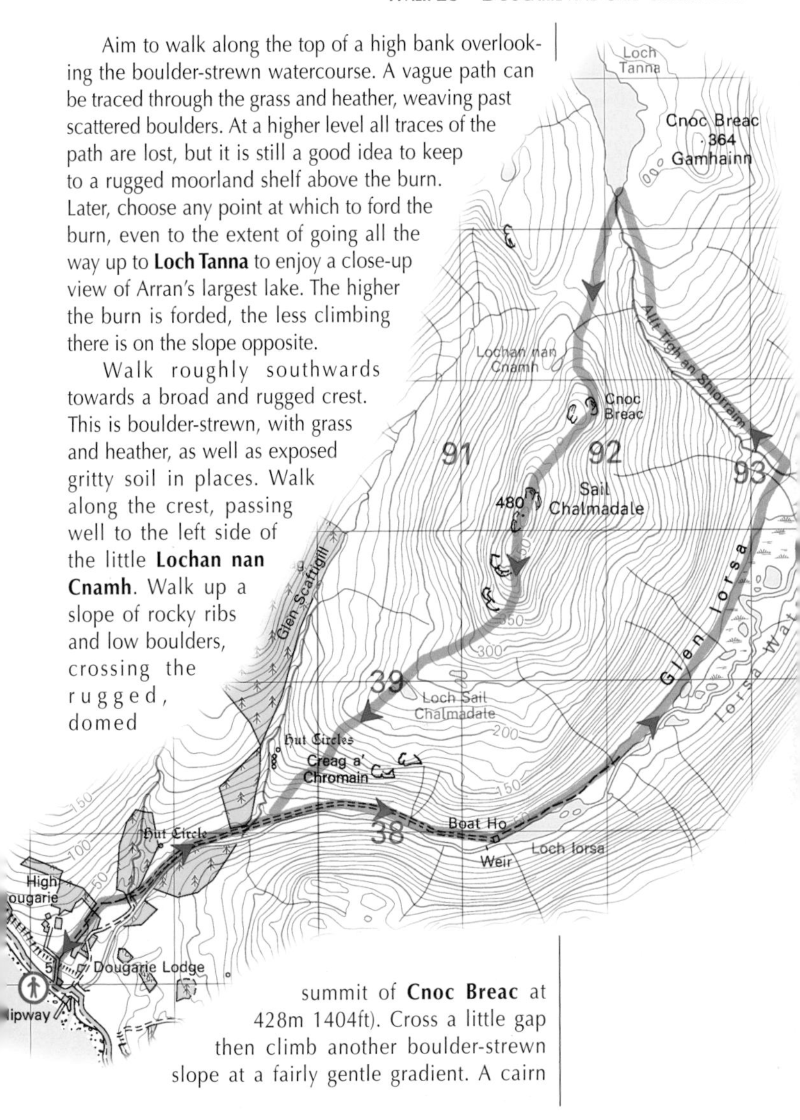

summit of **Cnoc Breac** at 428m 1404ft). Cross a little gap then climb another boulder-strewn slope at a fairly gentle gradient. A cairn

The view includes a host of higher summits arranged around Glen Iorsa. Looking seawards, it is possible to spot Jura, Kintyre, Antrim and even Ailsa Craig over a moorland shoulder.

stands on top of **Sail Chalmadale** at 480m (1575ft), surrounded by boulders poking through short heather. ◂

A narrow path is trodden away from the summit, running roughly southwards, but it soon vanishes. Keep walking until the lower parts of the ridge can be seen, bearing two small lochans. Drift a little to the left to descend steeply while avoiding hidden sloping slabs of granite. Swing back to the right, and later aim well to the right of the two lochans, the larger of which is **Loch Sail Chalmadale**. Bear in mind that they pass from sight until they are approached more closely on a broad moorland shoulder. Vague paths could be traced further downhill. The lower slopes, away from the rugged **Creag a' Chromain**, are largely of tussocky grass, heather, bracken and bog myrtle.

When the main track running through Glen Iorsa is gained, it is simply a matter of turning right and retracing the earlier steps of the day. Cross the concrete ford at the foot of **Glen Scaftigill** and pass through the gate in the tall deer fence. Follow the track to another ford and footbridge on the Allt na h' Airighe. A sign reads 'footpath to main road'. The path negotiates boggy patches and passes occasional marker posts, later joining a track. Go into a small wood on the left to follow the path onwards, later crossing a stile over a fence, then follow a wall beside fields. Cross a ladder stile over a wall, go down broken stone steps and follow an access road back to the main road at **Dougarie**.

DOUGARIE LODGE

The attractive whitewashed Dougarie Lodge was built towards the end of the 19th century as a shooting lodge. Although the red deer population on Arran had almost been wiped out by the beginning of the 19th century, there was considerable restocking and the northern half of the island was surrounded by a tall deer fence. At one time the exterior of Dougarie Lodge was covered in antlers. There is no access to the lodge, and walkers are directed along a nearby footpath that keeps well away from the building.

WALK 26

Circuit of Glen Iorsa

Start/Finish	Dougarie (NR 882 370)
Distance	30.5km (19 miles)
Total ascent	1930m (6330ft)
Time	10hrs
Terrain	Good valley tracks, but plenty of pathless, rocky and boggy moorland, followed by some well-trodden rocky ridge paths. Altogether a very long walk through remote and arduous mountains.
Refreshments	None closer than the Machrie Bay tearoom.

This is one of the toughest and most remote day's walks on Arran. Glen Iorsa is a broad, bleak and boggy glen slicing through northern Arran, without any habitations apart from Dougarie Lodge beside the sea. This long and arduous circuit takes in Sail Chalmadale, Loch Tanna, Beinn Tarsuinn and Loch na Davie. It includes ascents of Caisteal Abhail and the rocky Cir Mhòr. Bypassing the rocky ridge of A' Chir, the route climbs over Beinn Tarsuinn and Beinn Nuis before making a long descent towards Loch Iorsa. Paths are few and vague for the first half of the walk, although they're much clearer over the higher, rockier mountains. Walkers who attempt this long, hard walk should have a number of escape routes in mind. While a descent into Glen Iorsa is possible from many points, it could involve crossing very rugged, pathless terrain. Descents into other glens might be preferable.

There are small spaces to park cars at Dougarie, some distance either side of the bridge spanning Iorsa Water at its confluence with the sea. The whitewashed **Dougarie Lodge**, which is seen briefly near the bridge, is private. A nearby farm access road for **High Dougarie**, however, is signposted as 'footpath to Loch Iorsa'. The tarmac quickly gives way to a concrete track that soon bends left. Another sign on the bend indicates the footpath climbing straight up a flight of broken stone steps.

Dougarie Lodge is a late 19th-century shooting lodge

Cross a stile over a wall, then the path follows the wall beside fields, crossing a stile over a fence. Continue through a small wood, leaving it later to follow a track towards a rugged slope. Watch carefully for the line of the path, negotiating boggy patches and looking for occasional marker posts. The path reaches a bend on a track where a sign points back, reading 'footpath to main road'. Cross either a concrete ford or a footbridge over the Allt na h' Airighe and keep walking along the track parallel to the broad and bouldery Iorsa Water, which is the biggest river on the island.

The river cuts through masses of glacial rubble, whose ill-bedded layers can be seen alongside the track. Go through a gate in a tall deer fence and cross a concrete ford across a river draining Glen Scaftigill. When the river is in spate, wet feet are guaranteed at this point. A footbridge was once available upstream, but was swept away many years ago. The track continues across a slope of tussocky grass, heather and bog myrtle.

Once across, turn left to leave the track and pick up any vague paths climbing the lower slopes of Sail Chalmadale. Tussocky grass, heather, bracken and bog myrtle are crossed while keeping well to the left of rugged **Creag a' Chromain**. Pass to the left of **Loch Sail Chalmadale** and another small lochan on a moorland shoulder. The hill rises ahead, but there are sloping slabs of granite in view, so keep well to the right to outflank them and climb steeply. The higher crest is much gentler and there's even a vague path leading across short heather and boulders to the summit cairn on **Sail Chalmadale** at 480m (1575ft). There's a chance to study the whole of the route around Glen Iorsa, stretching from Loch Tanna to Caisteal Abhail and Beinn Nuis. It's a daunting prospect, considering how tough the ascent of this first summit has been.

Continue walking along the crest of the hill, heading down a boulder-strewn slope to cross a little gap. Walk over the rugged, domed summit of **Cnoc Breac**, at 428m (1404ft), and cross rocky ribs and boulders on the short descent towards **Lochan nan Cnamh**. Pass the lochan on its right-hand side and continue across a broad moorland slope, boulder-strewn in some parts and clothed in tussocky grass and heather in other parts. Aim for **Loch Tanna** and ford the outflowing burn

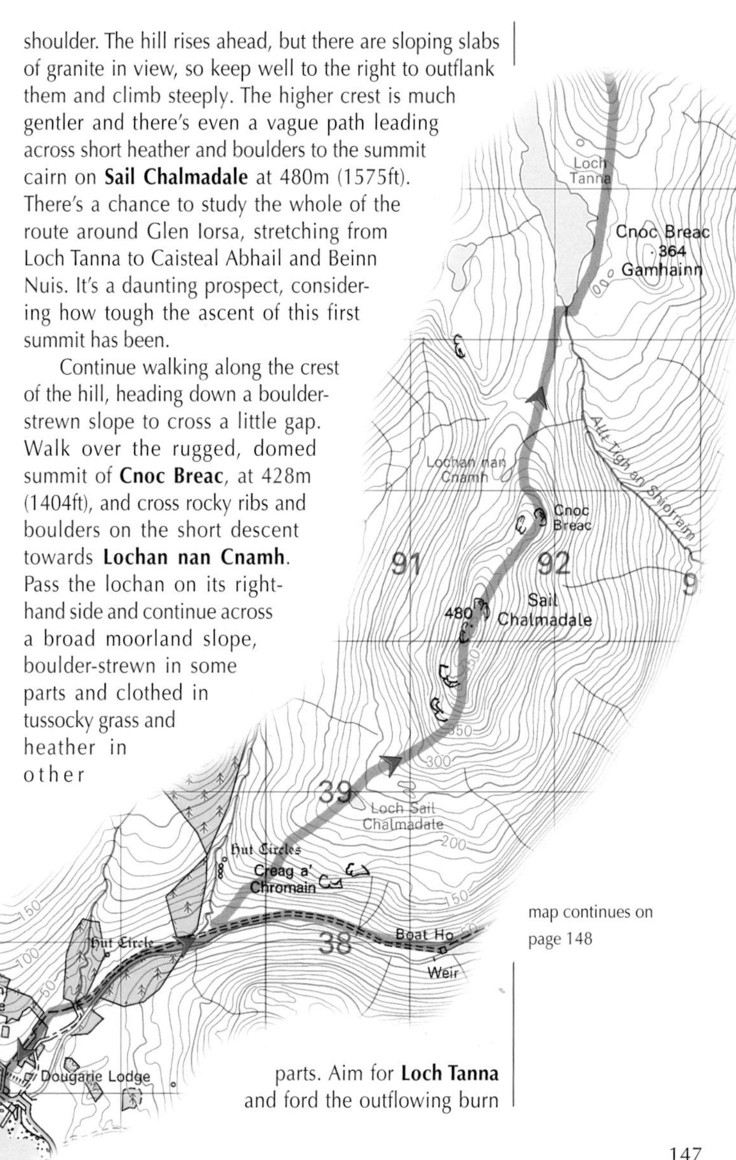

map continues on page 148

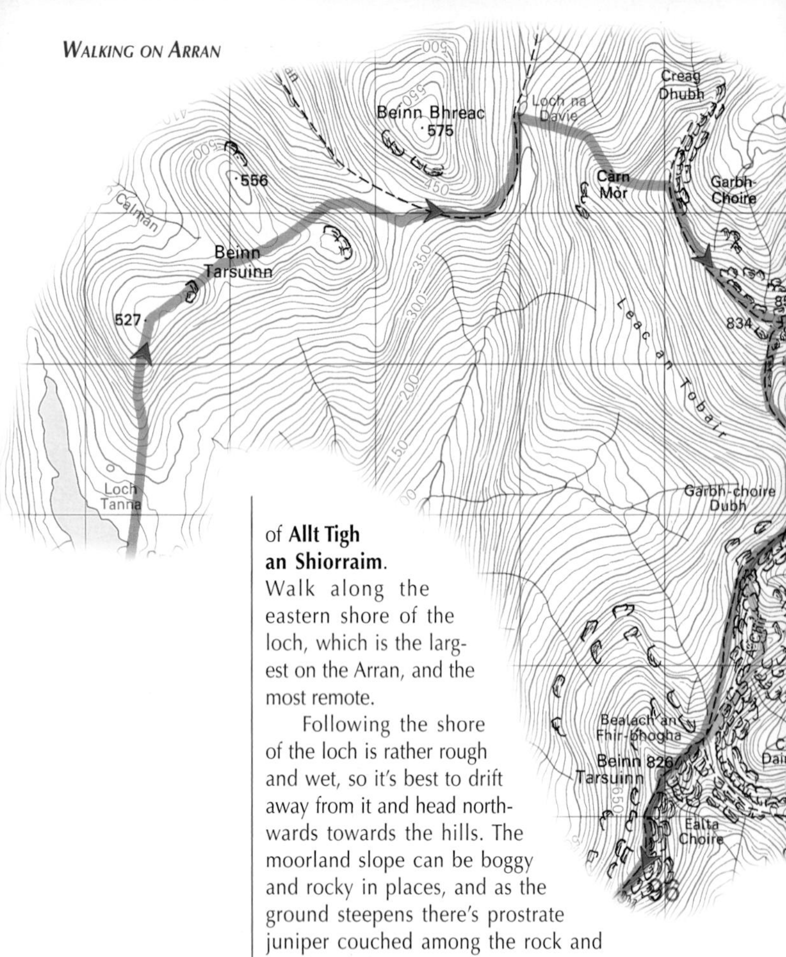

of **Allt Tigh an Shiorraim**. Walk along the eastern shore of the loch, which is the largest on the Arran, and the most remote.

Following the shore of the loch is rather rough and wet, so it's best to drift away from it and head northwards towards the hills. The moorland slope can be boggy and rocky in places, and as the ground steepens there's prostrate juniper couched among the rock and heather. **Beinn Tarsuinn** has two summits; the first is broad, gritty, boulder-strewn and features some low outcrops of granite. The only cairn is a small construction just off the 527m (1729ft) summit. Continue from this summit, down to a broad, boggy gap, then climb towards a higher part of Beinn Tarsuinn. Don't go to the 556m (1824ft) summit, but cross over a bouldery shoulder. Pick a way down a steep and bouldery slope to reach a

map continues on page 151

broad gap of boggy ground and stony patches over 400m (1310ft).

Towering above is the awesomely boulder-strewn **Beinn Bhreac**, but there is no need to climb it. Instead, turn right along a vague and stony path, cutting round a shoulder of the hill and dropping gently towards **Loch na Davie**, on a lower gap around 360m (1180ft). Cross in front of the little lough on boggy ground, reaching a firmer footing on the steep and bouldery slopes beyond.

This is a major turning point in the route, but there is much effort to be expended on the ascent of **Carn Mòr**, and a break of slope around 600m (1970ft) proves welcome. Continue climbing the pathless slope to emerge suddenly on a fine, sweeping, curved ridge overlooking the **Garbh-Choire**. ▶ Turn right up the ridge and eventually to the summit of **Caisteal Abhail** at 859m (2818ft). A handful of granite tors on the summit have the appearance of ruined castles.

This ridge is often referred to as the 'Dress Circle'.

Pick a way roughly southwards down from the summit and along a rocky ridge between the deep hollows of Coire nan Uamh and **Garbh-choire Dubh**. The next summit in line is the impressively steep and rocky pyramid of **Cir Mhòr**. Walkers should climb all the way to the 799m (2621ft) summit, but the walk is well advanced, so it is only fair to point out that a path cuts across the Glen Iorsa flank of the peak, omitting the summit.

Rising above the next gap are the rocky buttresses of **A' Chir**, where walkers would normally not tread. The full traverse of the A' Chir ridge is technically a rock climb, with some very exposed moves. Walkers start by climbing along the rocky crest, but must look carefully for a path off to the right, from some flat slabs on the Glen Iorsa flank of the mountain. A narrow, stony, rocky path sneaks across a rugged slope and passes beneath weeping boilerplate slabs of granite, which support only a few little rugs of heather. The path then climbs gradually to the gap of **Bealach an Fhir-bhogha**.

Towering above the gap are dark granite buttresses, which frown on humble walkers – especially those who are tired and still have a long walk ahead. A rocky, bouldery path keeps to the right of the main buttress, and although there are sometimes alternative lines available, all of them involve the use of hands for balance at some point.

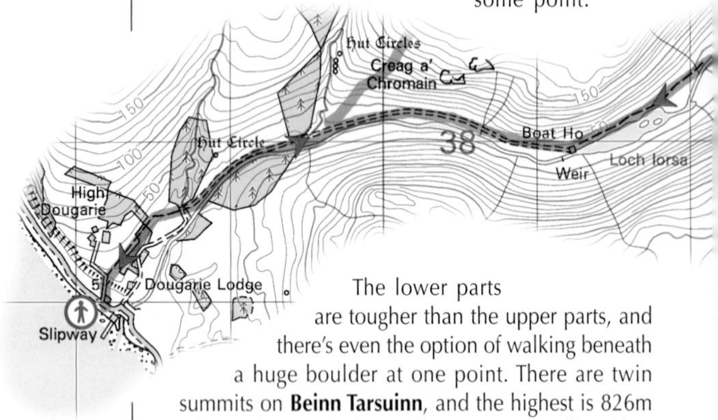

The lower parts are tougher than the upper parts, and there's even the option of walking beneath a huge boulder at one point. There are twin summits on **Beinn Tarsuinn**, and the highest is 826m (2710ft). Both summits feature low outcrops and boulders of granite.

A short, bouldery slope leads down to a dip, and on the next short ascent the human profile of the 'Old Man of Tarsuinn' will be seen to the left. A narrow ridge runs downhill and becomes covered in moss and short grass. Large rounded boulders are passed as the ridge broadens, then a narrow gap is crossed before a short ascent on a steep and bouldery slope leads onto the top of **Beinn Nuis**. A little cairn sits on the summit at 792m (2598ft). ◄

Views extend along the length of Glen Iorsa from this final summit, but the coast and the end of the walk still seem very distant.

Walk roughly westwards to leave, quickly swinging more south-west on a slope of short grass and boulders. Pass to the left of a wrinkly little tor of granite and cross a little gap below. After a short ascent, follow a rocky, blocky ridge downhill. The ridge broadens and becomes gritty, then more boulder-strewn and heathery. Below the rounded ridge is an expanse of moorland broken by the

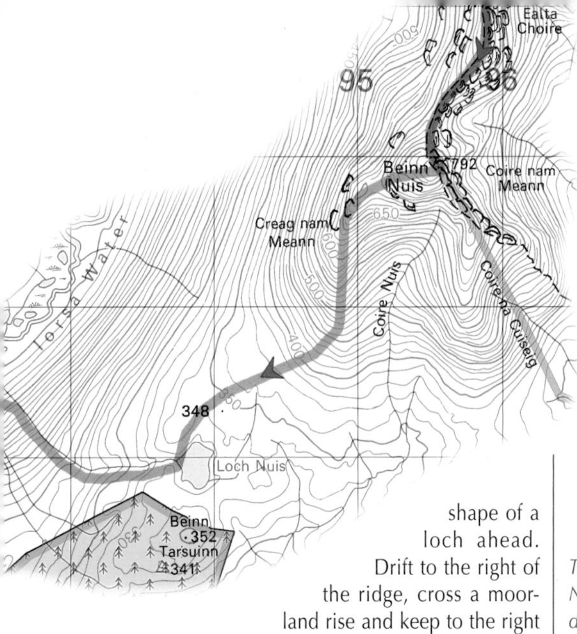

shape of a loch ahead. Drift to the right of the ridge, cross a moorland rise and keep to the right of **Loch Nuis**. A couple of rashes of boulders are passed

The view from Beinn Nuis before the long descent and walk out to Dougarie

Bear in mind, before descending, that if Iorsa Water is likely to be in spate after heavy rain you could switch to Walk 24 at Loch Nuis and head for an exit at Machrie.

on the moorland, and the outflow from the loch can be forded quite easily. ◂

Walk downstream beside the Allt Airidh Mhuirich and enjoy the sight of its little waterfalls as the slope steepens. Heather, bog myrtle and tussocky grass give way to bracken further downhill. Towards the bottom of the slope, drift to the left before the burn joins **Iorsa Water**. Watch carefully to spot shoals of reddish gravel where the river channel is braided and there is a chance of fording the river without getting wet feet.

Once across the river, turn left and pick up the course of a grassy, wet and boggy track, and follow it along the shore of **Loch Iorsa**. Bog myrtle grows among the grass and heather. At the foot of loch is a tiny boathouse and a gravel track. Follow the track downstream until a concrete ford is reached at the foot of Glen Scaftigill, which was forded much earlier in the day's walk. Ford it again and go through a gate in a tall deer fence beyond.

Follow the track to another ford and footbridge on the Allt na h' Airighe. A sign reads 'footpath to main road'. The path negotiates boggy patches and passes occasional marker posts, later joining a track. Go into a small wood on the left to follow the path onwards, later crossing a stile over a fence, then follow a wall beside fields. Cross a ladder stile over a wall, go down broken stone steps and follow an access road back to the main road at **Dougarie**.

Big rivers have to be forded on this walk, which swell after heavy rain

WALK 27

Imachar and Mullach Buidhe

Start/Finish	Between Whitefarland and Imachar (NR 864 413)
Distance	18km (11 miles)
Total ascent	890m (2920ft)
Time	5hrs 30mins
Terrain	Forest tracks at low level. Pathless moorland at mid level, needing care in poor visibility. Mountain paths at high level.
Refreshments	None closer than the Lighthouse café at Pirnmill.

A large forest plantation has been established on Ceann Reamhar and Roileag above Whitefarland and Imachar. While not being particularly attractive, it is largely tucked out of sight. It is served by clear gravel tracks that run fairly close to Mullach Buidhe. These forest tracks are used on the outward and return journeys, and the plan is to link them with a high-level walk over the top of Mullach Buidhe (sometimes referred to as Beinn Bharrain). Bear in mind that rugged and largely pathless slopes surround the mountain. The route has been structured to include the lonely Dubh Loch and Loch Tanna, as well as the unfrequented head of Glen Scaftigill. As some parts are quite rugged, this is a walk for the agile, sure-footed walker who can navigate competently in poor visibility.

Start on the main coastal road between the farmsteads at **Imachar** and **Whitefarland**. A track runs uphill from the road, flanked by double gates. Parking is not possible at this point, or for some distance either way along the road, but walkers using bus services can simply hop off at this point and start walking. The track climbs across a hillside that is variously vegetated, but mostly covered in grass and bracken. After zigzagging right and left, the track passes a prominent mast in a small compound beside two brick huts. Continue along the track, passing through a gate, then reaching a taller gate in a deer fence surrounding a forest. There is much more heather evident at this point.

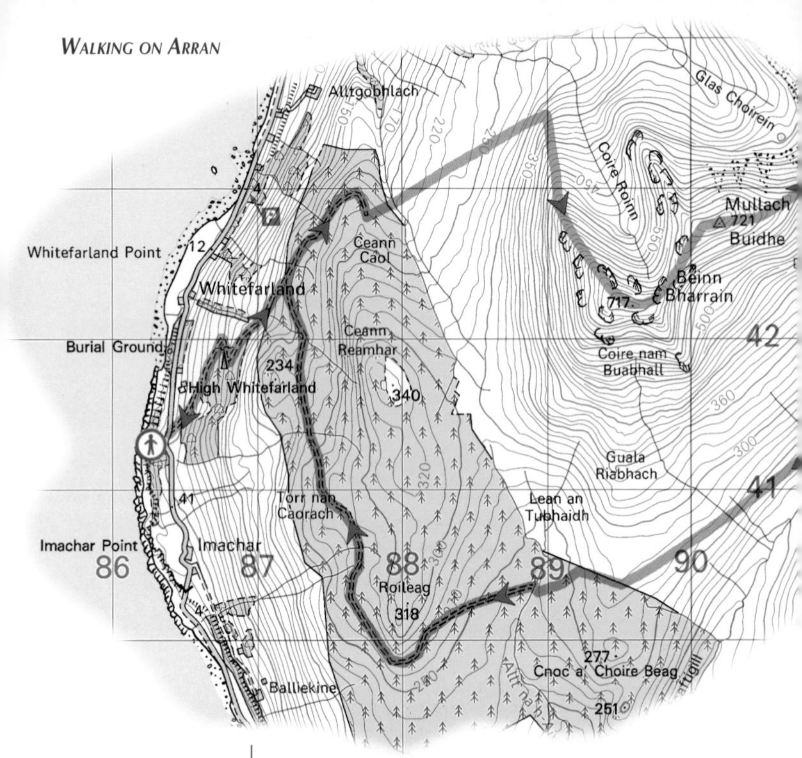

Follow the track up through the forest and keep left at a junction of tracks. The track follows a broad, heathery strip through the forest, then bends sharply to the right as it continues to climb. It expires suddenly on a broad, heathery ride near **Ceann Caol**. Turn left and follow another short ride down to the forest fence. There is no gate, although there is evidence that other people have walked this way. Thin walkers could squeeze beneath the tall deer fence, while more portly ones could climb at a straining post. Either way, agility is called for and this should be borne in mind before starting the walk.

Walk straight towards a burn in a rocky cut outside the forest. Look carefully and a rather narrow, precarious path will be spotted crossing from one side to the other.

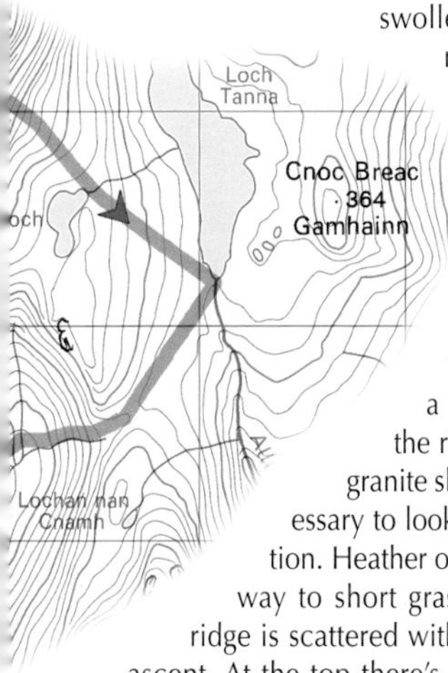

Cross with care, but note that it may be impassable when swollen with floodwater. Walk roughly north-east across a broad moorland slope, keeping well to the left of the huge mountain ahead. Aim to avoid the steep, boulder-strewn slopes and instead join the ridge to the left. Turn right and a path runs all the way up the ridge. It climbs and crosses granite slabs at first, where it is necessary to look carefully for its continuation. Heather on the steep path later gives way to short grass, although the rounded ridge is scattered with boulders throughout the ascent. At the top there's a small tor of tilted granite blocks, then the path is more vague as it crosses the broad summit. A cairn at 717m (2352ft) marks the highest part of the mountain. Some walkers refer to this as **Beinn Bharrain**, which is not strictly correct.

Walk across the short grass, passing low outcrops and boulders. Climb onto what appears to be a little tor, noting that there is a considerable gap on the far side. The steep and rocky slope bears a zigzag path leading down past granite slabs to a gap. The path climbs from the gap, and its narrow line can be traced past a couple of blocky tors to reach the summit of **Mullach Buidhe** at 721m (2365ft). There is a cairn and a trig point, with extensive views in clear weather.

Look carefully for the path leaving the summit, picking a way roughly east and north-east down a rounded ridge of scoured, gritty soil and short grass. The slope becomes less steep, but also more boulder-strewn and narrow. The lowest part of the ridge is a gap called Bealach an Fharaidh, where care should be taken to spot a path heading off to the right. Drop steeply down a rather worn and stony path. Anyone wanting to avoid this

Dubh Loch and Loch Tanna are seen on the moorlands below Mullach Buidhe

route could walk on the rough, boulder-strewn slopes to either side. When the slope begins to level out, masses of prostrate juniper can be seen among the boulders and heather. Head directly across a rugged, boggy moorland slope, passing the outflow of little **Dubh Loch** on the way to the foot of **Loch Tanna**. This is the largest lake on Arran, and also the most remote.

Head roughly south-west from the foot of Loch Tanna. The idea is to climb very gently across a rugged, boggy moorland to reach a broad gap between Beinn Bharrain and Sail Chalmadale. Cross this gap and descend to the head of Glen Scaftigill. The walking is fairly easy, although there is no trodden path at all. Cross grass, heather and bog myrtle on the gradual drift down towards the burn draining the glen, which is full of rock and boulders, so there are plenty of places to cross. After crossing, the ground on the far side is rather more rough and tussocky. Climb very gradually across the slopes of the glen towards a coniferous plantation seen straight ahead, reaching it around 280m (920ft). A tall deer fence surrounds the forest and there is a trodden path alongside it.

Turn right to follow the deer fence, and as it starts to descend, there is a gate on the left. Go through the gate and follow a ride into the forest for a short way. Turn right to walk down a grassy, mossy track through a wide, grassy, heathery strip between the trees. Cross a burn – the Allt na h-Airighe – and join a clear gravel track. Follow the track uphill through a broad, heathery ride. The track bends well to the right at the top of the rise at **Roileag**, and there are glimpses across Kilbrannan Sound to Kintyre.

The track descends very gradually across the forested slopes of **Torr nan Caorach** and **Ceann Reamhar**, crossing some unplanted swathes of moorland. A junction of gravel tracks is reached which was passed earlier in the day. Turn left to continue downhill, passing both the tall gate at the edge of the forest, and the next gate, before the track zigzags downhill past the mast. Simply continue downhill across the grass and bracken slope to end back on the main road.

A view of Mullach Buidhe while fording the Allt na h-Airighe inside the forest plantation

WALK 28

Pirnmill and Mullach Buidhe

Start/Finish	The Lighthouse café, Pirnmill (NR 872 441)
Distance	12km (7½ miles)
Total ascent	980m (3215ft)
Time	4hrs
Terrain	Rugged hillwalking, mostly on fairly good paths, but some parts are pathless.
Refreshments	The Lighthouse café at Pirnmill.

Mullach Buidhe, sometimes referred to as Beinn Bharrain, is the highest of the Pirnmill Hills grouped in the north-west of Arran. It rises steeply above the long, straggly little village of Pirnmill. There is good access from the village to a rugged moorland shelf. Paths are vague afterwards, although there's a fairly well-trodden path along the mountain ridge high above. It's worth climbing Beinn Bhreac as well as Mullach Buidhe in order to make the most of the high ridge, although the ascent to the ridge by way of Meall Donn is steep and unremitting. In clear weather, views from the ridge are remarkably extensive and take in all the highest peaks on Arran.

Start at The Lighthouse café in **Pirnmill**, beside the village store. Walk northwards along the road for a few paces and turn right up a track signposted as a footpath. Concrete quickly gives way to gravel and the track swings to the left, then turns right and runs uphill, crossing a cattle grid. When the track bends to the left, don't follow it, but turn right as signposted and cross a stile over a fence. A narrow, muddy path squeezes between densely planted birch trees, but a more open stand of oak is encountered at a higher level. There are glimpses of fine, slender waterfalls deep within a gorge.

Follow the path further uphill, crossing a stile, fording a muddy burn and later crossing a large ladder-stile over a deer fence. Climb alongside the fence until it turns a corner.

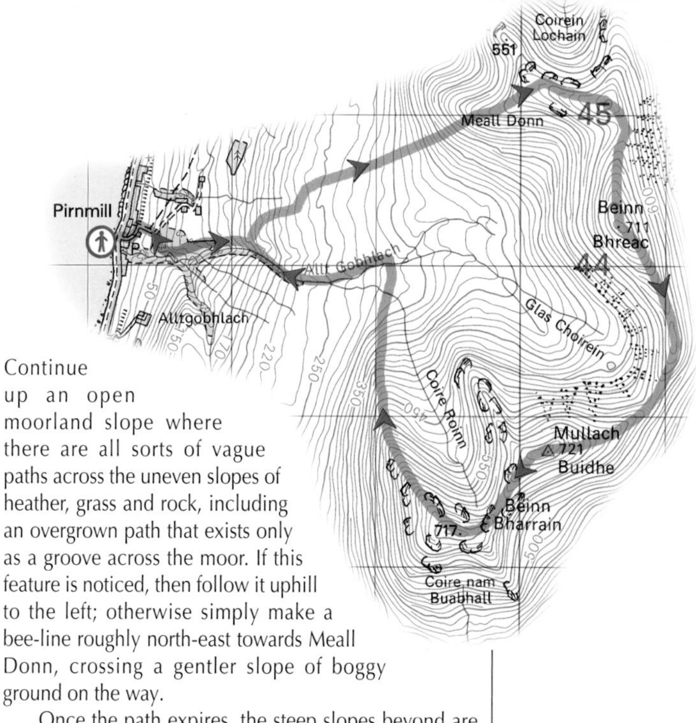

Continue up an open moorland slope where there are all sorts of vague paths across the uneven slopes of heather, grass and rock, including an overgrown path that exists only as a groove across the moor. If this feature is noticed, then follow it uphill to the left; otherwise simply make a bee-line roughly north-east towards Meall Donn, crossing a gentler slope of boggy ground on the way.

Once the path expires, the steep slopes beyond are covered in heather and boulders, without trodden routes. Choose any line uphill, but note that the ground is less boulder-strewn further to the left. The steep slope is unremitting, but taken steadily there is an eventual break of slope where the walking becomes easier at **Meall Donn**. Follow the rounded, heathery, bouldery crest onwards and upwards. A path is eventually gained on another broad crest overlooking Coire-Fhionn Lochan, joining Walk 29. Turn right and follow the crest gently uphill to a broad and bouldery summit at 653m (2142ft).

Continue straight along the rounded crest, using a path that proves quite easy despite the boulders. The path crosses a gap and leads to a large summit cairn on **Beinn Bhreac** at 711m (2333ft). There is a sudden view straight ahead, stretching beyond Arran to the distant, prominent pyramid of Ailsa Craig. Leave the summit and continue

Beinn Bhreac and Mullach Buidhe rise as rugged domes from the broad ridge

along the rounded, boulder-strewn ridge, following a path that is rather vague in places. The ridge levels out on a shoulder, then there are larger boulders to be crossed on the way down to the gap of Bealach an Fharaidh. Climb from the gap, stepping across some large boulders at first. The slope becomes less boulder-strewn, but rather steeper too, featuring scoured gritty soil and short grass. The top of **Mullach Buidhe** is fairly broad, bearing a cairn and trig point at 721m (2365ft).

Continue along the broad crest on short grass, following a vague path and passing a couple of blocky little granite tors. The path remains narrow, but is more clearly trodden down to the next gap. A steep slope ahead bears a zigzag path, which passes granite slabs on the rockier parts of a prominent tor. The top of this tor is a prominent summit in its own right, and this should be borne in mind in poor visibility. Drop down slightly from the tor and follow the path further across the broad summit, walking on short grass and passing low outcrops and boulders. A cairn at 717m (2352ft) marks the highest point. Some walkers refer to this as **Beinn Bharrain**, which is not strictly correct.

Drift to the right while crossing the broad summit, towards a small tor of tilted granite blocks. A path leaves the tor, running straight down a rounded ridge scattered with boulders. Later, the ground steepens and short grass gives way to heather. Look carefully for the line of the path after it runs onto granite slabs then follow it down onto a gentler sloping, but more rugged moorland, which can be boggy underfoot. Only a vague path crosses the lower moorland, so be sure to swing a little to the right to cross a river, the **Allt Gobhlach**, well before it plunges into a steep, wooded gorge.

Stay well clear of the gorge on the final stage of the descent, enjoying views of its waterfalls, aiming to reach the corner of the deer fence that was passed earlier in the day's walk. Cross the large ladder-stile over the deer fence, then follow the narrow path downhill alongside the fence. Cross a muddy burn and another stile as the path runs down through a birch and oak woodland, catching glimpses of the fine waterfalls in the gorge. The path has a muddy stretch before a stile gives way to a firm track. Turn left and follow the track back down to **Pirnmill**.

PIRNMILL

Penrioch was a farmstead of some antiquity from which the village of Pirnmill eventually grew. Apart from a history of smuggling, fishing was an important industry. The modern name of Pirnmill was derived from a mill that made bobbins, or 'pirns', from around 1780 to 1840. The ruins of the old mill can still be seen. The little village has only a few features and facilities. Listed from south to north they include: a war memorial, village store and post office, The Lighthouse café, Clisham B&B, Pirnmill Primary School and a corrugated iron church. The beach is quite rough and boulder-strewn.

WALK 29

Coire-Fhionn Lochan

Start/Finish	Mid Thundergay (NR 879 466)
Distance	9km (5½ miles)
Total ascent	660m (2165ft)
Time	3hrs
Terrain	A straightforward hill walk, mostly on good paths, but including some steep slopes.
Refreshments	None closer than a café at Pirnmill and a pub at Catacol.

There is a popular walk from Thundergay up to Coire-Fhionn Lochan, which can be extended into a short horseshoe walk on the hills overlooking the loch. Coire-Fhionn Lochan is sometimes rendered as 'Correin Lochain', which is a half-Anglicisation of the Gaelic pronunciation. While this walk is presented as a short hill walk, it can also double as an access route towards longer and tougher days on the hills. Some walkers who put in all the effort necessary to climb Meall Biorach may prefer to stay high and continue over Beinn Bhreac and Mullach Buidhe, descending to Pirnmill later, as described in Walk 28.

There is only limited parking at **Thundergay**, beside the coastal road. An access road, marked by a footpath signpost for 'Coire-Fhionn Lochan' and a small red postbox, serves a handful of houses at Mid Thundergay. Follow the stony access track as it winds uphill, giving way to a grassy surface past the last couple of houses. Go through a kissing gate as signposted for 'Coire-Fhionn Lochan'. A path runs up a grassy slope that has been planted with thousands of young deciduous trees. Cross a ladder-stile beside a tall gate in a deer fence.

The path runs across a heathery slope, with the dome of Meall nan Damh rising ahead. The path crosses a burn using a boulder stepping-stone, then swings to the right to face Meall Biorach. Continue upstream alongside the Uisge Soluis Mhòir, which features a series of little

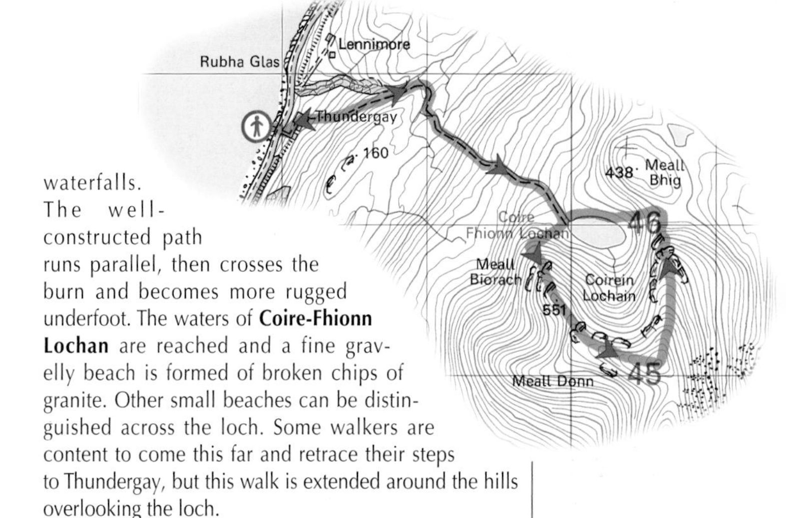

waterfalls. The well-constructed path runs parallel, then crosses the burn and becomes more rugged underfoot. The waters of **Coire-Fhionn Lochan** are reached and a fine gravelly beach is formed of broken chips of granite. Other small beaches can be distinguished across the loch. Some walkers are content to come this far and retrace their steps to Thundergay, but this walk is extended around the hills overlooking the loch.

An anti-clockwise circuit ensures that paths are easily spotted, especially paths used later on a steep descent. Start the circuit by turning right along the shore of the loch. Follow a narrow, gritty path gently uphill and away from the shore. The path swings suddenly to the right and cuts across steep, heathery slopes. As it climbs, it

Looking down on Coire-Fhionn Lochan and Kilbrannan Sound from the rugged crest

The little settlement of Thundergay looks across Kilbrannan Sound to Kintyre

becomes more boulder-strewn. Watch carefully for a turning to the left, and continue zigzagging uphill. The path takes a fairly easy course on the steep, rugged slope. At a higher level the gradient eases and there is a stretch along a level, rounded shoulder of low rocky outcrops, heather and gritty soil on **Meall Biorach**, at 551m (1898ft).

The path crosses a large, gently sloping slab of granite, then rises in stages towards the highest part of the route. There is often a good view back down to the loch. A broad summit at 653m (2142ft) is covered in large boulders and short grass. A number of vague paths converge on the summit, and by heading roughly northwards, the route begins its descent.

There are good views down to the loch from various points. A reasonably gentle, rounded ridge of outcropping slabs, gritty soil, sparse vegetation and scattered boulders leads downhill. Later, there is a steep slope of short heather leading down to a broad and boggy gap. Look out for a well-trodden path cutting across the gap. Turn left to follow this path downhill, back towards **Coire-Fhionn Lochan**. The path descends a rugged slope to reach the shore, then runs across the foot of a heathery slope to reach the outflowing Uisge Soluis Mhòir. Cross the burn and turn right to follow it downstream. The return route is simply a matter of retracing earlier steps of the day, back down to **Thundergay** and the coast road.

THUNDERGAY

Thundergay, or Thunderguy, was one of a series of farmsteads dotted along the western side of Arran, all of great antiquity. They included Thundergay, Penrioch, Altgobhlach, Imachar and Banleacainn. Stories relate that the tenants held their tenancy from the Scottish kings. Some are said to have obtained their tenancy from a grateful Robert the Bruce in respect of services rendered during his long and bitter campaign to secure the Scottish throne, although there is no real evidence to support this.

WALK 30

Catacol and Meall nan Damh

Start/Finish	Fairhaven, Glen Catacol (NR 910 489)
Distance	11km (7 miles)
Total ascent	650m (2130ft)
Time	5hrs 30mins
Terrain	A steep, rugged and pathless ascent, but paths and tracks are used later, with a road-walk at the end.
Refreshments	Catacol Bay Hotel at Catacol.

Meall nan Damh raises its rugged slopes almost directly south of Catacol. An ascent of its rocky dome can be combined with a descent alongside the lovely Coire-Fhion Lochan. Once the road is reached at Thundergay, if a handy bus happens to be passing, then it can be used to return to Catacol, but in any case the coastal walk along the main road is pleasant, pursuing a roller-coaster route and clinging to a rugged slope overlooking Kilbrannan Sound. It was the last part of the road encircling Arran to be completed, as the terrain was particularly difficult.

Fairhaven is a large white house a short way south of **Catacol**, where a bridge spans the river draining into **Catacol Bay**. There is a car park just on the south side of the bridge, close to Fairhaven. Start walking from the back of the car park, following a clear, grassy and stony path parallel to the river, the Abhainn Mòr. Go through a tall gate in a deer fence and cross a burn. Continue across a field where there is a large wooden hut. A narrower path continues across a squelchy area of heather and bog myrtle. There are a few trees on the hillside, and when these thin out, turn right and start climbing the rugged slope.

Heather and boulders have to be negotiated without the benefit of a trodden path. The rugged summit of **Meall nan Leac Sleamhuinn** can be seen at the top of the slope. While this is a useful feature to head towards at first, it is best to aim to the right of it. Later, the loftier dome of

Cobbly beach at Catacol, looking towards the hump of Meall nan Damh

Meall nan Damh comes into view and another change of course is made on a rugged moorland slope.

Turn right well before reaching the little pool of **Lochan a' Mhill** and cross the little burn flowing from it. Swing left and head south along a ridge where a steep slope of uniform heather gives way to a slightly gentler slope of low rocky outcrops and scattered boulders. In clear weather jagged peaks can be seen to the left, running from Caisteal Abhail to Beinn Nuis, while far away to the right, beyond Kintyre, are the Paps of Jura. The heather underfoot gets shorter and features little club-mosses,

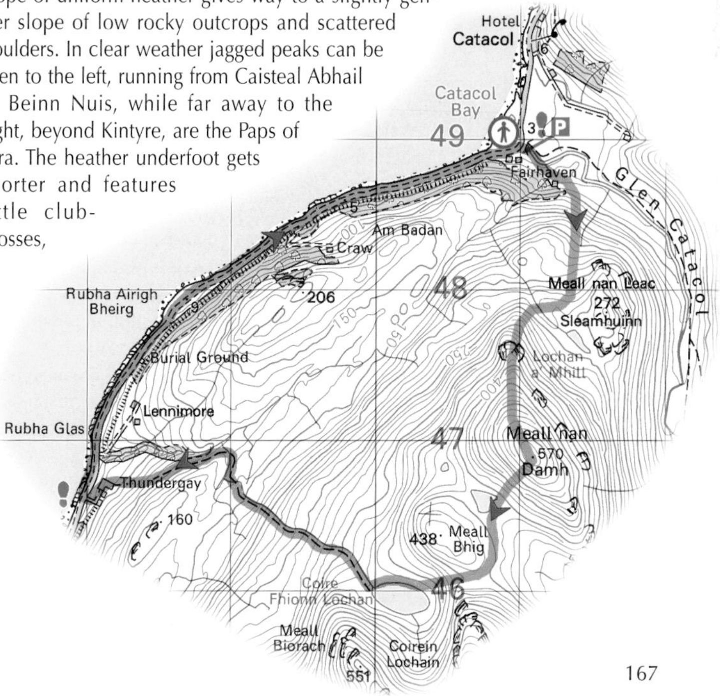

There are fine views all around Arran, but attention should be focussed on a gap beyond the moorland rise of Meall Bhig, where this route is heading.

while the gradient gradually eases. The ground becomes more boulder-strewn as a large cairn is passed. The larger summit cairn on **Meall nan Damh** is a bit further along and stands at 570m (1870ft). ◄

Leave the summit and pick a way downhill, roughly south-westwards, aiming to the left of a small lochan on a broad moorland gap. Take care on this steep descent, avoiding extensive outcrops of rock. The lochan lies just below 400m (1310ft), and the route forges straight across a moorland slope on the left-hand side of **Meall Bhig**. Tussocky bog on the slope features a narrow path leading to a tiny pool on the next gap.

A clear path cuts across the gap, so turn right to follow it into a splendid hollow in the hills. The path descends a rugged slope and runs beside the shore of **Coire-Fhionn Lochan**. Three bright, gritty beaches can be spotted, and an inspection of the beach at the outflow reveals it to be made of broken chips of granite. Cross the outflow and follow a path downstream. The burn is called Uisge Soluis Mhóir and it features a series of fine waterfalls. The path suddenly turns right and crosses the burn, then continues downstream on a better surface.

Later, turn left and cross the burn using a boulder stepping-stone. The path crosses a ladder-stile beside a tall gate in a deer fence. Continue down across a grassy slope that has been planted with thousands of young deciduous trees. Go through a kissing gate and a grassy track quickly joins a gravel track serving a few houses. Simply follow the bendy track down past more houses at **Thundergay**, reaching the main coastal road.

Turn right to follow the road, and the first burn crossed is the Uisge Soluis Mhóir again. The next feature of note is an old **burial ground**. The road clings precariously to a rugged slope, sometimes having cliffs above or below it, and contorted sea stacks can be spotted. There are plenty of trees clinging to the upper cliffs, with heather and bracken on the lower slopes. Halfway along the road, the access track running up to **Craw** will be noticed off to the right. When **Fairhaven** is reached the road finally levels out as the walk finishes.

WALK 31

Catacol and Beinn Bhreac

Start/Finish	Fairhaven, Glen Catacol (NR 910 489)
Distance	16.5km (10¼ miles)
Total ascent	1180m (3870ft)
Time	5hrs 30mins
Terrain	Rugged hill walking, often without trodden paths, so careful navigation is needed in poor visibility.
Refreshments	Catacol Bay Hotel at Catacol.

Beinn Bhreac offers a fine, high-level walk along a smooth, whaleback ridge. The rugged dome of Meall nan Damh can be crossed as an enormous stepping-stone on the way to Beann Bhreac and, after making a descent to lonely Loch Tanna, the two broad summits of Beinn Tarsuinn are included. There is a long descent into and through Glen Catacol to close the circuit. Beinn Bhreac is perched between the waters of Kilbrannan Sound and the highest peaks of Arran, so views in all directions prove most interesting in clear weather.

Fairhaven is a large white house a short way south of **Catacol**, where a bridge spans the river draining into **Catacol Bay**. There is a car park just on the south side of the bridge, close to Fairhaven. Start walking from the back of the car park, following a clear, grassy and stony path parallel to the river, the Abhainn Mòr. Go through a tall gate in a deer fence and cross a burn. Continue across a field where there is a large wooden hut. A narrower path continues across a squelchy area of heather and bog myrtle. There are a few trees on the hillside; when these thin out, turn right and start climbing the rugged slope.

Heather and boulders have to be negotiated without the benefit of a trodden path. The rugged summit of **Meall nan Leac Sleamhuinn** can be seen at the top of the slope. While this is a useful feature to head towards at first, it is best to aim to the right of it. Later, the loftier dome of

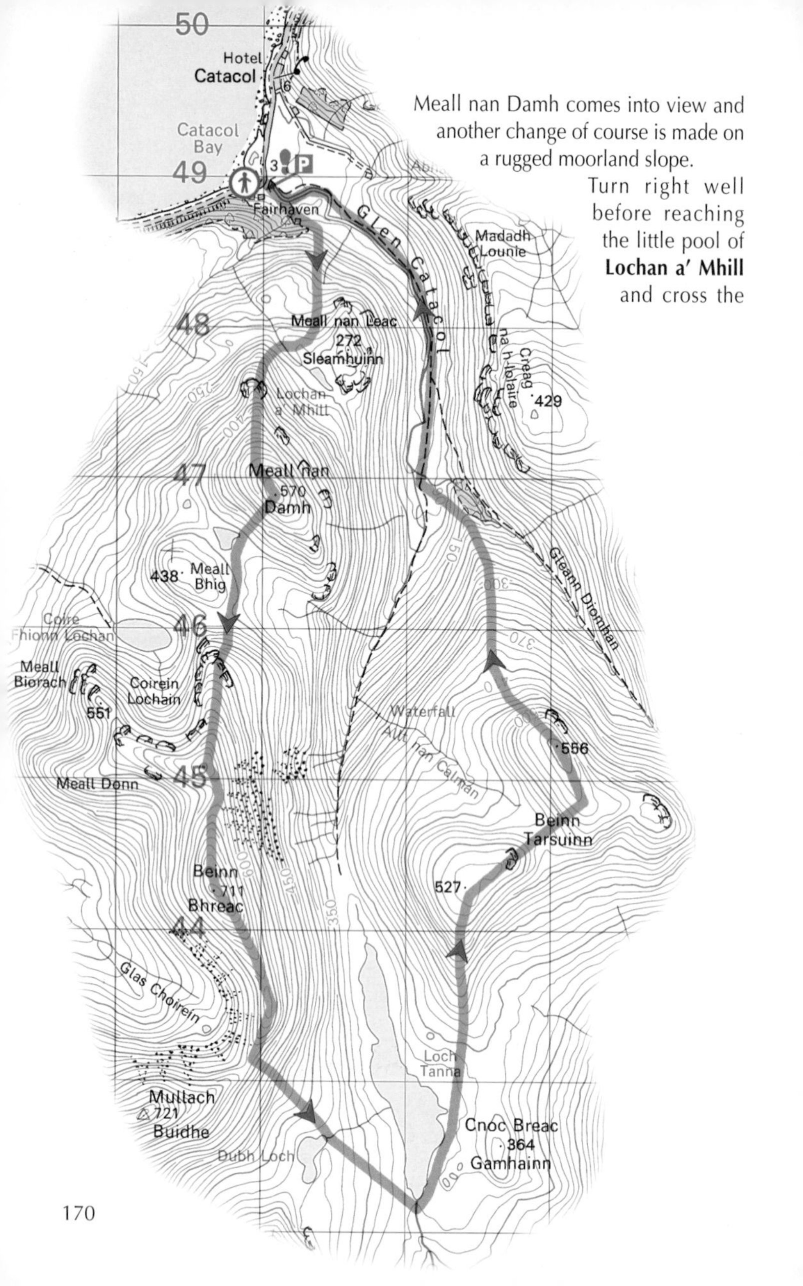

Meall nan Damh comes into view and another change of course is made on a rugged moorland slope.

Turn right well before reaching the little pool of **Lochan a' Mhill** and cross the

Looking back along the rugged crest towards the dome of Meall nan Damh

little burn flowing from it. Swing left and head south along a ridge where a steep slope of uniform heather gives way to a slightly gentler slope of low rocky outcrops and scattered boulders. In clear weather jagged peaks can be seen to the left, running from Caisteal Abhail to Beinn Nuis, while far away to the right, beyond Kintyre, are the Paps of Jura. The heather underfoot gets shorter and features little clubmosses, while the gradient gradually eases. The ground becomes more boulder-strewn as a large cairn is passed. The larger summit cairn on **Meall nan Damh** is a bit further along and stands at 570m (1870ft). ▸

There are fine views right around the island.

Leave the summit and pick a way downhill, roughly south-westwards, aiming to the left of a small lochan on a broad moorland gap. Take care on this steep descent, avoiding extensive outcrops of rock. The lochan lies just below 400m (1310ft), and the route forges straight across a moorland slope on the left-hand side of **Meall Bhig**. Tussocky bog on the slope features a narrow path leading to a tiny pool on the next gap.

A clear path cuts across the gap, but cross over it and climb straight uphill, heading southwards. A short, steep slope of heather gives way to a gentler slope of outcropping slabs, gritty soil, sparse vegetation and boulders. Follow this rounded shoulder further uphill, passing to one or the other side of a wrinkled outcrop at the top. There is a summit at 653m (2142ft), where a number of vague paths converge, and it's worth having a look down to **Coire-Fhionn Lochan**.

Continue straight along the rounded crest, using a path that proves quite easy despite the boulders. The path crosses a gap and leads to a large summit cairn on **Beinn Bhreac** at 711m (2333ft). There is a sudden view straight ahead, stretching beyond the Isle of Arran to the distant, prominent pyramid of Ailsa Craig. Leave the summit and continue along the rounded, boulder-strewn ridge, following a path that's rather vague in places. The ridge levels out on a shoulder, then there are larger boulders to be crossed on the way down to the gap of Bealach an Fharaidh.

Turn left and drop steeply down a rather worn and stony path. Anyone wanting to avoid this route could walk on the rough, boulder-strewn slopes to either side. When the slope begins to level out, masses of prostrate juniper can be seen among the boulders and heather. Head directly across a rugged, boggy moorland slope, passing the outflow of little **Dubh Loch** on the way to the foot of **Loch Tanna**. This is the largest lake on Arran, and also the most remote.

Cross the Allt Tigh an Shiorraim where it flows from Loch Tanna, then turn left to start walking towards Beinn Tarsuinn. Following the shore of the loch is rather rough and wet, so it's best to drift away from it and head northwards towards the hills. The moorland slope can be boggy and rocky in places, and as the ground steepens there is prostrate juniper couched among the rock and heather. **Beinn Tarsuinn** has two summits; the first is broad, gritty, boulder-strewn and features some low outcrops of granite. The only cairn is a small construction just off the 527m (1729ft) summit. Continue from this

A view along the length of Loch Tanna towards the dome of Meall nan Damh

summit, down to a broad, boggy gap, then climb towards a higher part of Beinn Tarsuinn, swinging left to reach the 556m (1824ft) summit, where there is a cairn. ▶

Aim north-west towards Meall nan Damh to start the descent down a steep slope of heather and boulders. Swing more northwards on a gentle, boggy slope before descending more steeply again on a rounded ridge. There's a vague path on the lower part of the descent. Swing to the left towards the end of the slope, aiming

There's a fine view along a jagged line of peaks from Beinn Nuis to Caisteal Abhail, while in the opposite direction the Paps of Jura appear beyond Meall nan Damh.

to pick up a clear path where **Glen Catacol** and **Gleann Diomhan** meet.

Turn right to follow the path and ford a bouldery river. The path generally runs close to a larger river, the Abhainn Mòr, which in turn often crosses slabs of granite where occasional boulders stand marooned. Small rapids and waterfalls can be enjoyed. The river has a more cobbly stretch and the ground alongside features a mixture of grass, heather, bracken and bog myrtle. When the river goes through a narrow constriction, the path climbs over an outcrop of banded rock. The final meanders of the river are faithfully traced and a tall kissing gate is passed before the main road is reached at a flat concrete bridge. Turn left to cross the bridge to return to the car park near **Fairhaven** where the walk started.

CATACOL

Catacol was no more than a poor clachan in the 1800s, but the land was acquired by the Hamiltons and things began to change. The illegitimate daughter of the eighth Duke, Ann Douglas, married Lord Rossmore from Ireland and received the lands around Catacol as a dowry. Lord Rossmore built a fine house where Catacol Farm now stands, as well as a church at Lenimore. There was no minister for the church at first, but when one was appointed a manse was built where the Catacol Bay Hotel now stands. The terrace of cottages known as the Twelve Apostles was built in the 1860s to house the people who were cleared from the older clachan. However, the people refused to live there and drifted elsewhere, and the terrace became known as Hungry Row until tenants were found. (There are 12 cottages, but 13 chimneys!) Facilities in the village are limited to the food, drink and accommodation provided by the Catacol Bay Hotel.

WALK 32

Catacol and Beinn Tarsuinn

Start/Finish	Fairhaven, Glen Catacol (NR 910 489)
Distance	16km (10 miles)
Total ascent	890m (2920ft)
Time	5hrs
Terrain	Apart from an initial low-level path, mostly rugged and often pathless hill walking.
Refreshments	Catacol Bay Hotel at Catacol.

Glen Catacol offers splendid access to the hills in the north-west of Arran. While many walkers feel obliged to climb the highest hills, there are a handful of lesser heights that prove to be just as rugged, if not more so in places. The sprawling Beinn Tarsuinn can be climbed, followed by the steep and bouldery Beinn Bhreac. The broad moorland crest beyond is punctuated by the little hump of Beinn Bhiorach and the larger hump of Meall Mòr. At the end of the walk is a splendid view along the length of Glen Catacol, not available from any other viewpoint. The lack of paths across these hills suggests that most walkers stay low in the glens, or traverse the higher mountains.

Fairhaven is a large white house a short way south of **Catacol**, where a bridge spans the river draining into **Catacol Bay**. There is a car park just on the south side of the bridge, close to Fairhaven. Start walking by crossing the bridge and turning right. A public footpath signpost offers destinations including Gleann Diomhan and Loch Tanna. Follow a broad, grassy, stony path alongside the river, the Abhainn Mòr, and go through a tall kissing gate in a deer fence. The path continues to run alongside the river, then rises to cross an outcrop of banded rock. The river runs through a narrow constriction below the outcrop. The path runs alongside a cobbly stretch of the river, passing areas of grass, heather, bracken and bog myrtle.

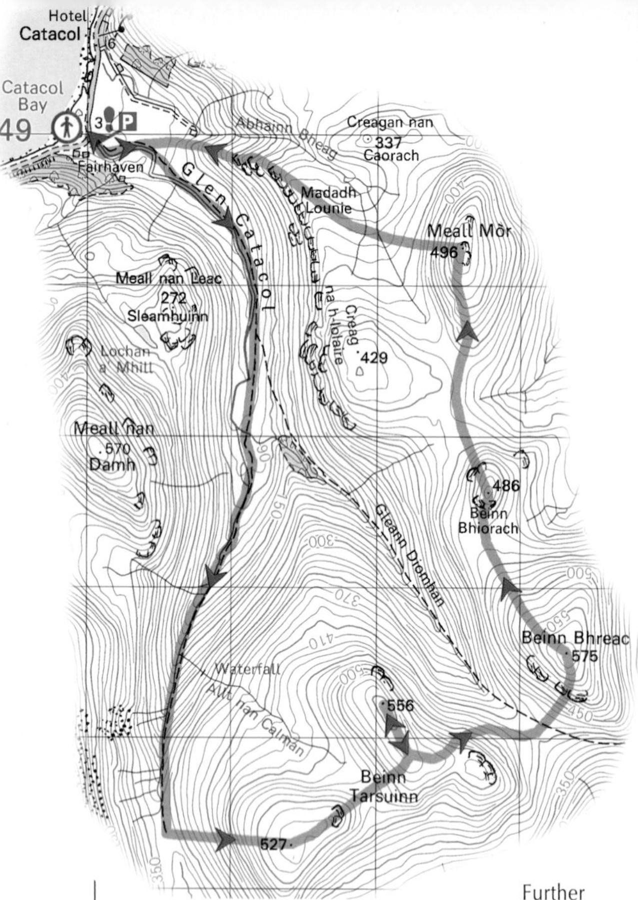

Further upstream, the river runs in rapids and waterfalls across bare slabs of granite where occasional boulders stand marooned. A couple of lesser paths branch off to the left, leading up into **Gleann Diomhan**, but don't follow them. A bouldery river needs to be forded and the path remains clear as it climbs towards the head of **Glen Catacol**. The surface is rather more bouldery and some sections can be boggy. The river often features small waterfalls and there are lengthy stretches where the water slides over clean beds of granite. Off to the left is a steeper waterslide on the **Allt nan Calman**. Follow the river upstream as it diminishes, passing a sprawling cairn before reaching another cairn on a broad, stony gap over 330m (1080ft). There is a view ahead of Loch Tanna, which is the largest and most remote lake on Arran.

Turn left to climb roughly east above the gap. There is a steep slope of heather and boulders before the gradient eases, with fewer boulders. At length a small cairn is passed on an outcrop of granite slabs, although this is not quite on the 527m (1729ft) summit of **Beinn Tarsuinn**.

Continue from this summit, down to a broad, boggy gap, then climb towards a higher part of the hill, swinging left to reach the 556m (1824ft) summit, where there is a cairn. ▶

There is a great view from here along a jagged line of peaks from Beinn Nuis to Caisteal Abhail, while in the opposite direction the Paps of Jura appear beyond Meall nan Damh.

The next summit is Beinn Bhreac, but it should not be approached directly across Gleann Diomhan. Instead, double back along the crest of Beinn Tarsuinn and gradually swing left until the direction is almost north-eastwards. Pick a way down a steep and bouldery slope to reach a broad gap of boggy ground and stony patches over 400m (1310ft).

Meall nan Damh is seen from a broad and boggy gap below Beinn Tarsuinn

Towering above is the awesomely boulder-strewn Beinn Bhreac, which is climbed fairly directly. The heather is quite deep and springy, interspersed with bilberry and crowberry, often concealing deep holes that need to be avoided. The boulder-strewn parts of the slope need great care as some of them are loose. On many parts it is necessary to use hands as well as feet to assist on the climb. The gradient eases near the top, with shorter heather, short grass and more deeply embedded boulders. The bouldery summit cairn on **Beinn Bhreac** stands at 575m (1886ft).

Leave the summit by walking north-west along a broad, rounded ridge. A large, square cairn is passed, then after crossing a broad moorland gap a short climb northward leads up an easy, bouldery slope. The top of **Beinn Bhiorach** is a bare peak of rock at 486m (1594ft).

Continue by carefully picking a way down a short, steep slope which has some rocky areas. Cross a broad gap and aim for the most prominent hill in view ahead. This is best approached by taking a direct line across an uneven slope of moorland. Climb straight up a blunt, rounded ridge, where scattered boulders on the heathery slope pose no problem. A cairn stands on the summit of **Meall Mòr** at 496m (1627ft), with another cairn further along the crest. There is a last chance to absorb the view before the descent.

Descend roughly westwards from the summit, picking a careful way down a very steep slope of heather, avoiding any areas of rock. Forge across an uneven tract of moorland, crossing a small burn in a shallow valley, then drifting to the right to reach the edge of **Madadh Lounie**. The rugged moorland underfoot gives way to a rounded spur of short heather descending steeply into **Glen Catacol**. ◂ Descend more steeply, bearing to the right along a narrow path to avoid a rock-step to the left. The path descends through a notch in the rock, then continues down a slope of bracken, later passing close to a large boulder of granite. The gradient eases and a wall can be followed onwards, soon joining a path that was used at the start of the day's walk. Follow the path

There's a splendid view along the length of the glen, which in its middle reaches is a perfect 'U' shape.

Madadh Lounie, in the background, is the last hill before the final descent

alongside the river, go through the tall kissing gate in the deer fence, and return to the main road and car park across the bridge near **Fairhaven**.

WALK 33

Lochranza and Meall Mòr

Start/Finish	Lochranza Castle (NR 931 506)
Distance	11km (6¾ miles)
Total ascent	650m (2130ft)
Time	3hrs 30mins
Terrain	Roads, tracks and paths at low level, giving way to rugged, pathless uplands.
Refreshments	Lochranza Hotel at Lochranza. Catacol Bay Hotel at Catacol. Restaurant at the Arran Distillery.

The rugged, rocky dome of Meall Mòr rises south of Lochranza. While a direct approach would be quite difficult, the hill can be climbed more easily on the way from Glen Catacol to Gleann Easan Biorach. The 'Postman's Path' is followed from Lochranza to Catacol, across a steep and well-wooded slope above the coastal road. Fine views are available on the ascent of Meall Mòr from Glen Catacol, although much of the upland moorland is rough and pathless, needing special care in poor visibility. The descent and return to Lochranza is by way of the boggy Gleann Easan Biorach.

The start of this walk could be anywhere in **Lochranza**, but Lochranza Castle makes a good reference point. Walk through the village in the direction of the pier on **Coillemore Point**, where the Claonaig Ferry departs. However, turn left beforehand up a track that serves a few houses. The track becomes grassier and is flanked by rhododendrons as it climbs to one final house. Before reaching the house, a path known as the 'Postman's Path' is waymarked to the right of a bend on the track. This is part of the Arran Coastal Way, and it runs uphill, passing to the right of the house and a ruin.

The path rises further, passing a junction, then reaching a 'Coastal Way' marker. Turn right and continue along a gravel path that provides a firm footing on a boggy slope. There are boggy patches ahead among patchy woodland,

The 'Twelve Apostles' are cottages beside the coast road at Catacol

and a power line will be noticed in a broad, open area. After passing lots of rhododendrons, cross a burn and follow the path onwards through woodland, reaching another open area. The path is fairly well-trodden and waymarked, and it crosses another couple of small burns before meeting the

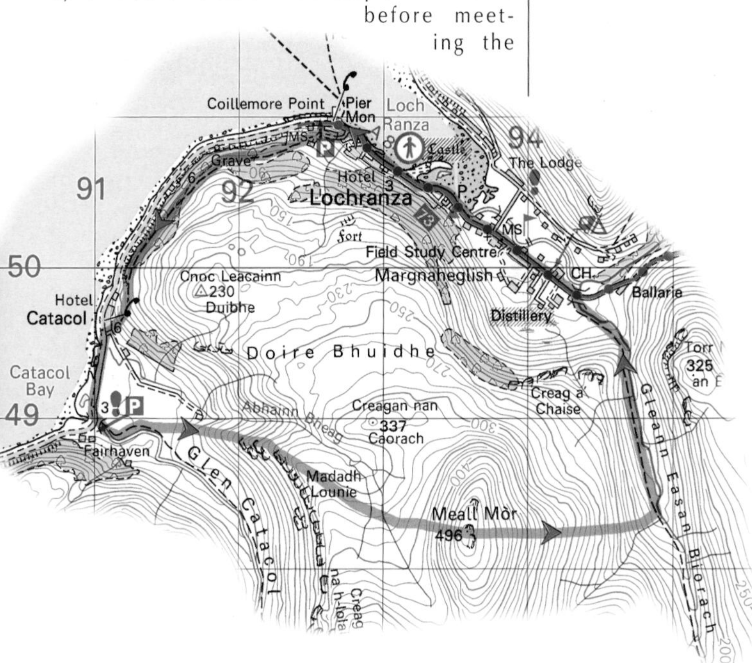

power line again. Head downhill and a long flight of stone steps leads to a gate, where a track quickly reaches the main coastal road at **Catacol**.

Turn left to follow the road away from the village, and there is a choice either of walking along the main road, or walking along a grassy and pebbly strip between the main road and the sea. Either way, a flat concrete bridge will be reached before a large white house called **Fairhaven**. Don't cross the bridge, but turn left to leave the road and follow a path indicated by a public footpath signpost. Follow a grassy and stony path alongside a river, the Abhainn Mòr, into **Glen Catacol**. Go through a tall kissing gate in a deer fence. The path continues alongside the river, then rises over an outcrop of banded rock. The river runs through a narrow constriction below the outcrop. The path runs alongside a cobbly stretch of the river, passing areas of grass, heather, bracken and bog myrtle.

When the open floor of the glen is reached, turn left away from the riverside path, then turn right to follow a wall in the direction of the rocky prow of Madadh Lounie, passing a prominent large boulder as the climbing commences. A narrow path should be located, which leaves the bracken-clad slope and climbs through a notch in the rock above. Keep strictly to the line of the path to negotiate the ascent of a rock-step. Once on top, note the splendid view along the length of Glen Catacol, which in its middle reaches is a perfect 'U' shape.

Continue climbing up a rounded spur of short heather, which gives way to more rugged moorland at a higher level. Leaving the edge of **Madadh Lounie**, drift left and forge straight across an uneven tract of moorland in the direction of Meall Mòr, crossing a small burn. Looking ahead, pick any line of ascent that seems to be free of rock. Strips of heather allow steep but relatively safe ascents. There is a cairn on the summit of **Meall Mòr** at 496m (1627ft), with another cairn further along the crest. Take a moment to savour the view before the descent, which is remarkably extensive despite the modest elevation.

Walk roughly eastwards to descend from the summit. The slope has outcrops of rock and boulders at first, although these later give way to rugged, boggy moorland slopes. There are no paths on the way downhill, and it is necessary to keep looking ahead to gauge the best line of descent. It is perhaps best to drift slightly to the left, in order to avoid being drawn into a watercourse on the lower slopes, which is mostly bare rock, but keep looking ahead to outflank obstacles in good time. Eventually a path is reached, so turn left and walk roughly parallel to the river draining **Gleann Easan Biorach**.

Enjoy a series of little waterfalls on the way down through the glen. The path often crosses boggy ground and squelchy grassland, but inflowing burns offer the chance to clean footwear from time to time. A firmer path is eventually joined where the river drops more steeply through a rocky gorge, where the path keeps left of a safety fence above a water intake. Small waterfalls and rock pools are overlooked by the rocky dome of **Torr Nead an Eoin**. The rocky path gives way to a level path, which runs between a bridge and a cottage to reach the main road near the **Isle of Arran Distillery**.

ISLE OF ARRAN DISTILLERY

The Isle of Arran Distillery was founded in 1995 and the buildings were completed in 1997. The site looks quite modern, but the roofing looks distinctly traditional. When the enterprise was being promoted, it was claimed to be the first legal distillery on the island for 160 years. Some say that when whisky was last distilled on Arran it was the best in Scotland. Connoisseurs can now judge for themselves, testing the single malts against others in Scotland. The distillery caters for visitors by offering tours, and incorporates a gift shop and restaurant. For details tel 01770 830264, www.arranwhisky.com

Turn left to follow the road back through the long and straggly village of **Lochranza**. After leaving the distillery the road passes a campsite, the Loch Ranza Field Studies Centre, St Bride's Church and a youth hostel to return to **Lochranza Castle**.

The route descends from the hills and passes the Isle of Arran Distillery

LOCHRANZA CASTLE

There are two parts to Lochranza Castle. First there was a medieval hallhouse, with a heavily defended lower doorway and an upper doorway with a removable ladder. The owner may have been Sween, who married into the royal house of Connacht and was Lord of Knapdale in Argyll. When Robert the High Steward became King of Scotland in 1371, Lochranza became a royal castle. A later period of building incorporated Sween's castle into a rather more decorative structure. The building was completed by one of the Montgomery Earls of Eglinton, who had received estates on the Isle of Arran from James II in 1452. New doorways were created and old ones were blocked, and this remains apparent from a close study of the fabric. The Montgomerys lost their estates to the Hamiltons in 1705 and much later the castle fell to ruins. One whole corner collapsed during a storm in 1897, but the fabric has now been consolidated and has plenty of interesting features and poky corners to explore.

WALK 34

Gleann Easan Biorach

Start/Finish	Lochranza Castle (NR 931 506)
Distance	16.5km (10¼ miles)
Total ascent	650m (2130ft)
Time	5hrs
Terrain	Mostly rough, boggy, bouldery paths that often run alongside rivers and burns.
Refreshments	Restaurants at the campsite and distillery. Catacol Bay Hotel at Catacol. Lochranza Hotel at Lochranza.

There is a popular circuit into the hills of northern Arran from Lochranza to Catacol. The route doesn't climb any hills, but works its way through the glens, crossing a couple of bleak and boggy gaps. Starting from Lochranza, the route climbs through Gleann Easan Biorach to reach Loch na Davie, then climbs over a gap on the slopes of Beinn Bhreac before descending through Gleann Diomhan and Glen Catacol. The 'Postman's Path' is followed from Catacol back to Lochranza. The paths in Gleann Easan Biorach, Glen Catacol and Gleann Diomhan can be used to reach a variety of hills in the north-west of Arran. Some are covered in other route descriptions in this guidebook.

The start of this walk could be anywhere in **Lochranza**, but Lochranza Castle makes a good reference point. Walk inland through the long and straggly village, passing a youth hostel, St Bride's Church, Loch Ranza Field Studies Centre, caravan and campsite and the Isle of Arran Distillery. ▶ Just beyond the distillery, beside a bridge, a public footpath signpost points right for Gleann Easan Biorach and Loch na Davie.

For information about the Distillery, see the end of Walk 33.

A level path runs beside a cottage and quickly gives way to a steep and stony path climbing alongside a rocky gorge. Keep right of a safety fence above a water intake. Small waterfalls and rock pools are overlooked by the rocky dome of **Torr Nead an Eoin**. The path continues climbing at a gentler gradient then runs more or less level across a

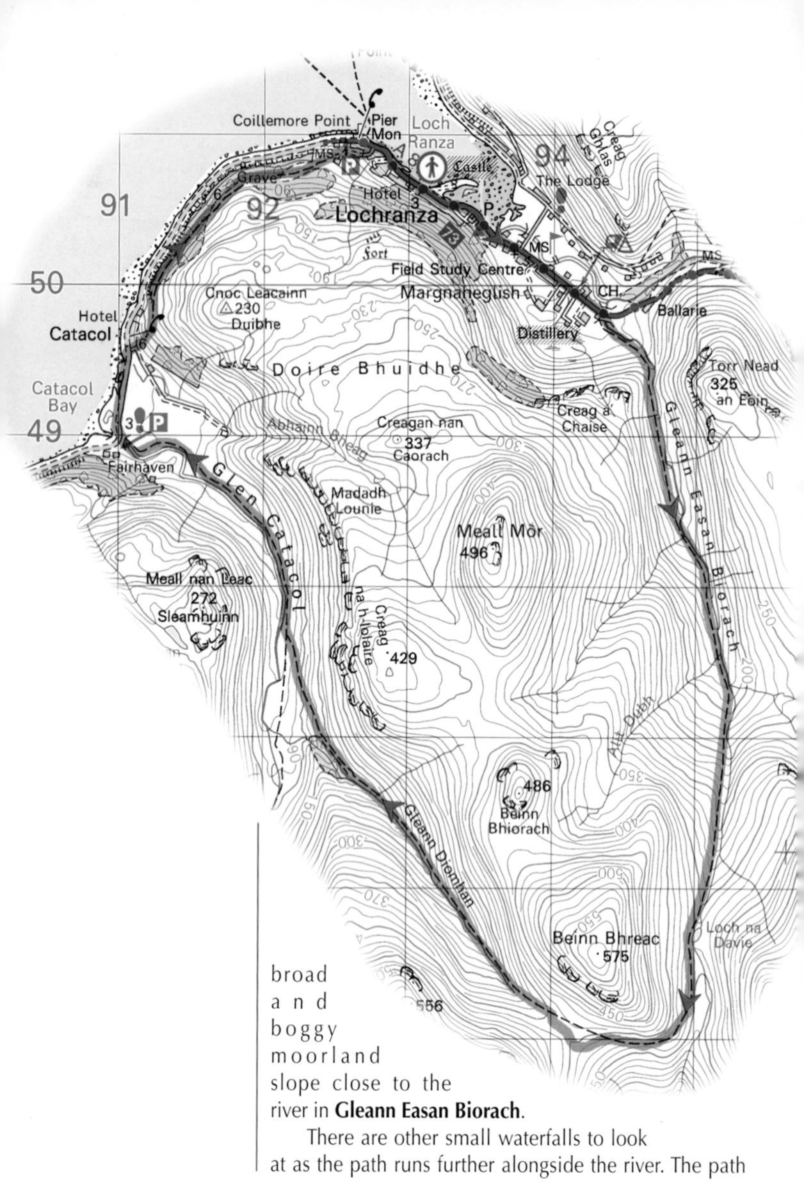

broad and boggy moorland slope close to the river in **Gleann Easan Biorach**.

There are other small waterfalls to look at as the path runs further alongside the river. The path

After leaving the Isle of Arran Distillery a path leads into Gleann Easan Biorach

often crosses boggy ground and squelchy grassland, but inflowing burns offer the chance to get footwear cleaned from time to time. The river often slides along a smooth bed of granite, and a tributary to the left has the same appearance. The path climbs a boulder-strewn, heathery slope, eventually reaching a heathery gap over 360m (1180ft), where the shallow waters of tiny **Loch na Davie** lie to the left. Dozens of small boulders poke from the water, while careful inspection of either end of the loch reveals that the water dribbles in opposite directions, into Gleann Easan Biorach and Glen Iorsa.

The path continues beyond the loch, passing a cairn and gradually swinging to the right to climb around the shoulder of **Beinn Bhreac**. A couple of smaller cairns help keep walkers on course when the path becomes narrow and vague. There is a gradual climb to a broad, boggy and stony gap over 400m (1310ft), with Beinn Bhreac to the right and Beinn Tarsuinn to the left. In poor visibility, be sure to spot the start of the path leading down into **Gleann Diomhan**. A narrow, stony path runs parallel to the burn, on its eastern side. ▶ The path is quite rugged in places on the way downhill. A stepped series of small

Inadvertently walking along the western side leads to great difficulties later.

waterfalls are followed by a longer fall tucked out of sight from the path. A granite gorge leads through an area surrounded by a tall deer fence. This is the Gleann Diomhan National Nature Reserve.

GLEANN DIOMHAN NATIONAL NATURE RESERVE

The securely fenced enclosure high in Gleann Diomhan seems incongruous in its wilderness setting, but it is necessary to prevent sheep and deer from damaging two rare species of tree that thrive there. *Sorbus arranensis* and *Sorbus pseudo-fennicus* both have a roothold in the glen. These trees are essentially whitebeam that have crossed with rowan, bearing clusters of berries when in fruit. They grow apparently from bare rock, needing very little soil to secure a root-hold. These two species are unique to Arran and a ladder stile allows access to walkers who wish to explore further.

Continue along the rough path beside the deer fence, continuing past a lower corner of the enclosure, before swinging to the right as it leaves the glen. The ground becomes firmer and drier, especially when areas of bracken are crossed. The path descends into **Glen Catacol** and joins a firm, clear path, which is followed by turning right.

The path generally runs close to a larger river, the Abhainn Mòr, which in turn often crosses slabs of granite where occasional boulders stand marooned. Small rapids and waterfalls can be enjoyed. The river has a more cobbly stretch and the ground alongside features a mixture of grass, heather, bracken and bog myrtle. When the river goes through a narrow constriction, the path climbs over an outcrop of banded rock. The final meanders of the river are faithfully traced and a tall kissing gate is passed before the main road is reached at a flat concrete bridge near a prominent white house called **Fairhaven**.

Walk through the village if a break is required at the Catacol Bay Hotel.

Turn right to follow the main coastal road towards the village of **Catacol**, or alternatively walk on the grass or pebbles along the shore. As soon as the first houses are reached, turn right along a track, but leave it at a gate as soon as its turns right. ▶ A path, known locally as the

'Postman's Path', climbs a long flight of stone steps and continues uphill as if following the posts of a power line.

Don't follow the power line too far, but watch for Arran Coastal Way marker discs, which indicate a path to the left. The path is fairly well-trodden and waymarked as it crosses a well-wooded slope and a couple of small burns. After passing through an open area another burn is crossed and there are lots of rhododendrons ahead. Another broad, open area is reached and the power line is seen again. There are boggy patches among patchy woodlands, then a gravel path provides a firm footing on a boggy slope.

At the end of the gravel path, a 'Coastal Way' marker indicates a left turn down a grassy path. Keep to the left of a house and a ruin, descending to join a grassy track. This is flanked by rhododendrons as it runs down to a broader track serving a few houses. Continue down to the main road near **Coillemore Point**, turning right to walk through **Lochranza**. The Lochranza Hotel is passed on the way back to Lochranza Castle.

LOCHRANZA

The long and straggly village of Lochranza sits beside a sea loch and for a long time the only real access was from the sea. It was named Ranza by Norse settlers, while Sir Walter Scott penned poetry about it in 'The Lord of the Isles'. There is a fine range of features and facilities. Working southwards through the village from the Claonaig Ferry slipway, these include: toilets, Arran Butcher, Caberfeidh Guest House, Kincardine Lodge B&B, Lochranza Hotel and Lochranza Castle. Next comes the Secret Garden Gallery, Lochranza and Catacol Village Hall and Lochranza Youth Hostel. These are followed by St Bride's Church, access to a surgery, Loch Ranza Field Studies Centre, Apple Lodge B&B, Lochranza Golf Club, caravan and campsite, Pavilion Restaurant and fire station. Last comes the Arran Distillery, with its gift shop and restaurant. Walkers who complete the full circuit described above will pass everything in Lochranza.

WALK 35

Lochranza and the Cock of Arran

Start/Finish	St Bride's Church, Lochranza (NR 937 502)
Distance	12.5km (7¾ miles)
Total ascent	360m (1180ft)
Time	4hrs
Terrain	Roads, tracks and rugged coastal paths. Some parts can be muddy and rocky.
Refreshments	Hotel bar and restaurants at Lochranza.

The walk around the Cock of Arran from Lochranza is one of the classic coastal walks on Arran. Lochranza is a long and straggly village that stretches inland from a charming sea loch. The romantic Lochranza Castle overlooks the waters from a narrow, grassy, pebbly point. The walk around the coast could be structured to link Lochranza with the distant village of Sannox, but this particular route description heads for the remote Laggan Cottage, then crosses back over the hills to return to Lochranza. The rest of the coastal walk is covered on Walk 37, in a circuit from Sannox.

This walk could start anywhere in **Lochranza**, but for the purpose of defining a location, start near St Bride's Church or the Loch Ranza Field Studies Centre. A signpost stands at a road junction, listing such all the places visited on this walk – the Fairy Dell, Ossian's Cave, the Cock of Arran and Laggan. Follow a minor road past the Lochranza Surgery, crossing a bridge and passing a golf course. At a junction with another minor road there are two public footpath signposts. Turn left to follow the road signposted for Fairy Dell and Ossian's Cave, passing cottages to reach a pebbly beach at the head of **Loch Ranza**.

Follow the road to a final turning place, where a track continues past a house. ◄ Follow a clear path round **Newton Point**, and it gradually

Before the end of the road, a path on the right climbs to The Whins, where crafts – especially decorated stones – are sold.

becomes rugged, running at the foot of a slope of patchy woodland, bracken and gorse. If groups of geologists are spotted on the rocky shore, they are no doubt inspecting a feature known as Hutton's Unconformity, where rocks of widely differing ages join at different angles.

HUTTON'S UNCONFORMITY

Hutton expounded his 'Theory of the Earth', in which mountains were continually being uplifted and eroded, although few of his contemporaries took the great man seriously. Geologists of Hutton's day were divided into the Vulcanists and Neptunists, according to whether they believed rocks were formed by volcanic action or deposited as sediments. Hutton's theory embraced both concepts and he became widely known as the 'Father of Geology'. On the rocky shore, ancient rocks are tilted very steeply, and even close to vertical, while younger sandstone lies almost horizontal on top of them. The two rock types differ in age by hundreds of millions of years.

Cross a couple of little burns and pass in front of a little white cottage at the foot of the wooded Fairy Dell, where there's short green grass above the rugged shore. Later, a huge boulder is

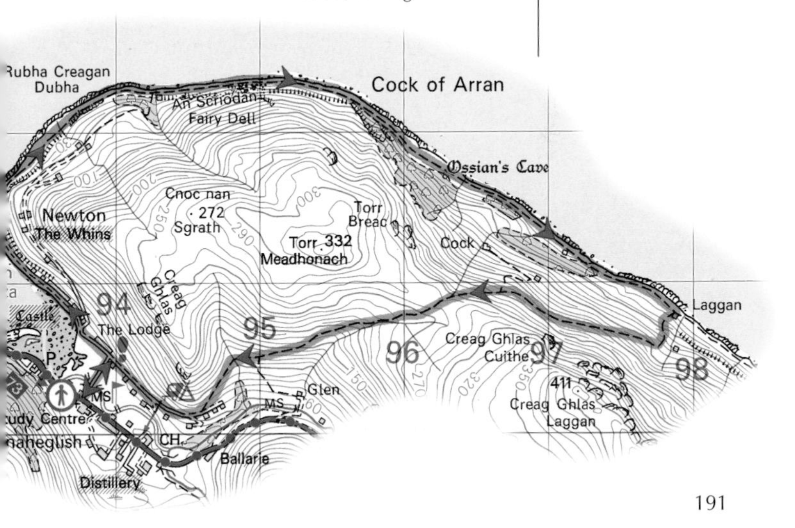

passed, where the slope and beach are littered with boulders of coarse conglomerate. This area is **An Scriodan**. Follow a well constructed path between the boulders. Further along, another large boulder features an overhanging projection that is good enough to offer shelter from rain.

Just before reaching the wall, Ossian's Cave lies uphill, but is difficult to reach.

The coastal path continues easily around the **Cock of Arran** along another ribbon of short green grass, and the ruins of a couple of stone huts might be noticed in the bracken alongside. One level stretch was used as a field in the past, and a curious natural igneous dyke forms a boundary wall between the field and the beach. The path crosses a drystone wall belonging to the abandoned Cock Farm, which is hidden from sight uphill. ◂

Keep to the path closest to the rocky shore, taking care over ankle-wrenching and muddy terrain. Some ruined buildings beside the sea once housed a little industrial site where coal was mined and saltpans were in use. The path crosses another rocky area, but gets a little easier later. Look out for a roughed-out circular millstone complete with a central hole just to the left of the path. The white form of **Laggan Cottage** appears quite suddenly after crossing a low outcrop of rock.

A view over the sea inlet of Loch Ranza on the way round to the Cock of Arran

Leave the isolated cottage by walking straight uphill, passing alongside its former kitchen garden. The path is a clear, grassy ribbon that zigzags uphill between areas of bracken. There are some drystone-walled enclosures off to the left, then the path swings to the right and cuts across a steep and roughly vegetated slope. Looking downhill, the ruins of **Cock Farm** and its old fields can be seen.

COCK FARM

The tumbled remains of Cock Farm are a sad reminder of how well populated the Isle of Arran once was. There were once over a hundred people living in the area now enclosed by Laggan and Cock Farm, yet not a single person lives there now. Cock Farm's greatest claim to fame concerns the Macmillan family. Malcolm Macmillan was born there in 1735 and he was the grandfather of Daniel Macmillan who founded the famous Macmillan publishing house. Malcolm was therefore the great-great grandfather of the mid-19th-century Prime Minister Harold Macmillan. Cock Farm was finally deserted in 1912 and now lies mouldering in a bracken-clad hollow.

As the path climbs it is flanked by heather and its surface becomes quite stony. At the top of the path a broad moorland gap is crossed, where a cairn stands alongside at 263m (863ft). ▶ The path is flanked by boggy ground on its downhill run, surfaced with stones in some parts and crossing bare rock in other parts. There is generally a view of the Isle of Arran Distillery all the way downhill. The only time this passes from view is where the path nips into a wooded ravine to cross a small burn using a footbridge.

Walk 37 turns left here for Creag Ghlas Laggan.

The path runs down onto a clear, broad track and turns right. The track continues gently downhill, eventually passing the entrance to Butt Lodge, which was once used by shooting parties and later served as a hotel. Turn left along the minor road used at the start of the walk, crossing the golf course and bridge to return to the main road near St Bride's Church in **Lochranza**.

WALK 36

Lochranza and Sail an Im

Start/Finish	Isle of Arran Distillery, Lochranza (NR 943 498)
Distance	17km (10½ miles)
Total ascent	1000m (3280ft)
Time	5hrs 30mins
Terrain	Good paths most of the way, followed by pathless moorland slopes.
Refreshments	Restaurants at the Isle of Arran Distillery and nearby campsite.

Few walkers would consider climbing Sail an Im without continuing along the fine mountain ridge to the summit of Caisteal Abhail. Even fewer walkers would consider climbing Sail an Im from Lochranza. In fact, an entertaining circuit is available, which uses traces of an old road over the Boguillie, linking Glen Chalmadale with North Glen Sannox. Sail an Im can then be climbed from the glen, with a return to Lochranza made directly along the broad moorland crest terminating at Torr Nead an Eoin. There is a surprise view of the village and the sea loch before the final steep descent.

Start at the **Isle of Arran Distillery**, set as far inland as the village of **Lochranza** extends. Follow the main road uphill from a humpback bridge, passing the farm of **Ballarie** while skirting round the lower slopes of Torr Nead an Eoin. Further up the road, turn left down a farm access road for **Glen**, either fording a river or crossing an adjacent footbridge. Turn right to follow the river upstream by walking along a track, passing a building and continuing along a path into **Glen Chalmadale**. The aim is to pick up an old road running up through the glen, but its course is unclear at first. Follow the river upstream, until forced uphill to pass a pronounced bend where there's a short, steep, wooded slope. A clearer path continues immediately beyond.

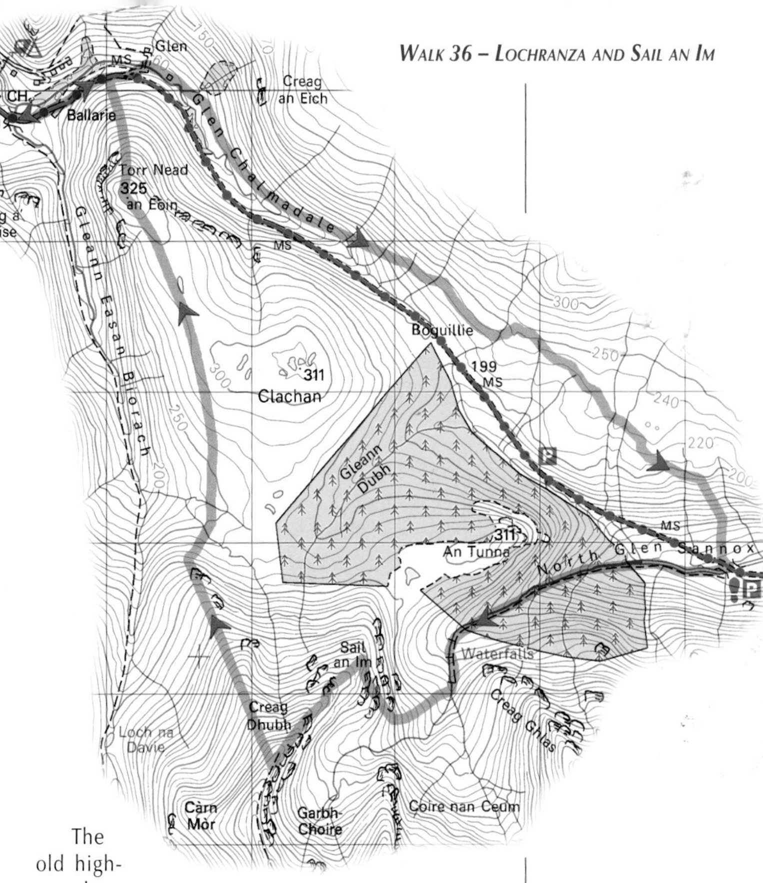

The old highway shows some traces of engineering, but is little trodden these days and some parts are quite vague. The old way rises roughly parallel to the current main road, but on the opposite side of the river. It rises gently across a slope of grass, bracken and heather. A handful of stunted trees are passed, then three small burns are crossed as the path continues to rise. A fourth burn is more powerful, filled with trees and fine waterfalls, and could result in wet feet after wet weather. The path continues a little more steeply uphill, climbing above the level of the main road over the **Boguillie**, but the gradient quickly eases on the higher moorlands and it crosses another path. The way ahead can be vague in places, crossing areas of grass and heather, but with care it is possible to distinguish the route.

THE BOGUILLIE

The 'new' road over the Boguillie was constructed between Lochranza and Sannox in 1843. Up to that point most traffic reaching Lochranza came from the sea; the tracks eastwards over the Boguillie or southwards via the Craw were simply too rough and narrow to travel easily. Even when the 'new' road was built, there were fords rather than bridges, and it was barely possible for two carts to pass each other.

The path is little more than a groove contouring across the moorland around 250m. It crosses a runnel of water, then drops to pass the lower corner of a fenced enclosure. The groove is little more than a boggy trough in places, but it is sometimes flanked by boulders and can be quite clear. A couple of little burns are crossed by their original stone slab bridges, and an outcrop of bedrock has a splash of white quartz. The old track turns downhill as a clear ribbon of boggy grass across a rugged moorland slope. The track may carry running water for a while, then there is a paved ford through a small burn. The route contours for a while across a steeper slope, then a right turn leads downhill, twisting and turning, but mainly heading towards a road bridge spanning North Sannox Burn. ◂

Note the fine waterfall pouring beneath the bridge.

Walk into a car park beside the bridge, where a path follows the river upstream into **North Glen Sannox**. Keep left at a path junction, as the path to the right ends abruptly on an island in the river. Follow a good path flanked by grass, heather and bog myrtle. Small burns are easily stepped across, then there is a gateway in a deer fence. The path continues between a stand of forest and the river, passing many fine waterfalls as it climbs. An old ladder stile stands beside a gateway at the top edge of the forest, where the path is often wet and muddy as it continues upstream, passing more **waterfalls**. ◂

There are fine views of Caisteal Abhail and the rocky cleft of Ceum na Caillich, or the Witch's Step.

Leave the path and ford the burn at some convenient point, then continue uphill, drifting gradually away from the river. The rugged face of Sail an Im is ahead, and by keeping to its left-hand side a relatively easy ascent can be made. A steep slope of heather and boulders also features low outcrops of granite, pitched at an angle easy enough to be walked up without difficulty. Turn left to reach the rounded, heathery summit of **Sail an Im**, which has a scattering of boulders at 508m (1667ft). There is a sudden view over to Lochranza.

Follow a narrow path that runs roughly south-west along a rounded ridge. The ascent is on grass and heather with some boulders and ribs of granite. Climb until a rounded granite hump is reached on top of the buttress of **Creag Dubh**, overlooking the Garbh-Choire at 644m (2113ft). It is possible to continue along the ridge to the summit of Caisteal Abhail, as described in Walk 38, but this route now changes course and proceeds directly back to Lochranza.

Walk roughly north-north-west as if dropping into Gleann Easan Biorach. In clear weather it is worth

There is a fine aerial view of Lochranza from the summit of Torr Nead an Eoin

surveying the terrain from a good height before negotiating it. Start the descent on a slope of grass, heather and boulders. The terrain is actually fairly easy at first, but later it is necessary to swing to the right and descend towards a broad, boggy gap high above the glen. Paths can be seen cutting across the bleak moorland slope, and any of them might be used if they seem helpful. The broad gap is usually wet underfoot and there are small burns to ford. There's a slight ascent on uneven heathery moorland, almost touching 300m (985ft) at **Clachan**. Small pools should be avoided and in clear weather a prominent hump can be seen at the end of the broad crest.

When the hump of **Torr Nead an Eoin** is finally climbed, a short ascent reveals a couple of small cairns at 325m (1066ft), overlooking Lochranza. It is worth walking a little further in the direction of Lochranza to enjoy a splendid bird's-eye view of the village, but note that it is not possible to descend directly as there are steep slopes of rock and little cliffs tucked out of sight. ◂

More distant views encompass much of northern Arran, as well as taking in the Paps of Jura beyond Kintyre.

The final descent should be made in the direction of a solitary white farmhouse of Glen, seen across the main road far below. The steep slope features short vegetation, although there is bracken at a lower level. A narrow path can be joined running alongside a fence. Keep to the right-hand side of it to walk straight down to the main road. Turn down the road, returning to the **Isle of Arran Distillery** on the outskirts of **Lochranza**. ◂

See Walk 33 for information about the distillery.

WALK 37

Sannox and Fionn Bhealach

Start/Finish	North Sannox picnic area (NS 014 466)
Distance	16km (10 miles)
Total ascent	670m (2200ft)
Time	5hrs
Terrain	Coastal tracks and paths, followed by moorlands with both clear and vague paths.
Refreshments	None closer than the golf club tearoom and hotel bar at Sannox.

The coastal walk around the northern part of Arran is a popular excursion. It is possible to walk all the way from Sannox to Lochranza along rugged coastal paths, but the route described below is a circular tour, taking in the Fallen Rocks, Millstone Point and Laggan Cottage, coming back over the top of Fionn Bhealach. The course of an old highway can be traced back towards Sannox, running parallel to the main road over the Boguillie. The start of the walk, North Sannox, is near Lag nan Sasunnach, where Cromwellian soldiers, killed in battle at Clach a' Chath, are said to be buried. This walk could be extended with reference to Walk 35.

There is a car park at the **North Sannox** picnic area, signposted as 'Sannox North' at a road junction near Sannox on the way to Lochranza. A car park and toilets are located at the end of a minor road, beside the sea. ▶ A track continues from the end of the tarmac road and enters a forest through a tall gate in a deer fence. Follow the track along what is actually a raised beach covered in vegetation. Deciduous trees screen views of the more regimented forest beyond. A rugged rock face in the trees was once a coastal cliff and features some small caves and undercut parts. Pass a prominent **beacon**, which indicates a 'measured mile' used for speed trials at sea, and follow a power line to the edge of the forest.

Alternatively, start and finish further up the road from the North Glen Sannox car park.

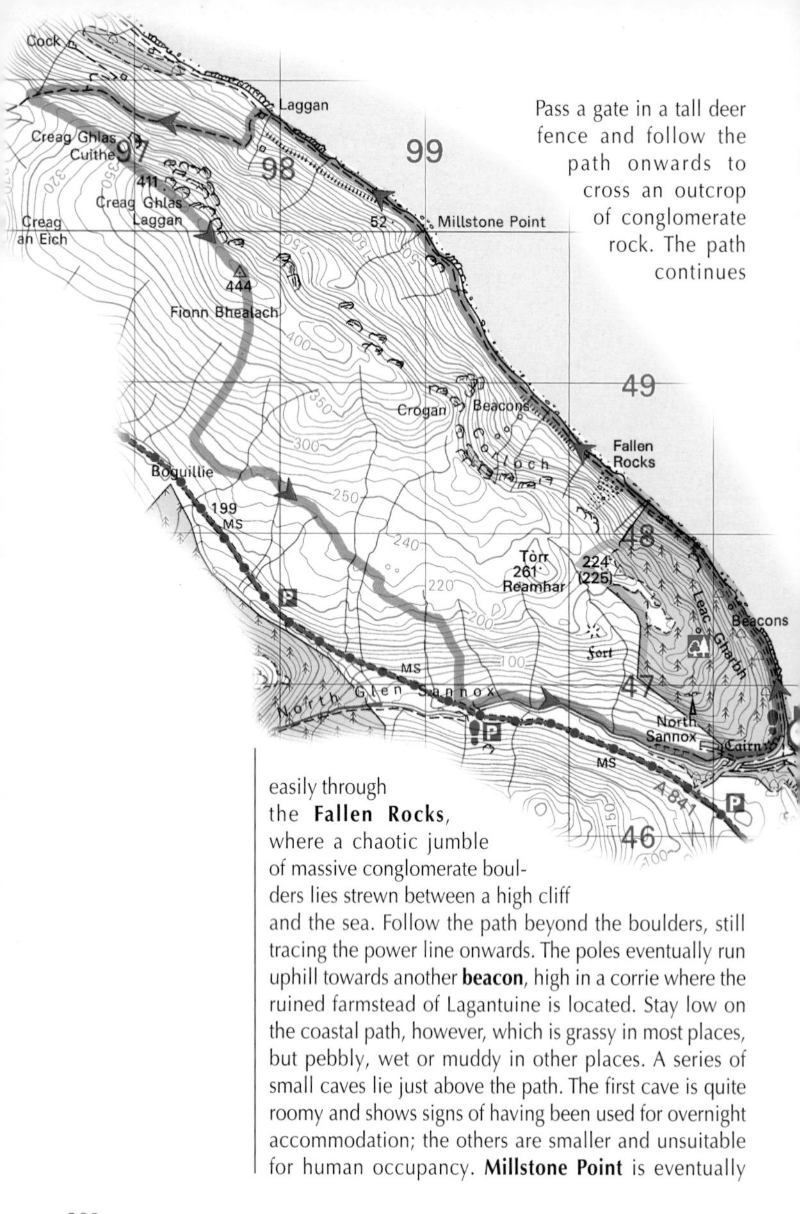

Pass a gate in a tall deer fence and follow the path onwards to cross an outcrop of conglomerate rock. The path continues easily through the **Fallen Rocks**, where a chaotic jumble of massive conglomerate boulders lies strewn between a high cliff and the sea. Follow the path beyond the boulders, still tracing the power line onwards. The poles eventually run uphill towards another **beacon**, high in a corrie where the ruined farmstead of Lagantuine is located. Stay low on the coastal path, however, which is grassy in most places, but pebbly, wet or muddy in other places. A series of small caves lie just above the path. The first cave is quite roomy and shows signs of having been used for overnight accommodation; the others are smaller and unsuitable for human occupancy. **Millstone Point** is eventually turned and the little whitewashed **Laggan Cottage** is seen ahead. The path remains easy all the way to the cottage.

Turn left and walk straight uphill, passing alongside a former kitchen garden. The path is a clear, grassy ribbon that zigzags uphill between areas of bracken. There are some drystone-walled enclosures off to the left, then the path swings to the right and cuts across a steep and roughly vegetated slope. Looking downhill, the ruins of **Cock Farm** and its old fields can be seen.

COCK FARM

The tumbled remains of Cock Farm are a sad reminder of how well populated Arran once was. There were once over a hundred people living in the area now enclosed by Laggan and Cock Farm, yet not a single person lives there now. Cock Farm's greatest claim to fame concerns the Macmillan family. Malcolm Macmillan was born there in 1735 and he was the grandfather of Daniel Macmillan who founded the famous Macmillan publishing house. Malcolm was therefore the great-great grandfather of the mid-19th-century Prime Minister Harold Macmillan. Cock Farm was finally deserted in 1912 and now lies mouldering in a bracken-clad hollow.

As the path climbs it is flanked by heather and its surface becomes quite stony. At the top of the path a broad moorland gap is crossed, where a cairn stands alongside at 263m (863ft). ▶ Turn left to leave the path and walk along a moorland crest of heather and grass. There are vague sheep paths or quad bike tracks, but it is just as easy to stay on the crest. The gently rounded top of **Creag Ghlas Laggan** is crossed at 411m (1348ftft), before the main summit of **Fionn Bhealach** is reached, where a trig point stands at 444m (1457ft).

Walk 35 continues straight ahead, down to Lochranza.

Continue along the moorland crest to start the descent, but head off to the right and pick a way down a rugged moorland slope, crossing areas of heather and grass, which may be boggy in places. If it is spotted, join a path that has been broadened by quad bike use and follow it down towards the main road near **Boguillie**.

Watch carefully to spot traces of an old highway cutting across the slope around 240m (785ft). Depending on where this is intersected, it might be little more than a groove, but if spotted, turn left to follow it. It climbs a little and crosses a runnel of water, then drops to pass the lower corner of a fenced enclosure. The groove is little more than a boggy trough in places, but it is sometimes flanked by boulders and can be quite clear.

A couple of little burns are crossed by their original stone slab bridges, and an outcrop of bedrock has a splash of white quartz. The old track turns downhill as a clear ribbon of boggy grass across a rugged moorland slope. The track may carry running water for a while, then there is a paved ford through a small burn. The route contours for a while across a steeper slope, then a right turn leads downhill, twisting and turning, but mainly heading towards a road bridge spanning North Sannox Burn. ◂

A car park across the bridge offers an alternative start/finish for this walk.

Don't cross the bridge, but turn left and follow the river downstream. A path squeezes between the river and a tall deer fence, eventually passing below a farm at

North Sannox Burn passes beneath a road bridge

A path runs downstream beside North Sannox Burn to return to North Sannox

North Sannox, where pony-trekking is offered. There are usually horses, ponies and donkeys grazing in the fields. The riverside becomes more and more wooded and the path rises to join the farm access road. Turn right to walk down to a minor road, and turn left to follow the road back to the **North Sannox** picnic area and car park.

SANNOX

The Sannox area is one of many places on Arran with abundant ancient remains, dating from the Neolithic and Bronze Age. The name Sannox is believed to have Viking origins and the area remained well settled, with numerous clachans and shielings. The Congregational Church was built in 1822, but the area was cleared of much of its population a few years later. It is known that many of them settled in Megantic County in Canada. The only real industry was a small barytes mine, which was opened in Glen Sannox in 1840. In 1862 the 11th Duke of Hamilton closed it as it was becoming an eyesore, but it reopened during the Great War and finally closed when it was exhausted in 1938. It had its own little railway running to a pier, but this was removed, leaving only the ruins of a few buildings.

Sannox has only a small range of features and facilities, including: Corrie Golf Club and tearoom, Sannox Bay Hotel and restaurant and Gowanlea Guest House.

WALK 38

North Glen Sannox Horseshoe

Start/Finish	North Glen Sannox car park (NR 993 468)
Distance	10.5km (6½ miles)
Total ascent	910m (2985ft)
Time	3hrs 30mins
Terrain	Easy low-level paths give way to steep and rocky slopes, later involving some exposed and arduous scrambling.
Refreshments	None closer than the golf club tearoom and hotel bar at Sannox.

There is a fine horseshoe walk around North Glen Sannox, starting with an easy walk along the floor of the glen. After a rugged climb onto Sail an Im, the route climbs high around the 'Dress Circle' ridge to reach the summit of Caisteal Abhail. This much is fairly straightforward, but the continuation involves crossing the notorious cleft of Ceum na Caillich, or the Witch's Step, calling for a good head for heights and scrambling skills. In wet weather the Witch's Step becomes more dangerous than it already is, and walkers would be well advised to retrace their steps or head north from Caisteal Abhail down the rugged ridge between Garbh Coire and Coire nan Ceum for a safer descent.

Start at a car park beside a bridge in **North Glen Sannox**, on the road between Sannox and Lochranza. Have a look at a waterfall pouring beneath the bridge. Follow a path out of the car park and keep left at a path junction, as the path to the right ends abruptly on an island in the river. Follow a good path flanked by grass, heather and bog myrtle. Small burns are easily stepped across, then there is a gateway in a deer fence. The path continues between a stand of forest and the river, passing many fine waterfalls as it climbs. An old ladder stile stands beside a gateway at the top edge of the forest, where the path is often wet and muddy as it continues upstream, passing more **waterfalls**. ◂

There are fine views of Caisteal Abhail and the rocky cleft of Ceum na Caillich, or the Witch's Step.

Looking down the bare rocky riverbed in North Glen Sannox

Leave the path and ford the burn at some convenient point, then continue uphill, drifting gradually away from the river. The rugged face of Sail an Im is ahead, and by keeping to its left-hand side a relatively easy ascent can be made. A steep slope of heather and boulders also features low outcrops of granite, pitched at an angle easy enough to be walked up without difficulty. Turn left to reach the rounded, heathery summit of **Sail an Im**, which has a scattering of boulders at 508m (1667ft).

Follow a narrow path that runs roughly south-west along a rounded ridge. The ascent is on grass and heather with some boulders and ribs of granite. Climb until a rounded granite hump is reached on top of the buttress of **Creag Dubh**, overlooking the Garbh-Choire at 644m (2113ft). Walk 36 heads north from here to Lochranza. Continue climbing at a fairly gentle gradient along the ridge, which levels out on **Càrn Mòr** and gradually bends to the left as it rises towards Caisteal Abhail. ▸

Some walkers call this ridge the 'Dress Circle', and it offers splendid views in clear weather.

The top of **Caisteal Abhail** features a handful of blocky granite tors which have the appearance of ruined castles. On a fine day they offer a host of interesting scrambling routes. The main summit is on one of these tors, ending

A final projecting slab of granite is an airy perch on the summit of Caisteal Abhail

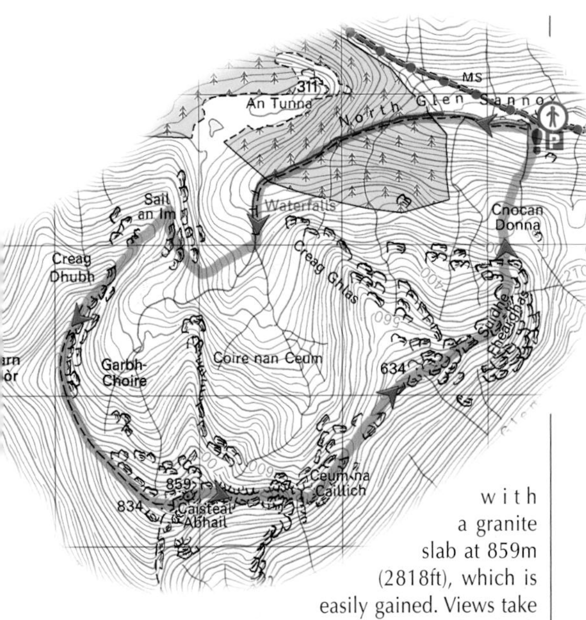

with a granite slab at 859m (2818ft), which is easily gained. Views take in all the intricate details of Cir Mhòr and the ridges leading to Goatfell and Cioch na h'Oighe. Further afield the rest of Arran is well displayed in its setting in the Clyde. Several portions of the mainland, Kintyre, Jura and Antrim can be seen.

Leave the summit of Caisteal Abhail by tracing a ridge path roughly eastwards. The path passes a couple of blocky tors, which adventurous walkers might like to scramble across. The path runs out onto a deceptively gentle, grassy shoulder, then drops down more ruggedly to a boulder-strewn gap. Rising above this gap is a rocky, blocky saw-tooth ridge, which is best avoided by tracing a path across the Glen Sannox flank of the ridge. Just before reaching the Witch's Step, another bouldery tor furnishes a short scramble.

Crossing **Ceum na Caillich**, or the Witch's Step, calls for care and attention, a good head for heights and a willingness to use hands as well as feet. The descent into the gap is on granite slabs that drop quite steeply. Always look for signs of previous passage, and use the available hand and footholds. Don't drop down to any place without being confident that the move can be reversed. While the broad slabs can be unnerving, there are useful steps encountered on the final few steps down into the gap.

The gap is a worn, yet sharply defined ridge. Towering above it is a steep and blocky peak of granite, which walkers will be pleased to hear they don't need to climb. Exit to the left of the gap, picking a way down a rather worn gully. Look to the right for a short scramble uphill, which shows obvious signs of use. A narrow path picks its way round a steep and rocky slope. There is another short scramble up some jammed boulders, then the path works its way back towards the main ridge.

The ridge is fairly narrow as it descends, and a good path cuts through the heather and crosses ribs of granite. A large boulder is passed before the next gap is reached. The path then climbs along a broader ridge featuring short grass, heather, low outcrops and boulders of granite. A minor summit is crossed, followed by a little gap, then a worn and gritty path runs up onto **Suidhe Fhearghas**,

Taking a break on the way down the steep and rocky slopes of Suidhe Fhearghas

whose summit is around 660m (2165ft). ▸ This point is mostly rock with a little short grass and heather. A pointed block projects over Glen Sannox, which makes the summit more easily identified in mist. Views take in the whole of Glen Sannox, with distant Beinn a' Chliabhain filling the deep gap of The Saddle.

Some OS maps mark a lower shoulder at 634m (2080ft).

The path runs plainly down the ridge in a series of giant steps separated by short level stretches. There are low outcrops and boulders among the grass and heather, while areas of rotting granite make the path rather gritty. Towards the end of the ridge lies a spread of gritty ground followed by a broad, low outcrop of granite. Beyond that point there is a sudden steepening towards Sannox. The path swings to the left and runs steep and stony down a rugged slope. Note that there is a slab of rock to be crossed towards the foot of the slope. This can be avoided by taking action well in advance. Look out for a rowan tree in a gully and cut off to the left well above it, following a path which introduces a loop into the descent. This loop later swings right and runs beneath the slab.

There is a broad, boggy, heathery gap at the foot of this slope, where paths can be distinguished heading to left and right. ▸ Turn left, but note that the path is rather vague, and it is important to keep well to the left of a couple of hummocky, heathery hills at **Cnocan Donna**. Looking over the edge in clear weather, the car park where the walk started in **North Glen Sannox** can be seen. Closer to hand, and still below, the very tops of some trees can be seen. Keep to the right of these trees once they are reached and walk down the heathery slope alongside. Heather gives way to bracken on the steep slope and a vague path runs straight down to the car park. A little squelchy ground is crossed before the car park and main road are reached.

Turning right offers a descent to Sannox.

WALK 39

Glen Sannox Horseshoe

Start/Finish	Glen Cottage, Sannox (NS 016 454)
Distance	16km (10 miles)
Total ascent	1700m (5575ft)
Time	6hrs
Terrain	Rough and rocky mountain walking, mostly along rugged, but well-trodden paths. Some parts involve exposed and arduous scrambling.
Refreshments	Sannox Bay Hotel and Corrie Golf Club tearoom in Sannox.

The Glen Sannox Horseshoe offers a day of high adventure and the circuit is one of Arran's mountain classics. Note at the outset that the route involves several rocky scrambles. The four most serious are the ascent of Cioch na h'Oighe, the descent from North Goatfell, the ascent of Cir Mhòr and the traverse of Ceum na Caillich, or the Witch's Step. Time could be lost at each of these points, especially if travelling as part of a group. An escape from The Saddle into Glen Sannox is itself a scramble down the steep and rocky Whin Dyke. In foul weather, the Glen Sannox Horseshoe should not be attempted, but in clear, dry weather competent, tough scramblers will find it a most entertaining round.

Start at **Sannox**, at a small car park and bus shelter in-between the Sannox Bay Hotel and Sannox Bridge. Almost directly across the road stands Glen Cottage, where a footpath signpost points along a track. Go through a tall gate and follow a narrow tarmac track. It seems to head directly for Cioch na h'Oighe, which towers above, but quickly bends to the right at a small **cemetery**. The track is stony underfoot as it continues gently up through another gate. Tall white navigation **beacons** stand either side of the track, then there is a fine view around **Glen Sannox** which includes Cioch na h'Oighe, Cir Mhòr, Caisteal Abhail and Suidhe Fhearghas. All will be climbed in due course.

The track climbs more gently and has a line of beech trees to the right. ▶ The ruins of old mine buildings are passed, then a rocky burn called the Allt a' Chapuill is reached, beside an area of spoil from an old barytes mine. There is no need to ford it, but turn left and follow a path upstream. This narrow path climbs a rugged slope of grass, heather, bracken and bog myrtle. There are a series of small waterfalls in the burn, although these are sometimes obscured by birch trees overhanging a rocky gorge.

A footbridge is signposted down to the right, and the route crosses it at the end of the day.

When the last of the trees beside the burn are passed, the path fords the burn and appears to move away from it, but later continues upstream. The path runs across a squelchy bowl of moorland, aiming more directly towards Cioch na h'Oighe. The gentle gradient is followed by a steeper, boulder-strewn, heathery slope, but still with a trodden path. There are more waterfalls on the ascent.

Don't follow the Allt a' Chapuill all the way up into **Coire na Ciche**, but turn right across a slope of heather and boulders. The aim is to pick up the course of a narrow, gravelly path that slices across the steep face of Cioch na h'Oighe. The path is quite clear at close quarters, but it is difficult to spot from below, and might be missed altogether by walkers who climb too high. Follow the narrow path across the steep slope, which has no real difficulties.

The path turns a corner and enjoys a view into Glen Sannox, but it is important not to be drawn into the glen. Instead, look out for a clear, narrow path that starts zigzagging steeply uphill to the left. This path climbs up towards a sloping face of rock, where it appears to terminate. Looking upwards, there appears to be a difficult scramble ahead, but retrace steps for a few paces to locate the start of an easier scramble.

The rock is bare, but there are good hand and footholds. The path continuing uphill is rather vague in places, but it can be traced without too much difficulty. The course of the trodden path often zigzags and any scrambles up rocky outcrops tend to be short and fairly easy. In fact, there is nothing as difficult as the first scramble at the start of this steep climb. The path later begins to move across the slope, so that views at one point overlook

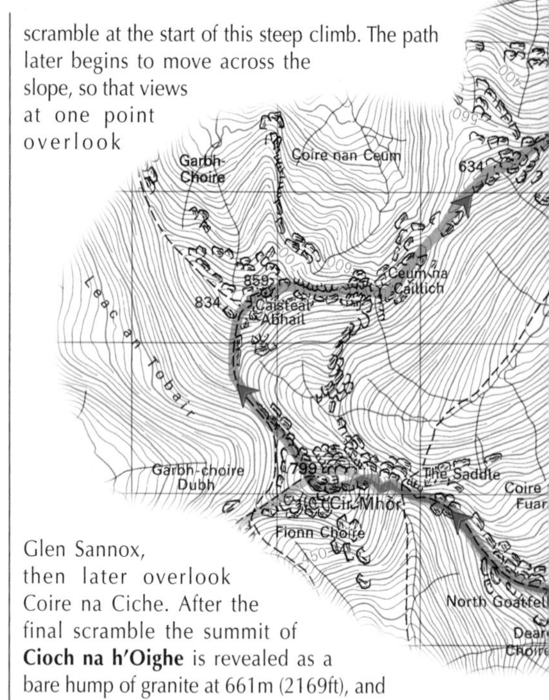

Glen Sannox, then later overlook Coire na Ciche. After the final scramble the summit of **Cioch na h'Oighe** is revealed as a bare hump of granite at 661m (2169ft), and

The tiny shape of a walker stands on Cioche na h'Oighe, or the 'maiden's breast'

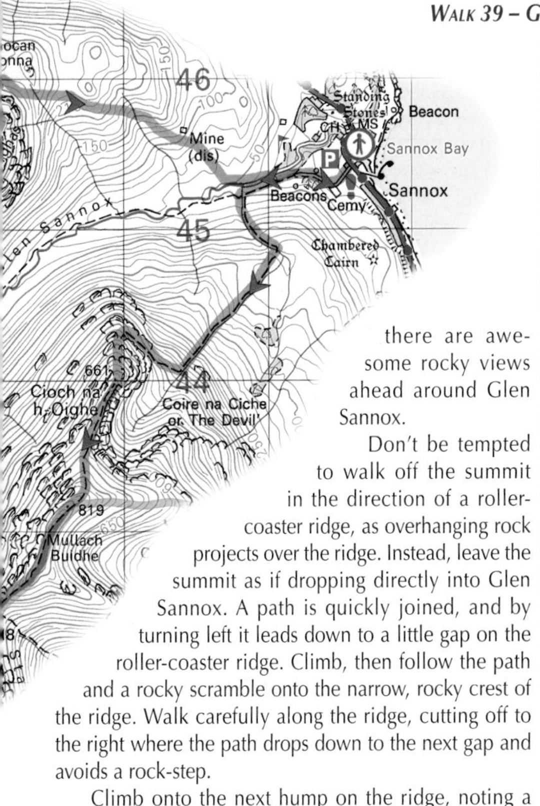

there are awesome rocky views ahead around Glen Sannox.

Don't be tempted to walk off the summit in the direction of a roller-coaster ridge, as overhanging rock projects over the ridge. Instead, leave the summit as if dropping directly into Glen Sannox. A path is quickly joined, and by turning left it leads down to a little gap on the roller-coaster ridge. Climb, then follow the path and a rocky scramble onto the narrow, rocky crest of the ridge. Walk carefully along the ridge, cutting off to the right where the path drops down to the next gap and avoids a rock-step.

Climb onto the next hump on the ridge, noting a small, creeping juniper on the way. The next two notches in the ridge are linked by a path, which picks its way across the flank overlooking Glen Sannox. Both notches feature strange upstanding spikes of granite. Continue along the rocky crest, crossing the highest part of the roller-coaster ridge. Follow a well-worn path across a broad gap. The path climbs up to some blocky slabs on the flanks of Mullach Buidhe, then continues up a slope littered with large, low boulders. Pick a way uphill fairly easily between the boulders, then there is an easier grassy slope at a higher level. A broad crest of grass and low boulders has a good path that continues onwards.

There are a couple of jumbled rocky outcrops overlooking Glen Sannox, but a more ordered pyramidal outcrop is the highest point on **Mullach Buidhe** at 830m (2723ft).

There is a clear view ahead around Glen Sannox and towards Goatfell. The ridge path runs down past embedded boulders to reach a gap below North Goatfell. There are two paths ahead, and the one to the right is used to reach the summit of North Goatfell. The path climbs steeply up a grassy slope, passing rocks to reach the crest of the fell. Turn left to reach the bare granite summit of **North Goatfell** at 818m (2684ft).

An escape is possible by switching to Walk 41.

Descending from North Goatfell to The Saddle requires care. ◄ First, drop down a chaotic arrangement of boulders, then walk further down to cross an exposed step. Head down some rotten ribs and grooves of granite, where some security can be gained from wedging the body in the grooves. A buttress located ahead features a curious rocky projection on the Glen Sannox side, but pass it on the Glen Rosa side to continue downhill. There are areas of rotten granite where gritty material is strewn across the slopes. Follow a worn path onto a bouldery ridge where there are fewer problems. A short, level, easy stretch is found on a heathery shoulder. Pick a way along a little ledge of rock overlooking Glen Sannox, then drop down a slope of clean granite. There is rotten, crumbling granite to cross before landing on the gap of **The Saddle** at 432m (1417ft). Ahead rise the awesome rocky slopes of Cir Mhòr. ◄

An escape is possible by reversing Walk 40 to return to Sannox.

Climbing from The Saddle is relatively easy at first, where slopes of heather and granite slabs are pitched at a good gradient. The slope becomes steeper and trickier, with outcropping rock, slabs, boulders and loose stones and grit. A brief, easier interlude follows along a well-trodden path. Above lies the final part of the ascent, which needs great care. Very steep granite proves to be rotten, and worn down to treacherous boulders and grit. The boulders are sometimes jammed in heaps or wedged in gullies, but there are some loose specimens too. The nature of this ascent is always going to be subject to change and must always be approached with extreme caution. Every hand and foothold needs to be checked for stability. Above is the fine rock peak of **Cir Mhòr** at 799m (2621ft.)

Leave the summit by picking a way downhill carefully on rock and boulders. Look for traces of a path heading towards a gap on the way to Caisteal Abhail. The path is clearer on the final stages of the descent, crossing the gap and passing a cairn. Continue uphill, following the path along a blunt ridge and passing a couple more cairns. The top of **Caisteal Abhail** is a rocky tor ending with a granite slab at 859m (2818ft), which is easily gained and offers fine views. ▸ Views take in all the intricate details of Cir Mhòr and the ridges leading to Goatfell and Cioch na h'Oighe. Further afield the rest of Arran is well displayed in its setting in the Clyde. Several portions of the mainland, Kintyre, Jura and Antrim can be seen.

A handful of blocky granite tors have the appearance of ruined castles and offer interesting scrambling routes.

Leave the summit of Caisteal Abhail by tracing a ridge path roughly eastwards. The path passes a couple of blocky tors, which adventurous walkers might like to scramble across. The path runs out onto a deceptively gentle, grassy shoulder, then drops down more ruggedly to a boulder-strewn gap. Rising above this gap is a rocky, blocky saw-tooth ridge, which is best avoided by tracing a path across the Glen Sannox flank of the ridge. Just before reaching the Witch's Step, another bouldery tor furnishes a short scramble.

Crossing **Ceum na Caillich**, or the Witch's Step, calls for care and attention, a good head for heights and a willingness to use hands as well as feet. The descent into the gap is on granite slabs that drop quite steeply. Always look for signs of previous passage, and use the available hand and footholds. Don't drop down to any place without being confident that the move can be reversed. While the broad slabs can be unnerving, there are useful steps encountered on the final few steps down into the gap.

The gap is a worn, yet sharply define ridge. Towering above it is a steep and blocky peak of granite, which walkers will be pleased to hear they don't need to climb. Exit to the left of the gap, picking a way down a rather worn gully. Look to the right for a short scramble uphill, which shows obvious signs of use. A narrow path picks its way round a steep and rocky slope. There is another short scramble up some jammed boulders, then the path works its way back towards the main ridge.

The ridge is fairly narrow as it descends, and a good path cuts through the heather and crosses ribs of granite. A large boulder is passed before the next gap is reached. The path then climbs along a broader ridge featuring short grass, heather, low outcrops and boulders of granite. A minor summit is crossed, followed by a little gap, then a worn and gritty path runs up onto **Suidhe Fhearghas**, whose summit is around 660m (2165ft). ◂ This point is mostly rock with a little short grass and heather. A pointed block projects over Glen Sannox, which makes the summit more easily identified in poor visibility. Views take in the whole of Glen Sannox, with distant Beinn a' Chliabhain filling the deep gap of The Saddle.

Some OS maps mark a lower shoulder at 634m (2080ft).

The path runs plainly down the ridge in a series of giant steps separated by short level stretches. There are low outcrops and boulders among the grass and heather, while areas of rotting granite make the path rather gritty. Towards the end of the ridge lies a spread of gritty ground

Cir Mhòr, Caisteal Abhail and the rocky ridge hiding the awkward Witch's Step

followed by a broad, low outcrop of granite. Beyond that point there is a sudden steepening towards Sannox. The path swings to the left and runs steep and stony down a rugged slope. Note that there is a slab of rock to be crossed towards the foot of the slope. This can be avoided by taking action well in advance. Look out for a rowan tree in a gully and cut off to the left well above it, following a path that introduces a loop into the descent. This loop later swings right and runs beneath the slab.

There is a broad, boggy, heathery gap at the foot of this slope, where paths can be distinguished heading to left and right. ▶ Turn right and follow the path down slopes of heather, crossing patches of bracken, to reach the lower slopes of grass and bracken. Note the spoil heaps of old barytes mines and aim for the top of these. A broad mine track can be followed down towards Sannox Burn. Turn left around the corner of a tall deer fence, walking along a path between the fence and the river. Turn right to cross over a wide wooden bridge and walk up to a track beside a stand of beech trees. Turn left to follow the track out of **Glen Sannox**, retracing the earliest steps of the day to reach the main road beside Glen Cottage.

Turning left offers a descent to North Glen Sannox.

WALK 40

Glen Sannox to Glen Rosa

Start	Glen Cottage, Sannox (NS 016 454)
Finish	Ferry terminal, Brodick (NS 022 359)
Distance	15.5km (9¾ miles)
Total ascent	550m (1805ft)
Time	5hrs
Terrain	Easy walking through the glens, although the ground beside the paths is often boggy. Scrambling is required on The Saddle.
Refreshments	Sannox Bay Hotel and Corrie Golf Club tearoom in Sannox. Café Rosaburn at the Arran Heritage Museum. Plenty of choice in Brodick.

The walk from Glen Sannox to Glen Rosa is a popular route through the high mountains on Arran. Being linear, it is best completed using bus services. Catch a bus to Sannox at the start of the day, then walk back through the glens at leisure to return to Brodick. There are good paths in the glens, although some parts are boggy underfoot. The climb out of Glen Sannox is a rocky scamble through the leaning gully of the Whin Dyke. The Saddle is slung between some of the highest mountains on the island, but this walk simply heads down through Glen Rosa. When the main road is reached, a bus might be caught back to Brodick, but it takes little extra time to walk there.

Start at **Sannox**, at a small car park and bus shelter in-between the Sannox Bay Hotel and Sannox Bridge. Almost directly across the road stands Glen Cottage, where a footpath signpost points along a track. Go through a tall gate and follow a narrow tarmac track. It seems to head directly for Cioch na h'Oighe, which towers above, but quickly bends to the right at a small **cemetery**. The track is stony underfoot as it continues gently up through another gate. Tall white navigation **beacons** stand either side of the track, then there is a fine view around **Glen Sannox**

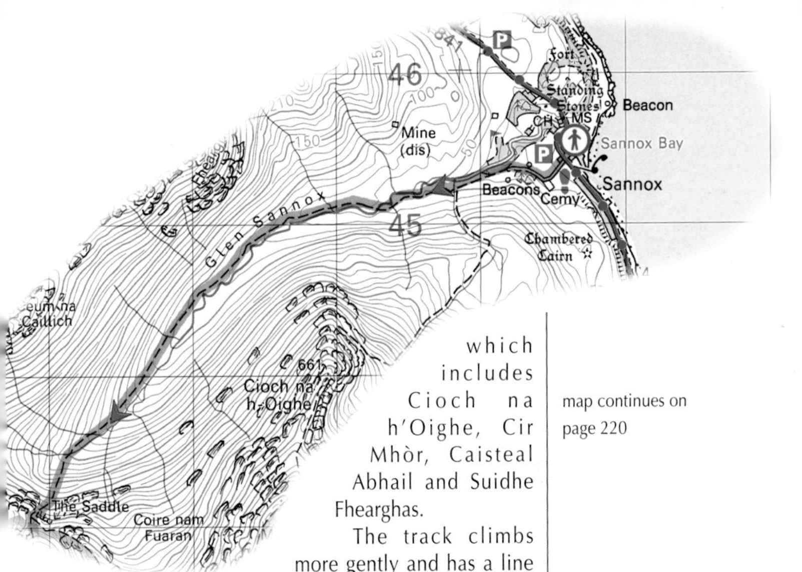

which includes Cioch na h'Oighe, Cir Mhòr, Caisteal Abhail and Suidhe Fhearghas.

map continues on page 220

The track climbs more gently and has a line of beech trees to the right. ▶ The ruins of old mine buildings are passed, then a rocky burn called the Allt a' Chapuill is reached, beside an area of spoil from an old barytes mine. Ford it, and continue walking until Sannox Burn is reached. This is the main river in the glen, and it is crossed using seven chunky stepping-stones.

A footbridge is signposted down to the right. Use this if heavy rain has swollen the river, then continue upstream.

Once across, the path running along the length of Glen Sannox is usually firm, dry and practically level. However, the ground to either side can be rugged and boggy. Enjoy the feeling of moving further and further towards the wild head of the glen, where high mountains tower on all sides. The lowest gap seen in the mountains ahead is The Saddle, and the path climbs towards it. Much of the path has been reconstructed and is plain and obvious to follow, fording little burns at the head of the glen, then climbing more and more steeply.

As height is gained, the path swings to the right and enters a steep, sloping, rocky gully, known as the Whin Dyke. The ascent is an awkward scramble at times, requiring care and the use of hands. Take greater care towards the top, where the ground is crumbling in places

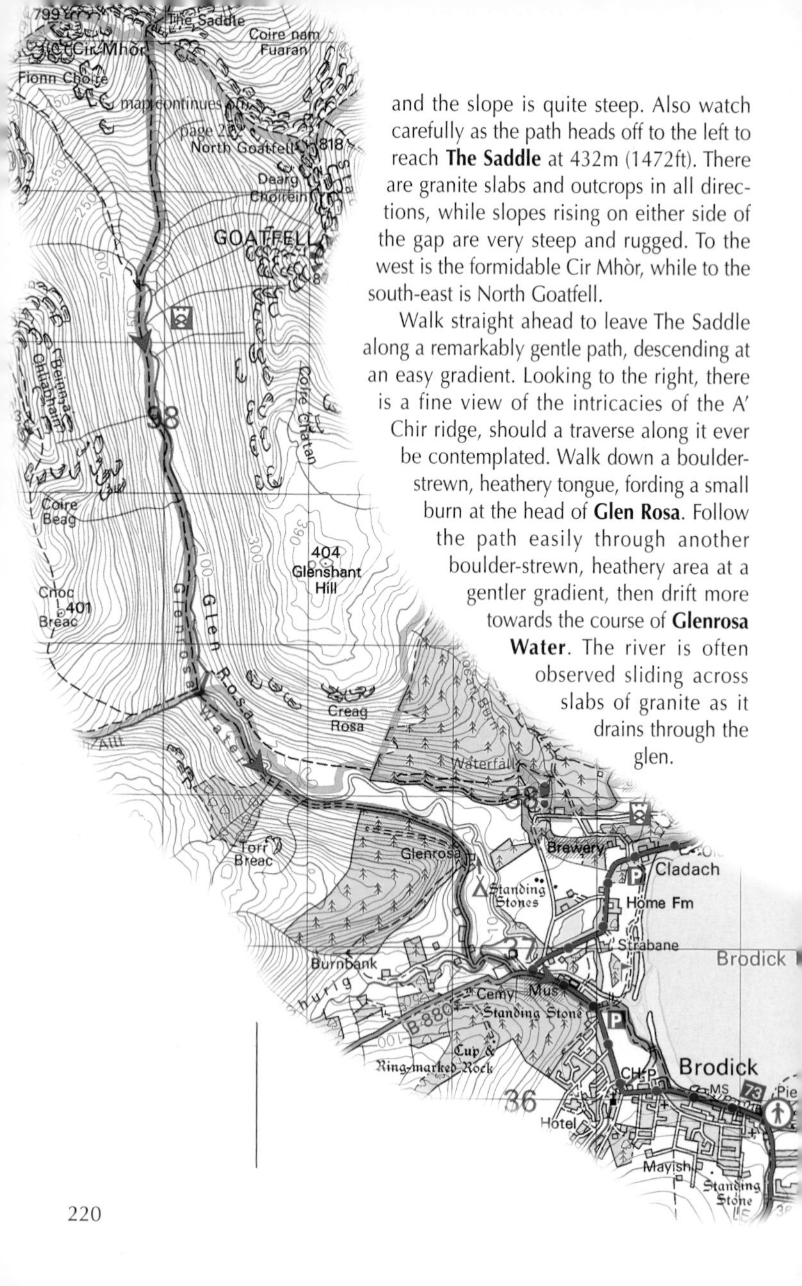

map continues on page 222

and the slope is quite steep. Also watch carefully as the path heads off to the left to reach **The Saddle** at 432m (1472ft). There are granite slabs and outcrops in all directions, while slopes rising on either side of the gap are very steep and rugged. To the west is the formidable Cir Mhòr, while to the south-east is North Goatfell.

Walk straight ahead to leave The Saddle along a remarkably gentle path, descending at an easy gradient. Looking to the right, there is a fine view of the intricacies of the A' Chir ridge, should a traverse along it ever be contemplated. Walk down a boulder-strewn, heathery tongue, fording a small burn at the head of **Glen Rosa**. Follow the path easily through another boulder-strewn, heathery area at a gentler gradient, then drift more towards the course of **Glenrosa Water**. The river is often observed sliding across slabs of granite as it drains through the glen.

The bouldery Glenrosa Water is full of small waterfalls and interesting rapids

Keep to the path, whose surface is usually firm and dry, although the ground to either side is usually wet and boggy. The path follows the river downstream and passes a large boulder of granite. Look out for an attractive waterfall, which plunges into a deep pool in a rocky gorge overhung by birch trees. The path moves away from Glenrosa Water and crosses a wide wooden footbridge over the **Garbh Allt**, which is full of little waterfalls. From this point, it is simply a matter of following a clear and obvious track leading out of Glen Rosa. Go through a kissing gate in a tall deer fence, shortly followed by another gate. A campsite lies down to the left beside the river. ◂ Follow a narrow minor road past a few houses and farms at **Glenrosa**, crossing a bridge over a river to reach a junction with The String road.

To stay at the campsite, simply pitch your tent and someone will be along later, or tel 07985 566004. Note that the river can flood low-lying ground.

Turn left along the road, then right at a junction with the nearby main road for Brodick. The road passes the **Arran Heritage Museum**, followed by Brodick Primary School. Turn left opposite the school to follow a track flanked by bushes. This later swings right and runs beside a golf course. It is known as the Fisherman's Walk and crosses a footbridge before passing a play park and car park, reaching the main road again beside a Co-op store in **Brodick**. Turn left and follow a path beside the road, which becomes a fine promenade through a pleasant green above a rocky shore. It leads all the way to the bus station and ferry terminal. ◂

For a list of facilities along the road through Brodick, see Walk 1.

WALK 41

Sannox, Goatfell and Corrie

Start/Finish	Glen Cottage, Sannox (NS 016 454)
Distance	14.5km (9 miles)
Total ascent	1190m (3905ft)
Time	5hrs
Terrain	Rough and rocky mountain walking, mostly along rugged but well-trodden paths. Some parts involve exposed and arduous scrambling.
Refreshments	Sannox Bay Hotel and Corrie Golf Club tearoom at Sannox. Corrie Hotel at Corrie.

A rugged, entertaining horseshoe route climbs high above the villages of Sannox and Corrie. It embraces the summits of Cioch na h'Oighe, Mullach Buidhe, North Goatfell and Goatfell. The initial climb involves short rock scrambles and an airy rock ridge. The route is not recommended in wet or windy conditions, and in mist care is needed with navigation. Escapes are possible from the higher parts of the route, but on the ascent of Cioch na h'Oighe it is necessary to stick to the route described. Short-cutting is asking for trouble and early descents are inadvisable before Mullach Buidhe. In clear weather, there is a chance to get to grips with the granite and enjoy amazing views into the rocky heart of northern Arran. The route described ends with a short road walk between Corrie and Sannox. This could be completed at the start of the walk, the end of the walk, or omitted entirely by catching a bus between the two villages.

Start at **Sannox**, at a small car park and bus shelter in-between the Sannox Bay Hotel and Sannox Bridge. Almost directly across the road stands Glen Cottage, where a footpath signpost points along a track. Go through a tall gate and follow a narrow tarmac track. It seems to head directly for Cioch na h'Oighe, which towers above, but quickly bends to the right at a small **cemetery**. The track is stony underfoot as it continues gently up through another gate. Tall white navigation **beacons** stand either side of the track, then there is a fine view around **Glen Sannox** which includes Cioch na h'Oighe, Cir Mhòr, Caisteal Abhail and Suidhe Fhearghas. All will be climbed in due course.

The track climbs more gently and has a line of beech trees to the right. The ruins of old mine buildings are passed, then a rocky burn called the Allt a' Chapuill is reached, beside an area of spoil from an old barytes mine. There is no need to ford it, but turn left and follow a path upstream. This narrow path climbs a rugged slope of grass, heather, bracken and bog myrtle. There are a series of small waterfalls in the burn, although these are sometimes obscured by birch trees overhanging a rocky gorge.

When the last of the trees beside the burn are passed, the path fords the burn and appears to move away from it, but later continues upstream. The path runs across a squelchy bowl of moorland, aiming more directly towards Cioch na h'Oighe. The gentle gradient is followed by a steeper, boulder-strewn, heathery slope, but still with a trodden path. There are more waterfalls on the ascent.

Don't follow the Allt a' Chapuill all the way up into **Coire na Ciche**, but turn right across a slope of heather and boulders. The aim is to pick up the course of a narrow, gravelly path that slices across the steep face of Cioch na h'Oighe. The path is quite clear at close quarters, but it is difficult to spot from below, and might be missed altogether by walkers who climb too high. Follow the narrow path across the steep slope, which has no real difficulties.

The path turns a corner and enjoys a view into Glen Sannox, but it is important not to be drawn into the glen. Instead, look out for a clear, narrow path that starts zigzagging steeply uphill to the left. This path climbs up towards a sloping face of rock, where it appears to terminate. Looking upwards, there appears to be a difficult scramble ahead, but retrace steps for a few paces to locate the start of an easier scramble.

The rock is bare, but there are good hand and footholds. The path continuing uphill is rather vague in places, but it can be traced without too much difficulty. The course of the trodden path often zigzags and

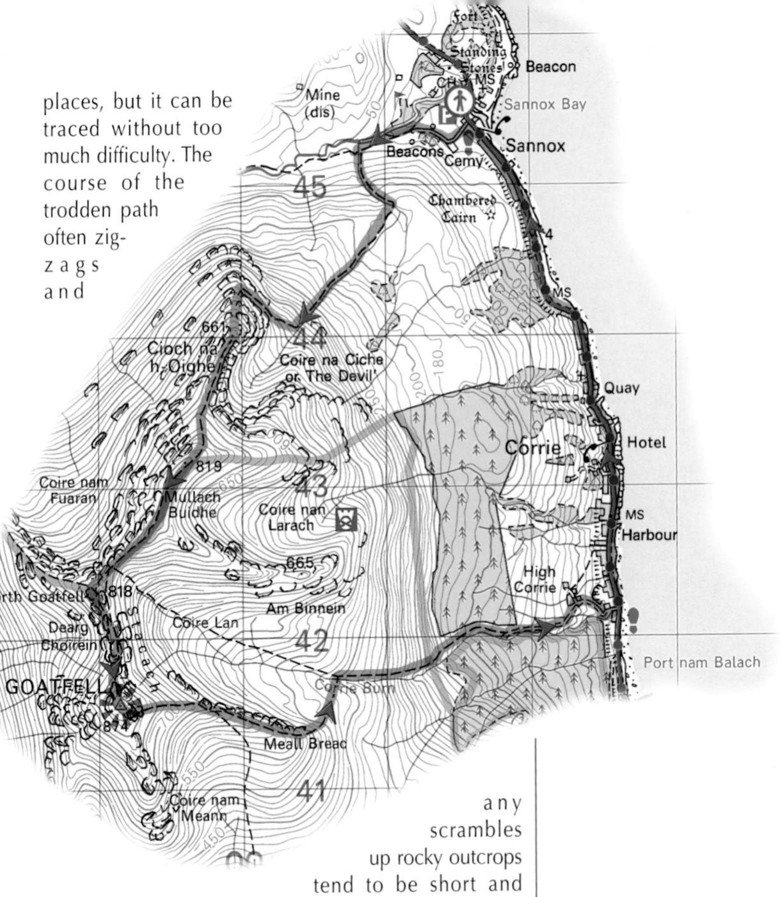

any scrambles up rocky outcrops tend to be short and fairly easy. In fact, there is nothing as difficult as the first scramble at the start of this steep climb. The path later begins to move across the slope, so that views at one point overlook Glen Sannox, then later overlook Coire na Ciche. After the final scramble the summit of **Cioch na h'Oighe** is revealed as a bare hump of granite at 661m (2169ft), and there are awesome rocky views ahead around Glen Sannox.

Don't be tempted to walk off the summit in the direction of a roller-coaster ridge, as overhanging rock projects

Looking along the rugged ridge from Mullach Buidhe towards North Goatfell

over the ridge. Instead, leave the summit as if dropping directly into Glen Sannox. A path is quickly joined, and by turning left it leads down to a little gap on the roller-coaster ridge. Climb, then follow the path and a rocky scramble onto the narrow, rocky crest of the ridge. Walk carefully along the ridge, cutting off to the right where the path drops down to the next gap and avoids a rock-step.

Climb onto the next hump on the ridge, noting a small, creeping juniper on the way. The next two notches in the ridge are linked by a path, which picks its way across the flank overlooking Glen Sannox. Both notches feature strange upstanding spikes of granite. Continue along the rocky crest, crossing the highest part of the roller-coaster ridge. Follow a well-worn path across a broad gap. The path climbs up to some blocky slabs on the flanks of Mullach Buidhe, then continues up a slope littered with large, low boulders. Pick a way uphill fairly easily between the boulders, then there is an easier grassy slope at a higher level. A broad crest of grass and low boulders has a good path that continues onwards. There are a couple of jumbled rocky outcrops overlooking Glen Sannox, but a more ordered pyramidal outcrop is the highest point on **Mullach Buidhe** at 830m (2723ft).

There is a clear view ahead around Glen Sannox and towards Goatfell. The ridge path runs down past embedded boulders to reach a gap below North Goatfell. There are two paths ahead, and the one to the right is used to reach the summit of North Goatfell. The path climbs steeply up a grassy slope, passing rocks to reach the crest of the fell. Turn left to reach the bare granite summit of **North Goatfell** at 818m (2684ft).

Follow the narrow, blocky ridge onwards, stepping down from the rock to gain an easy path that crosses a grassy gap over 760m (2495ft). A pyramidal tor of wrinkled granite rises above the gap, on the **Stacach** ridge, where three options are available. One route is an almost direct ascent, to the left of some large, jammed boulders. A less direct route uses giant steps to the right of the boulders. Both these options are exposed scrambles. Walkers can also walk round the base of the pyramid, on the left side overlooking the sea. Anyone climbing over the top of the tor will need to scramble down the other side. There are a couple more rocky bosses to scramble over if required. Anyone on the lower path can avoid all the rocky parts of the ridge by staying always on the seaward side of the ridge. A fourth route on the Glen Rosa flank might also be considered, although this is quite badly eroded.

The last part of the ridge is mostly a jumble of boulders through which the path continues. The summit of **Goatfell** is reached quite suddenly and is composed of a bare table of granite bearing a few large boulders. There is a trig point at 874m (2867ft), with a view indicator provided by the Rotary Club of Kilwinning. This is the highest peak on Arran. ◄

Views are extensive and stretch far into mainland Scotland as well as embracing the Highlands, islands and Northern Ireland.

To leave the summit, follow the ridge path eastwards. The ground is boulder-strewn, and the path is quite rugged as it weaves between boulders and blocky outcrops. There is a more level shoulder on **Meall Breac**, where the main path down to Brodick heads off to the right. However, keep straight on along the broad and boulder-strewn crest, then descend a bouldery, heathery slope, where the path is patchy in places and a couple of steps down may require the use of hands. Watch for the path drifting off to the left, down towards **Corrie Burn**.

The rugged path fords Corrie Burn among a jumble of boulders, but should present no problems except in times of severe flooding. Continue downstream using a reconstructed path running parallel to the burn. The path leads down to a kissing gate in a tall deer fence. The path roughly follows the river through a broad clearing flanked by forest plantations, and many parts of the path have been reconstructed, although a few rugged bits remain.

A clear track is joined, which becomes a narrow tarmac road as it passes a small covered reservoir. Walk steeply down past **High Corrie** to the main coastal road and turn left to follow it through the long and straggly village of **Corrie**. ◄ Food and drink might be obtained at the Corrie Hotel, and buses can be caught along the road.

If ever attempting this walk in reverse, the road junction is signposted for Goatfell.

CORRIE

A 'runrig' farm (one with no one permanent tenant) was recorded in Corrie in 1449, and by 1773 it was divided into three farms. In addition to farming there were quarries above the village, providing cut stone and lime. There was a decline in the population during the clearances around 1830, but enough people remained for churches and a school to be built. The Free Church, now closed, dates from 1848. The 11th Duke of Hamilton provided a school in 1870, while the parish church dates from 1886. There was once a Congregational Church too. Corrie has a number of features and facilities which, listed from south to north include: Corrie and Sannox Village Hall and surgery, car park, a small harbour with sheep sculptures, then a long stretch of houses. Next comes Corrie Croft Bunkhouse, craft shops and the Corrie Hotel. Further on, beyond another long stretch of houses, is a tiny harbour with a war memorial, yet another harbour, the Parish Church and Corrie Primary School.

Those who wish to walk back to Sannox should head all the way through Corrie, passing a boulder-strewn and rocky shoreline with three small harbours. After leaving the long and straggly village, a huge boulder stands to the left of the road at Clach a' Chath, or the Cat Stone. ▶

Cromwellian soldiers were killed at Clach a' Chath and their bodies are said to be buried at Lag nan Sasunnach near Sannox.

The coastal road features only occasional glimpses of the sea as it is quite well wooded, but watch for seals hauled out on boulders, basking in the sun. There is a rugged, wooded cliff to the left, and a wooded raised beach to the right. Walking off the road proves to be very difficult and is not recommended. After passing an outcrop of rough conglomerate rock, the village of **Sannox** is reached. Follow the road straight through, passing the Sannox Bay Hotel to return to the small car park opposite Glen Cottage. ▶

For a list of facilities in Sannox, see Walk 37.

WALK 42

Glen Rosa and Beinn Tarsuinn

Start/Finish	Glen Rosa campsite (NS 001 376)
Distance	14.5km (9 miles)
Total ascent	1030m (3380ft)
Time	5hrs
Terrain	Rough and rocky mountain walking, mostly along rugged but well-trodden paths. Some lower parts can be boggy.
Refreshments	None closer than the Arran Heritage Museum, Duchess Court and Brodick.

An interesting little horseshoe circuit can be completed around Coire a' Bhradain on the western side of Glen Rosa. It makes a fine circuit in its own right, or it could be used by walkers who set out on the Glen Rosa Horseshoe walk, but realise that they are not going to be able to complete the full round. Beinn Nuis, Beinn Tarsuinn and Beinn a' Chliabhain form the 'nails' in the horseshoe, and an impressive traverse around the head of Coire Daingean is also included. A couple of sections of the Garbh Allt have been surrounded by tall deer fences to prevent sheep and deer from grazing. The intention is to enable the scanty tree cover beside the burn to regenerate.

This walk starts from the Glen Rosa campsite. To reach the campsite from Brodick, follow the main coastal road out of town, then turn left along the Blackwaterfoot road. Turn right almost immediately along a narrow minor road signposted for Glen Rosa. If using buses, the nearest stop is at the Arran Heritage Museum, but with advance notice, the driver might drop passengers at the Glen Rosa road-end. The narrow road passes a few houses and farms and the tarmac expires at the riverside campsite. Parking is limited and taking a car as far as the campsite should be avoided if at all possible. ◂

To stay at the campsite, simply pitch your tent and someone will be along later, or tel 07985 566004. Note that the river can flood low-lying ground.

A clear and obvious track continues from the end of the tarmac road at the campsite. Follow it alongside a wood and go through two gates. After passing through the second gate, the track stays low through **Glen Rosa**, overlooking **Glenrosa Water**. The track rises and falls, twists and turns, but is generally firm, stony and dry underfoot. Cross a wide wooden footbridge and admire the waterfalls tumbling down the **Garbh Allt**. There are also fine views of the pyramidal peak of Cir Mhòr which dominates the head of Glen Rosa, and the pinnacles either side of Ceum na Caillich – the Witch's Step – which actually lie in neighbouring Glen Sannox.

After crossing the footbridge, turn left and pick up a path climbing roughly parallel to the Garbh Allt. Patches of bog myrtle near the bridge give way to bracken and heather as height is gained on the steep and boulder-strewn slope. A fenced enclosure is entered at a kissing gate and the path continues climbing. The rough surface offers better walking than the tussocks of grass alongside.

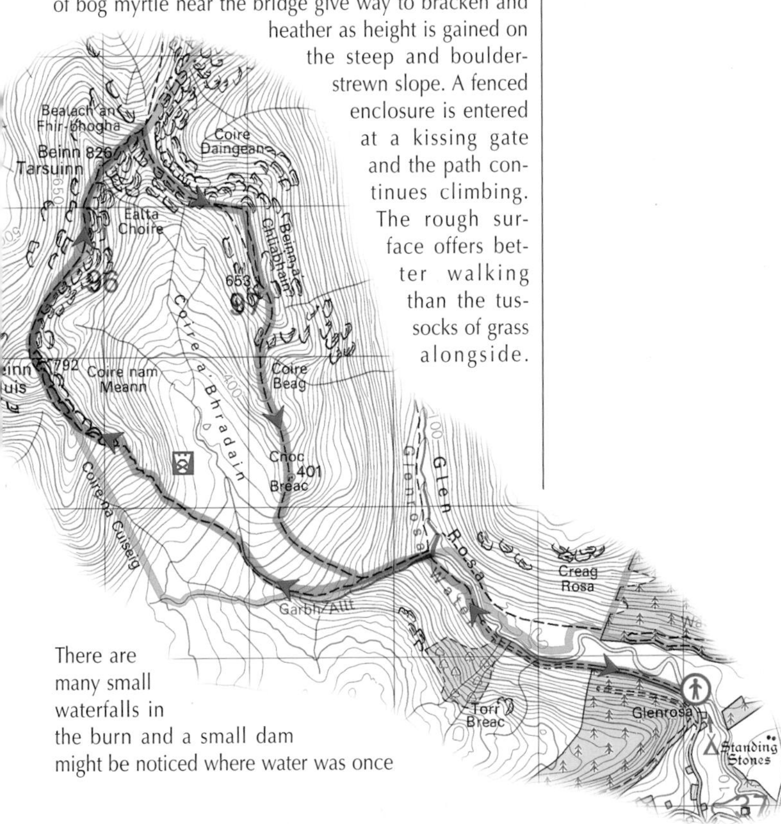

There are many small waterfalls in the burn and a small dam might be noticed where water was once

Precipitous cliffs fall from the summit of Beinn Nuis into Coire a' Bhradain

collected and piped down through the glen. Another kissing gate is passed and the path continues beside the burn. The waterfalls often roar down rocky slopes, while at a higher level the path crosses a gentler moorland and the burn runs through a small rocky gorge.

Go through a kissing gate to enter another fenced enclosure surrounding the gorge. There are views around the fine little horseshoe of peaks encircling **Coire a' Bhradain**. Look out for the path crossing the gorge and fording the burn. In very wet weather it might be inadvisable to cross. Another kissing gate allows an exit from the fenced enclosure, then the path climbs towards mountains. ◂

Ahead lies the pyramidal Beinn Nuis to the left, followed by Beinn Tarsuinn in the middle and Beinn a' Chliabhain to the far right. Goatfell, visible throughout the ascent, is seen over a shoulder of Beinn a' Chliabhain.

The path heads away from the burn and crosses a boggy moorland slope before climbing more steeply. After passing small slabs of granite, the path drifts to the right and follows a rib of granite. The way uphill is usually clearly trodden, except where the route crosses slabs of granite. These outcrops are set at an easy angle. Looking across the gap between Beinn Tarsuinn and Beinn a' Chliabhain, the peaks of A' Chir and Cir Mhòr can be seen.

A less rocky shoulder is climbed and the path is clear. It threads its way past low, rounded tors and boulders, before a final pull up to the summit of **Beinn Nuis**. Large boulders of granite protrude from the 792m (2598ft) summit and there is a small cairn. Views encompass Glen Rosa, with a glimpse of Glen Sannox over the gap of The Saddle. Southern Arran is well displayed, but has few significant features. The Pirnmill Hills rise in a mountainous barrier beyond Loch Tanna.

A path descends from the summit of Beinn Nuis, picking its way down a steep and bouldery slope to a gap before continuing along the high ridge. There are fine views of rocky buttresses overlooking Glen Rosa, then the path runs along the side of the ridge overlooking Glen Iorsa to avoid a bouldery scramble. On the next uphill stretch there is a tremendous view along the length of Glen Iorsa, featuring its little loch towards the sea, its awesomely boggy stretches along its floor, and the meandering course of its river.

Continuing uphill, many large, rounded boulders are passed. The ridge broadens and is clothed in short grass and moss, then it narrows and rises again. Just before a dip in the ridge the Old Man of Tarsuinn presents a sort of human profile off to the right.

OLD MAN OF TARSUINN

The Old Man of Tarsuinn is a comical natural sculpture projecting from the ridge between Beinn Nuis and Beinn Tarsuinn. Its profile resembles that of Popeye, or some other gnarled seafarer, which is appropriate as the figure appears to gaze out to sea. After a couple of visits, walkers should be able to spot the Old Man even from distant Brodick, although from that distance it is a mere pimple on the rocky ridge.

Cross the dip and climb a final, short, boulder-strewn slope to reach the summit of **Beinn Tarsuinn** at 826m (2710ft). There are twin summits with no real difference between them, and both have low outcrops and boulders of granite. Views ahead tend to make A' Chir merge into Cir Mhòr, but it is important to remember that these two peaks are quite separate and that there is no walking route directly from one to the other.

A path runs steeply downhill from Beinn Tarsuinn and there is a need to grapple with some big boulders and outcrops of granite. Sometimes there is a choice of paths, and at one point there is even the option of walking beneath a huge boulder. After much squeezing and slithering the bottom of the slope is reached and the gap of **Bealach an Fhir-bhogha** is gained. From certain points on the gap it is possible to see the pyramidal form of Ailsa Craig and the humps of the Paps of Jura, both out to sea in the distance, but in opposite directions.

To leave Bealach an Fhir-bhogha, turn sharp right to spot a path contouring beneath a monstrous granite face overlooking **Coire Daingean** and Glen Rosa. The path is narrow and clings to a steep slope, but it is continuous throughout. Looking upwards, tottering blocks of granite can be seen, and there is a long, dark slit slicing through the rock face. The path runs downhill on a crumbly slope, then rises to gain the crest of the ridge between Beinn

Looking from Beinn a' Chliabhain towards A' Chir, Caisteal Abhail and Cir Mhòr

Tarsuinn and Beinn a' Chliabhain. Throughout the traverse, there are fine views into Glen Rosa.

Turn left along the rocky crest, following a path that soon crosses a gentle, grassy gap. Note that the well-trodden path proceeds by cutting across the western slopes of Beinn a' Chliabhain. If a summit bid is to be made, then it is necessary to start climbing to the left to stay on the ridge. Grass, heather and boulders give way to a fine rocky ridge. The summit of **Beinn a' Chliabhain** rises to 653m (2142ft) and offers fine views around Glen Rosa from an airy perch. There is a last chance to sample distant views, which stretch from Antrim to Galloway and Ayrshire and include Ailsa Craig and Holy Isle.

Continue along the ridge path, which joins the path skirting along the flank of the mountain. The path is clear and stony, braided in places, running down a broadening, boulder-strewn moorland slope. The gradient eases later, where boggy ground and granite slabs are followed by a bouldery cairn. Continue to trace the path down broad, boggy slopes of tussocky grass. The path swings to the left as it approaches the Garbh Allt, and it reaches a kissing gate at the corner of a fenced enclosure.

All that remains is to retrace the earlier steps of the day. Follow the steep and rugged path downhill alongside the waterfalls of the **Garbh Allt** and pass through another kissing gate at the bottom of the fenced enclosure. Turn right to cross the footbridge over the Garbh Allt, then follow the clear track through **Glen Rosa** to return to the campsite.

WALK 43

Western Glen Rosa

Start/Finish	Glen Rosa campsite (NS 001 376)
Distance	18km (11 miles)
Total ascent	1200m (3935ft)
Time	5hrs 30mins
Terrain	Rough and rocky mountain walking, mostly along rugged but well-trodden paths, with some rock scrambling. Some lower parts can be boggy.
Refreshments	None closer than the Arran Heritage Museum, Duchess Court and Brodick.

Tough walkers who are prepared to start early and finish late on a good, clear day would be able to manage the long walk around the Glen Rosa Horseshoe. Others would need to tackle the round in two halves. The western half is the toughest, requiring a long ascent, some steep and rugged slopes, and even some scrambling on steep rock at times. The wrinkly rock faces of A' Chir are beyond the capabilities of more cautious walkers, and the full traverse of the rocky ridge is really the domain of rock climbers. However, an optional ascent of A'Chir is described for walkers who wish to bring its summit underfoot.

Starting from the Glen Rosa campsite gives walkers a headstart on this route. Those who drive into the glen could have difficulty securing a parking space. However, some walkers are prepared to walk in by road from Brodick.

This walk starts from the Glen Rosa campsite. To reach the campsite from Brodick, follow the main coastal road out of town, then turn left along the Blackwaterfoot road. Turn right almost immediately along a narrow minor road signposted for Glen Rosa. If using buses, the nearest stop is at the Arran Heritage Museum, but with advance notice, the driver might drop passengers at the Glen Rosa road-end. The narrow road passes a few houses and farms and the tarmac expires at the riverside campsite. Parking is limited and taking a car as far as the campsite should be avoided if at all possible. ▶

To stay at the campsite, simply pitch your tent and someone will be along later, or tel 07985 566004. Note that the river can flood low-lying ground.

A clear and obvious track continues from the end of the tarmac road at the campsite. Follow it alongside a wood and go through two gates. After passing through the second gate, the track stays low through **Glen Rosa**, overlooking **Glenrosa Water**. The track rises and falls, twists and turns, but is generally firm, stony and dry underfoot. Cross a wide wooden footbridge and admire the waterfalls tumbling down the **Garbh Allt**. There are also fine views of the pyramidal peak of Cir Mhòr, which dominates the head of Glen Rosa, and the pinnacles either side of Ceum na Caillich – the Witch's Step – which actually lie in neighbouring Glen Sannox.

After crossing the footbridge, turn left and pick up a path climbing roughly parallel to the Garbh Allt. Patches of bog myrtle near the bridge give way to bracken and heather as height is gained on the steep and boulder-strewn slope. A fenced enclosure is entered at a kissing gate and the path continues climbing. The rough surface offers better walking than the tussocks of grass alongside. There are many small waterfalls in the burn and a small dam might be noticed where water was once collected and piped down through the glen. Another kissing gate is passed and the path continues beside the burn. The waterfalls often roar down rocky slopes, while at a higher level the path crosses a gentler moorland and the burn runs through a small rocky gorge.

Go through a kissing gate to enter another fenced enclosure surrounding the gorge. There are views around the fine little horseshoe of peaks encircling **Coire a' Bhradain**. Look out for the path crossing the gorge and fording the burn. In very wet weather it might be inadvisable to cross. Another kissing gate allows an exit from the fenced enclosure, then the path climbs towards mountains. ▶

Ahead lies the pyramidal Beinn Nuis to the left, followed by Beinn Tarsuinn in the middle and Beinn a' Chliabhain to the far right. Goatfell, visible throughout the ascent, is seen over a shoulder of Beinn a' Chliabhain.

The path heads away from the burn and crosses a boggy moorland slope before climbing more steeply. After passing small slabs of granite, the path drifts to the right and follows a rib of granite. The way uphill is usually clearly trodden, except where the route crosses slabs of granite. These outcrops are set at an easy angle. Looking across the gap between Beinn

Tarsuinn and Beinn a' Chliabhain, the peaks of A' Chir and Cir Mhòr can be seen.

A less rocky shoulder is climbed and the path is clear. It threads its way past low, rounded tors and boulders, before a final pull up to the summit of **Beinn Nuis**. Large boulders of granite protrude from the 792m (2598ft) summit and there is a small cairn. Views encompass Glen Rosa, with a glimpse of Glen Sannox over the gap of The Saddle. Southern Arran is well displayed, but has few significant features. The Pirnmill Hills rise in a mountainous barrier beyond Loch Tanna.

A path descends from the summit of Beinn Nuis, picking its way down a steep and bouldery slope to a gap before continuing along the high ridge. There are fine views of rocky buttresses overlooking Glen Rosa, then the path runs along the side of the ridge overlooking Glen Iorsa to avoid a bouldery scramble. On the next uphill stretch there is a tremendous view along the length of Glen Iorsa, featuring its little loch towards the sea, its awesomely boggy stretches along its floor, and the meandering course of its river.

Continuing uphill, many large, rounded boulders are passed. The ridge broadens and is clothed in short grass and moss, then it narrows and rises again. Just before a dip in the ridge the Old Man of Tarsuinn presents a sort of human profile off to the right. Cross the dip and climb a final, short, boulder-strewn slope to reach the summit of **Beinn Tarsuinn** at 826m (2710ft). There are twin summits with no real difference between them, and both have low outcrops and boulders of granite. Views ahead tend to make A' Chir merge into Cir Mhòr, but it is important to remember that these two peaks are quite separate and that there is no walking route directly from one to the other.

A path runs steeply downhill from Beinn Tarsuinn and there is a need to grapple with some big boulders and outcrops of granite. Sometimes there's a choice of paths, and at one point there's even the option of walking beneath a huge boulder. After much squeezing and slithering, the bottom of the slope is reached and

The natural granite sculpture of the Old Man of Tarsuinn looks out over the glens

the gap of **Bealach an Fhir-bhogha** is gained. From certain points on the gap it is possible to see the pyramidal form of Ailsa Craig and the humps of the Paps of Jura, both out to sea in the distance, but in opposite directions.

Two paths continue beyond Bealach an Fhir-bhogha – one climbing right, to the summit of A' Chir and one staying lower, keeping to the left of A' Chir. Most walkers will keep left and avoid the summit.

Optional ascent of A' Chir

Those who wish to include the summit of A' Chir in this walk should note that there is steep and exposed scrambling even on the easiest ascent.

Take the path forking to the right and running uphill. This stays on the Glen Iorsa side of the rugged ridge, gaining the crest of the ridge at a notch overlooked by a monstrous buttress of rock. Take a path to the left, then scramble up boulders and slabs. Another path at a higher level picks its way along a narrow ledge on a sloping boilerplate slab overlooking Glen Iorsa. It gains the rocky crest and reaches another notch.

It is possible to scramble down into the notch in a couple of places, but the rock can be damp and greasy, and a slip could have disastrous consequences. This awkward descent can be avoided by backtracking a little along the ridge, then dropping down to another thin path on the Glen Iorsa side. The path leads along a ledge, which runs into a gully just below the notch. To the left of this gully is an exposed rock scramble on sloping slabs, allowing the crest to be regained. Once this has been accomplished, walk and scramble towards the summit of **A' Chir**, which is a monstrous perched boulder at 745m (2444ft). Walkers may be excused for not tackling this final obstacle!

Continuing along the ridge towards **Cir Mhòr** is fraught with difficulties and is actually graded as a rock climb. Anyone experiencing hardship scrambling to the summit of A' Chir would not be able to cover the rest of the ridge. ▶ Cautious explorers who have reached the summit of A' Chir but don't want to be drawn along the rest of the ridge should retrace steps faithfully to **Bealach an Fhir-bhogha**. The descent is trickier than the ascent and it needs more care. The first full traverse of the A' Chir ridge was accomplished in January 1892.

While experienced rock climbers might manage without a rope, others should rope up for safety. Experienced rock climbers with ropes could coax less accomplished climbers along the ridge.

Keeping left, the path runs beneath boilerplate slabs of granite, which flank **A' Chir** on the Glen Iorsa side. The path is narrow in places, although it should always be distinguishable ahead. It dips downhill to pass beneath the foot of the slabs. This is something of a 'weeping wall' with clean granite slabs dripping or running with water, and only a few rugs or carpets of heather able to grow on the steep rock. The path rises from the base of the slabs and reaches a little notch, offering a view back along the more difficult parts of the ridge. The path continues in the direction of Cir Mhòr.

A short rock-step gives access to an inclined table of rock on the rugged crest of the ridge. The path runs down to a broad, bouldery gap, where a small cairn sits on the lowest part, marking a useful escape path into Coire Buidhe, if an ascent of Cir Mhòr is not required on this particular outing.

Alternative descent to Glen Rosa (saves 1km (½ mile), 200m (655ft) of ascent and 30mins)
Head down to the right from the small cairn. The first part of the path consists of steep, loose, stony material. Later, there is a gentler path, before another drop leads down through **Fionn Choire** and finally into **Glen Rosa**.

Follow the path as it wriggles up a bouldery slope. At one point another path heads off to the left, running directly towards Caisteal Abhail, so be careful not to be drawn along it in poor visibility. The final part of the climb is even steeper and the rocky summit of **Cir Mhòr** is gained only by grappling with hands. From the 799m (2621ft) stance there are amazing views around the ridges of Glen Rosa and Glen Sannox. The peaks of Goatfell, Cioch na h'Oighe and Caisteal Abhail all feature prominently, as well as the A' Chir ridge. The more distant Pirnmill Hills are seen across Glen Iorsa.

The descent from Cir Mhòr to The Saddle needs exceptional care. Looking down from the summit, only a couple of portions of the path near the top can be seen. What is not apparent is the nature of the terrain. Very steep granite proves to be rotten and worn down to a treacherously boulder-strewn, gritty condition. The boulders are sometimes jammed in heaps or wedged in gullies, but there are some loose specimens too. The nature of this descent is always going to be subject to change and must always be approached with extreme caution.

The first part of the descent is steep and horrible, with every hand and foothold needing to be checked for stability, then there is a brief, easy interlude along a well-trodden path. Another steep and rugged drop picks a way down a steep slope where there is outcropping rock, slabs, boulders and loose stones and grit. This steep and tricky slope continues all the way down to **The Saddle** at 432m (1417ft). Only on the final parts of the

The fine ridge between Cir Mhòr and Caisteal Abhail

descent are there any easy gradients, where slopes of heather and slabs pitche d at an easier angle lead onto the gap. Anyone wishing to complete the full Glen Rosa Horseshoe can switch to Walk 44 and pick up the route description from The Saddle.

Walk straight ahead to leave The Saddle along a remarkably gentle path, descending at an easy gradient. Walk down a boulder-strewn, heathery tongue, fording a small burn at the head of **Glen Rosa**. ▸ Follow the path easily through another boulder-strewn, heathery area at a gentler gradient, then drift more towards the course of **Glenrosa Water**. The river is often observed sliding across slabs of granite as it drains through the glen.

The 'alternative descent' joins here.

Keep to the path, whose surface is usually firm and dry, although the ground to either side is usually wet and boggy. The path follows the river downstream and passes a large boulder of granite. Look out for an attractive waterfall, which plunges into a deep pool in a rocky gorge overhung by birch trees. The path moves away from Glenrosa Water and crosses a wide wooden footbridge over the

Garbh Allt, which is full of little waterfalls. From this point, it is simply a matter of following a clear and obvious track leading out of Glen Rosa. Go through a kissing gate in a tall deer fence, shortly followed by another gate. The campsite lies down to the left beside the river.

GLEN ROSA

Facilities in Glen Rosa are limited to the Glen Rosa Campsite and a few self-catering cottages. Practically all of the Glen Rosa Horseshoe, and some land outside its bounds, is owned and managed by the National Trust for Scotland. The extent of their holdings in the mountains is around 2835 hectares (7000 acres).

The walk ends with a descent through Glen Rosa

WALK 44

Eastern Glen Rosa

Start/Finish	Arran Heritage Museum (NS 008 367)
Distance	18km (11 miles)
Total ascent	1000m (3280ft)
Time	5hrs 30mins
Terrain	Rough and rocky mountain walking, mostly along rugged but well-trodden paths, with some rock scrambling. Easy road-walking at the start and finish.
Refreshments	Café at the Arran Heritage Centre. Plenty of choice in Brodick.

The Glen Rosa horseshoe can be completed in a long, hard day's walk by tough and experienced hill walkers. Other walkers may prefer to tread more cautiously and complete the horseshoe walk in two easier halves. Note the use of the word 'easier' and not 'easy'. The Glen Rosa Horseshoe can never be easy and there are some very steep and exposed rocky slopes. Some basic scrambling is required in places. The western half of the horseshoe features some of the more arduous scrambles, while the eastern half is easier on the hands. The walk includes Goatfell, which is the highest mountain on Arran and offers the most extensive views. Parking is awkward on the roads used at the start and finish, so this route is structured from the nearest bus stops.

There are bus stops at the **Arran Heritage Museum** outside Brodick. Follow the main road to a nearby junction and turn left as signposted for Blackwaterfoot. Turn right almost immediately as signposted for Glen Rosa. Bus drivers might stop here if given due notice. A narrow road crosses a river, passes a few houses and farms, reaching a house called **Glenrosa**. The tarmac ends at the riverside Glen Rosa Campsite. Parking is limited here. ▶

To stay at the campsite, simply pitch your tent and someone will be along later, or tel 07985 566004. Note that the river can flood low-lying ground.

A clear and obvious track continues from the end of the tarmac road at the campsite. Follow it alongside a wood and go through two gates. After passing through

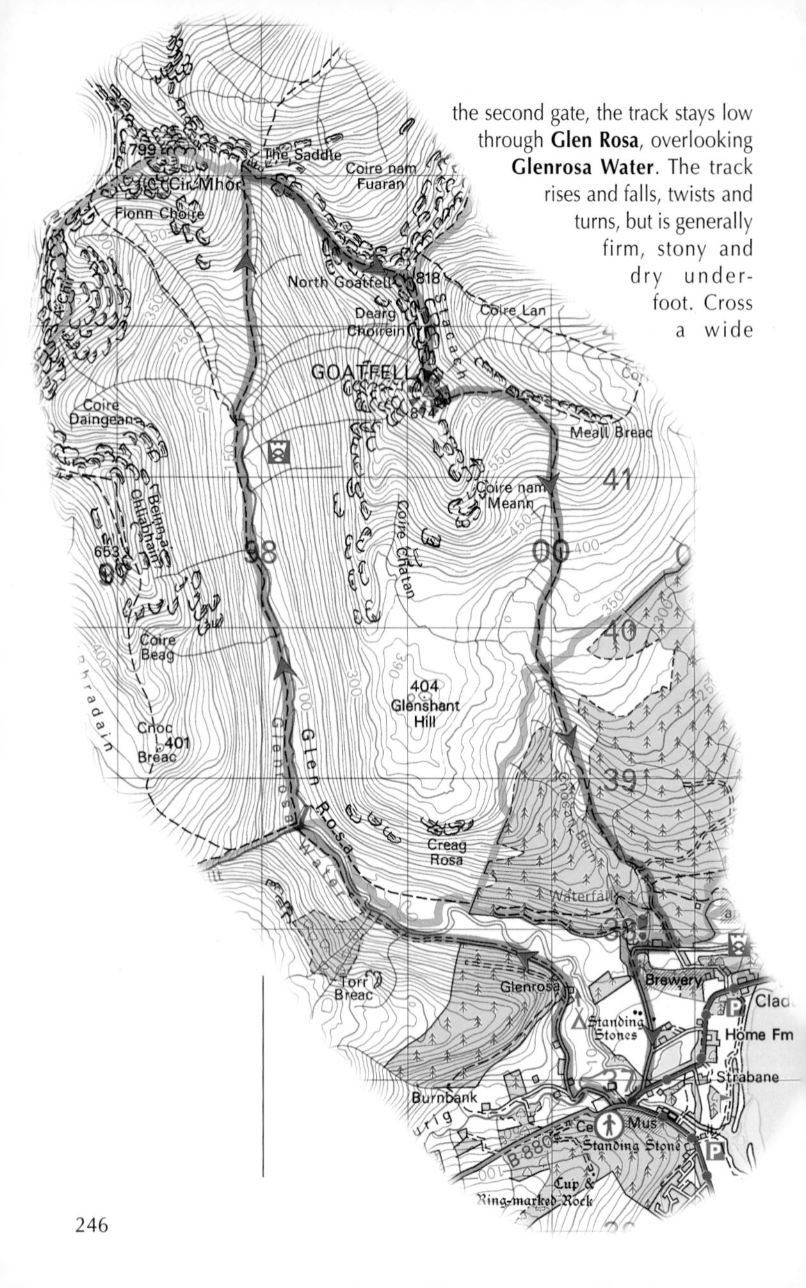

the second gate, the track stays low through **Glen Rosa**, overlooking **Glenrosa Water**. The track rises and falls, twists and turns, but is generally firm, stony and dry under-foot. Cross a wide

A long walk is required through Glen Rosa before any mountains are climbed

wooden footbridge and admire the waterfalls tumbling down the Garbh Allt.

Follow the path ahead, drifting closer to Glenrosa Water. Look out for an attractive waterfall, which plunges into a deep pool in a rocky gorge overhung by birch trees. The path is usually firm and dry, although the ground to either side is usually wet and boggy. Pass a large boulder of granite and later ford a small burn at the head of Glen Rosa. Walk up a boulder-strewn, heathery tongue, and the gradient eases as the path approaches **The Saddle**, at 432m (1417ft), which is flanked by low outcrops of granite. There is a fine view over into Glen Sannox.

Turn right to follow the path climbing towards North Goatfell. This crosses the lowest part of the gap, which is strewn with grit and gravel. Clean, hard granite gives way to rotten, crumbling granite as the ridge is followed higher. More clean granite follows and there are splendid views back towards the peak of Cir Mhòr. There is one point where it is necessary to pick a way across a little ledge of rock overlooking Glen Sannox. Beyond is a short, level, easy stretch on a heathery sholder. The path then climbs uphill on a boulder-strewn ridge with no real difficulties for a while.

Steep and rocky ridges fall from North Goatfell to The Saddle and Cir Mhòr

On a higher part of the ridge there is a worn path on a grassy slope, then more rock becomes apparent towards the top. The rock is rotten and gritty material has been washed down towards Glen Rosa. A buttress ahead has a curious rocky projection on the Glen Sannox side, so pass it on the Glen Rosa side and regain the crest of the ridge at a notch. Ribs and grooves of granite, although rotten, offer some security on an uphill scramble. There is an exposed step to negotiate before the next uphill pull. The final climb crosses a chaotic arrangement of boulders and reaches an inclined slab, which is the summit of **North Goatfell** at 818m (2684ft).

Follow the narrow, blocky ridge onwards, stepping down from the rock to gain an easy path that crosses a grassy gap over 760m (2495ft). A pyramidal tor of wrinkled granite rises above the gap, on the **Stacach** ridge, where three options are available. One route is an almost direct ascent, to the left of some large, jammed boulders. A less direct route uses giant steps to the right of the boulders. Both these options are exposed scrambles. Walkers can also walk round the base of the pyramid, on the left side overlooking the sea. Anyone climbing over the top of the tor will need to scramble down the other side.

There are a couple more rocky bosses to scramble over if required. Anyone on the lower path can avoid all the rocky parts of the ridge by staying always on the seaward side of the ridge. A fourth route on the Glen Rosa flank might also be considered, although this is quite badly eroded.

The last part of the ridge is mostly a jumble of boulders through which the path continues. The summit of **Goatfell** is reached quite suddenly and is composed of a bare table of granite bearing a few large boulders. There is a trig point at 874m (2867ft), with a view indicator provided by the Rotary Club of Kilwinning. This is the highest peak on Arran. ▶

Views are extensive and stretch far into mainland Scotland as well as embracing the Highlands, islands and Northern Ireland.

To leave the summit, follow the ridge path eastwards. The ground is boulder-strewn, and the path is quite rugged as it weaves between boulders and blocky outcrops. There is a more level shoulder on **Meall Breac**, where the main path down to Brodick heads off to the right. The path descends steeply in **Coire nam Meann**, then eases. Later, the surrounding moorland is mostly wet, grassy, heathery and boulder-strewn, but the path has been restored and features pitched stonework, drains and a good, firm surface. The surrounding moorland is mostly wet, grassy, heathery and boulder-strewn. On some short stretches the path runs over granite slabs.

Go through a gate in a tall deer fence, then cross a footbridge over a water channel cut across the hillside. Smaller streams are crossed as the path continues down the rugged slopes. Forest stands far away from the path, but scattered stands of birch are passed, and further downhill a slope of bracken and heather is passed, where rhododendron scrub has been cut back.

The path joins a bend on a track, so continue straight ahead downhill through forest. ▶ Stay on the track, regardless of a series of paths marked to right and left. Eventually, a narrow tarmac road is reached. Turn right to follow the road, which soon bends left and later reaches a junction with a main road. Turn right to cross Rosa Bridge, then turn left to return to the **Arran Heritage Museum**.

Walk 2 is a short circular route that follows part of this track.

APPENDIX A

Route summary table

Walk	Title	Start	Finish	Distance	Total ascent	Time	Page
1	Goatfell and Brodick	Ferry terminal, Brodick	Ferry terminal, Brodick	16.5km (10½ miles)	850m (2790ft)	5hrs	32
2	Brodick Castle and Country Park	Brodick Castle	Brodick Castle	5km (3 miles)	180m (590ft)	1hr 30mins	37
3	Brodick and the Clauchland Hills	Ferry terminal, Brodick	Ferry terminal, Brodick	11km (7 miles)	380m (1245ft)	3hrs 30mins	42
4	Sithein and Glen Cloy	Cnoc na Dail	Cnoc na Dail	14km (8¾ miles)	610m (2000ft)	4hrs 30mins	46
5	Lamlash and the Clauchland Hills	Pier, Lamlash	Pier, Lamlash	10.5km (6½ miles)	300m (985ft)	3hrs 15mins	50
6	Sithein and The Ross	Pier, Lamlash	Pier, Lamlash	12.5km (7¾ miles)	480m (1575ft)	4hrs	55
7	Lamlash to Brodick	Pier, Lamlash	Ferry terminal, Brodick	6.5km (4 miles)	200m (655ft)	2hrs	59
8	Holy Isle from Lamlash	North Jetty, Holy Isle	North Jetty, Holy Isle	7km (4½ miles)	350m (1150ft)	2hrs 30mins	62
9	Tighvein and Monamore Glen	Dyemill car park, Monamore Glen	Dyemill car park, Monamore Glen	10km (6¼ miles)	490m (1605ft)	3hrs	68
10	Glenashdale and Urie Loch	Whiting Bay	Whiting Bay	17km (10½ miles)	620m (2035ft)	5hrs 30mins	72

Walk	Title	Start	Finish	Distance	Total ascent	Time	Page
11	Glenashdale Falls and Giants' Graves	Whiting Bay	Whiting Bay	6km (3¾ miles)	250m (820ft)	2hrs	78
12	Lamlash and Kingscross	Lamlash Parish Church	Lamlash Parish Church	13km (8 miles)	380m (1245ft)	4hrs	82
13	Eas Mór and Loch Garbad	Car park, Eas Mór	Car park, Eas Mór	5km (3 miles)	200m (655ft)	1hr 30mins	87
14	Lagg to Kildonan coastal walk	Lagg Hotel	Village hall, Kildonan	8.5km (5¼ miles)	200m (655ft)	2hrs 30mins	89
15	Kilmory forest circuit	Kilmory	Kilmory	13.5km (8½ miles)	260m (855ft)	4hrs to 7hrs	94
16	Sliddery and Cnocan Donn	Sliddery	Sliddery	13.5km (8½ miles)	360m (1180ft)	4hrs 30mins	99
17	Tighvein and Glenscorrodale	The Ross, Glenscorrodale	The Ross, Glenscorrodale	12.5km (7¾ miles)	460m (1510ft)	4hrs	104
18	The Ross and Cnoc a' Chapuill	The Ross, Glenscorrodale	The Ross, Glenscorrodale	16km (10 miles)	400m (1310ft)	5hrs	109
19	Shiskine and Clauchan Glen	Shiskine	Shiskine	10.5km (6½ miles)	360m (1180ft)	3hrs 30mins	113
20	Balmichael and Ard Bheinn	Balmichael Centre	Balmichael Centre	13km (8 miles)	650m (2130ft)	4hrs	117
21	The String and Beinn Bhreac	Glenloig, The String road	Glenloig, The String road	12km (7½ miles)	680m (2230ft)	4hrs	122
22	Blackwaterfoot and King's Cave	Harbour, Blackwaterfoot	Harbour, Blackwaterfoot	10km (6¼ miles)	200m (655ft)	3hrs	126

Walk	Title	Start	Finish	Distance	Total ascent	Time	Page
23	Machrie Moor Stone Circles	Nr Machrie Water	Nr Machrie Water	4.5km (2¾ miles)	40m (130ft)	1hr 30mins	131
24	Dougarie and Beinn Nuis	Dougarie	Dougarie	23km (14¼ miles) or 16km (10 miles)	900m (2950ft) or 400m (1310ft)	7hrs 30mins or 5hrs	134
25	Dougarie and Sail Chalmadale	Dougarie	Dougarie	16.5 km (10¼ miles)	555m (1820ft)	5hrs	141
26	Circuit of Glen Iorsa	Dougarie	Dougarie	30.5km (19 miles)	1930m (6330ft)	10hrs	145
27	Imachar and Mullach Buidhe	Between Whitefarland and Imachar	Between Whitefarland and Imachar	18km (11 miles)	890m (2920ft)	5hrs 30mins	153
28	Pirnmill and Mullach Buidhe	Pirnmill	Pirnmill	12km (7½ miles)	980m (3215ft)	4hrs	158
29	Coire-Fhionn Lochan	Mid Thundergay	Mid Thundergay	9km (5½ miles)	660m (2165ft)	3hrs	162
30	Catacol and Meall nan Damh	Glen Catacol	Glen Catacol	11km (7 miles)	650m (2130ft)	5hrs 30mins	166
31	Catacol and Beinn Bhreac	Glen Catacol	Glen Catacol	16.5km (10¼ miles)	1180m (3870ft	5hrs 30mins	169
32	Catacol and Beinn Tarsuinn	Glen Catacol	Glen Catacol	16km (10 miles)	890m (2920ft)	5hrs	175
33	Lochranza and Meall Mór	Lochranza Castle	Lochranza Castle	11km (6¾ miles)	650m (2130ft)	3hrs 30mins	180

Walk	Title	Start	Finish	Distance	Total ascent	Time	Page
34	Gleann Easan Biorach	Lochranza Castle	Lochranza Castle	16.5km (10¼ miles)	650m (2130ft)	5hrs	185
35	Lochranza and the Cock of Arran	St Bride's Church, Lochranza	St Bride's Church, Lochranza	12.5km (7¾ miles)	360m (1180ft)	4hrs	190
36	Lochranza and Sail an Im	Isle of Arran Distillery, Lochranza	Isle of Arran Distillery, Lochranza	17km (10½ miles)	1000m (3280ft)	5hrs 30mins	194
37	Sannox and Fionn Bhealach	North Sannox	North Sannox	16km (10 miles)	670m (2200ft)	5hrs	199
38	North Glen Sannox Horseshoe	North Glen Sannox	North Glen Sannox	10.5km (6½ miles)	910m (2985ft)	3hrs 30mins	204
39	Glen Sannox Horseshoe	Sannox	Sannox	16km (10 miles)	1700m (5575ft)	6hrs	210
40	Glen Sannox to Glen Rosa	Sannox	Ferry terminal, Brodick	15.5km (9¾ miles)	550m (1805ft)	5hrs	218
41	Sannox, Goatfell and Corrie	Sannox	Sannox	14.5km (9 miles)	1190m (3905ft)	5hrs	223
42	Glen Rosa and Beinn Tarsuinn	Glen Rosa campsite	Glen Rosa campsite	14.5km (9 miles)	1030m (3380ft)	5hrs	230
43	Western Glen Rosa	Glen Rosa campsite	Glen Rosa campsite	18km (11 miles)	1200m (3935ft)	5hrs 30mins	236
44	Eastern Glen Rosa	Arran Heritage Museum	Arran Heritage Museum	18km (11 miles)	1000m (3280ft)	5hrs 30mins	245

APPENDIX B

Arran Coastal Way

Start/Finish	Ferry terminal, Brodick (NS 022 359)
Distance	105 to 113km (66 to 70 miles), depending on route choices
Time	Up to one week
Terrain	Very varied, including easy road-walks and tracks, a variety of paths, and beach walks that vary from easy to very difficult. Some stretches are far inland, such as the ascent of Goatfell.
Refreshments	Plenty of choice in the larger coastal villages, but less in the smaller villages. Brodick, Cladach, Corrie, Sannox, Lochranza, Catacol, Pirnmill, Machrie, Blackwaterfoot, Lagg, Kildonan, Whiting Bay and Lamlash.

This is not intended to be a detailed route description, but simply serves to highlight the fact that a complete coastal walk around the Isle of Arran is available. The route is mostly signposted and waymarked, but it is still evolving, so expect changes. It could be completed comfortably within a week, but bear in mind that while some stretches are easy, other stretches are quite difficult. A road completely encircles the island and often runs very close to the coast. In some places, in order to avoid long road-walks, the route moves far inland. Indeed, one stretch even climbs to the top of Goatfell! At the other extreme, some stretches can be covered at high tide, so be sure to check the tide times. Walkers can either trek from village to village around the coast, or operate from a single base and 'commute' to and from the route using bus services. As many stretches of the Arran Coastal Way are covered in this guidebook, the simplified route description below refers readers to walks in the book for further details. See also *The Ayrshire and Arran Coastal Paths*, by Keith Fergus, published by Cicerone, and the website www.coastalway.co.uk

Day 1: Brodick to Sannox – 12 to 15.5km (7½ to 9¾ miles)

Stepping ashore at the ferry terminal in Brodick, simply follow a coastal promenade north, switching to the Fisherman's Path to Cladach. From there, a low-level option wanders through Brodick Country Park and continues through forest to Corrie, then follows the main coastal road to Sannox. However, there is also a high-level route from Cladach to the summit of Goatfell, followed by a descent to Corrie. For more details, refer to Walk 1 and Walk 41.

Looking across a placid Brodick Bay towards the towering peak of Goatfell

Day 2: Sannox to Lochranza – 16km (10 miles)
This stage involves the least amount of road-walking on the Arran Coastal Way. Leave Sannox for North Sannox, and follow a coastal track and a rugged path past the Fallen Rocks and Millstone Point to reach Laggan Cottage. A shortcut over the hill to Lochranza is possible, but the rugged coastal path can be followed round Cock of Arran to Newton Point, before a road-walk leads into Lochranza. For more details, refer to Walk 37 and Walk 35.

Day 3: Lochranza to Imachar – 14.5km (9 miles)
Leave Lochranza and follow the 'Postman's Path' across a wooded slope to Catacol. There is little opportunity to avoid the road-walk to Thundergay and Pirnmill, as there are no coastal paths, and the beaches are very rocky and boulder-strewn. Beyond Pirnmill, a stretch of coast can be followed past Whitefarland and Imachar, rejoining the road. For more details, refer to Walk 33, Walk 30, Walk 29 and Walk 28.

Day 4: Imachar to Blackwaterfoot – 16km (10 miles)
The main coastal road has to be followed from Imachar to Dougarie and Machrie. The road then moves inland onto Machrie Moor, which is rich in archaeological remains. Eventually, the road can be left in favour of a forest path, followed by a quality stretch of coastal path passing the King's Cave and The Doon, on the way to Blackwaterfoot. For more details, refer to Walk 24 and Walk 22.

Some beaches are boulder-strewn, so roads offer easier walking

Swans pass Lamlash pier, with Holy Isle beyond

Day 5: Blackwaterfoot to Lagg – 13km (8 miles)

The Arran Coastal Way runs close to the coast as it heads south from Blackwaterfoot. There are a few easy tracks and paths, as well as some easy beach walks. However, there are also some very rugged stretches that are rocky or boulder-strewn, particularly around Brown Head. There are escape routes up to the road at Corriecravie, and in any case the coastal path heads inland to Sliddery, then follows the main road to Lagg. For more details, refer to Walk 16.

Day 6: Lagg to Whiting Bay – 15 to 19km (9½ to 11¾ miles)

This is one of the toughest stages on the Arran Coastal Way. A pleasant and easy path leaves Lagg, but it quickly becomes quite difficult along the coast. Getting round the foot of Bennan Head, passing the Black Cave, requires the tide to be out. Easy walking through Kildonan is followed by increasingly tough walking around Dippin Head, where the tide needs to be out. Apart from a few easy stretches of path, there is plenty of difficult walking before Whiting Bay is reached. In order to avoid difficulty, there is an inland alternative from Kildonan to Whiting Bay, taking advantage of a high-level forest track. For more details, refer to Walk 14.

Day 7: Whiting Bay to Brodick – 19km (11¾ miles)

The high-level forest track can be used to continue from Whiting Bay to Lamlash, in preference to more rugged coastal walking around Kingscross Point, where the tide needs to be out for most of the way. Beyond Lamlash, a coastal road gives way to a coastal track to Clauchlands Point. A rugged coastal path can be followed towards Corriegills Point, then the route steps inland to continue through fields to Strathwhillan, ending with a short road-walk back into Brodick to finish at the ferry terminal. For more details, refer to Walk 10, Walk 12, Walk 5 and Walk 3.

APPENDIX C

Useful contacts

Tourist information centres

Ayr
Ayrshire and Arran Tourism
Burns House
Burns Statue Square
Ayr
KA7 1UT
www.ayrshire-arran.org

Arran
The Pier
Brodick
Isle of Arran
KA27 8AU
tel 01770 303774
www.visitarran.com
email info@visitarran.com

Transport to Arran

Glasgow International Airport
www.glasgowairport.com

Prestwick International Airport
www.glasgowprestwick.com

Virgin Trains
www.virgintrains.co.uk

Transpennine Express
www.tpexpress.co.uk

Caledonian Sleeper
www.sleeper.scot

ScotRail
www.scotrail.co.uk

Caledonian MacBrayne
www.calmac.co.uk

Transport around Arran

Stagecoach West Scotland
www.stagecoachbus.com

Strathclyde Passenger Transport (SPT)
www.spt.co.uk

Holy Isle Ferry
tel 01770 700463,
01770 600998,
or mobile 07970 771960

Traveline Scotland
tel 0871 200223
www.travelinescotland.com

Emergency services

In an emergency, to call the Police, Ambulance, Fire Service, Mountain Rescue or Coastguard, tel 999, or the European emergency number 112.

For non-urgent matters, contact the Police Station at Lamlash, tel 01770 302573.

For non-urgent medical matters, contact the Medical Centre at Lamlash, tel 01770 600777.

Access

Scottish Outdoor Access Code
Copies of the code are available from Scottish Natural Heritage and tourist information centres
www.outdooraccess-scotland.com

Arran Access Trust
Senior Ranger
National Trust for Scotland
Brodick Country Park
KA27 8HY
tel 01770 302462
www.arran-access-trust.org.uk

Arran Coastal Way
Forest Office
Auchrannie Road
Brodick
KA27 8BZ
Tel 01770 303926
www.coastalway.co.uk

Arran Hillphone
Tel 01770 302363 for a recorded message alerting walkers to areas where deer stalking is taking place from mid-August to mid-October.

Organisations and centres

Scottish Natural Heritage
Great Glen House
Leachkin RoadInverness
IV3 8NW
tel 01463 725000
www.snh.org.uk

National Trust for Scotland
Hermiston Quay5 Cultins Road
Edinburgh
EH11 4DF
tel 0131 4580200
www.nts.org.uk

Brodick Castle
Isle of Arran
KA27 8HY
tel 01770 302202

Ranger Service (for guided walks)
Brodick Castle
Isle of Arran
KA27 8HY
tel 01770 302462

Forestry Commission Scotland
Silvan House
231 Corstophine Road
Edinburgh
EH12 7AT
tel 0300 0675000
scotland.forestry.gov.uk

Auchrannie Road
Brodick,
KA27 8BZ
tel 01770 302218
scotland.forestry.gov.uk/visit/arran

Isle of Arran Heritage Museum
Rosaburn
Brodick
KA27 8DP
tel 01770 302636
www.arranmuseum.co.uk

The Holy Isle
Holy Isle
Lamlash Bay
KA27 8GB
tel 01770 601100
www.holyisland.org

Arran Adventure Centre
Auchrannie Resort
Auchrannie Road
Brodick
KA27 8BZ
tel 01770 302234
auchrannie.co.uk/pamper-play/adventure.html

Arran Outdoor Centre
Lamlash
Isle of Arran
KA27 8PL
tel 01770 600532
www.arranoutdoor.com

Loch Ranza Field Studies and Activity Centre
Lochranza
KA27 8HL
tel 01770 860637
www.pgl.co.uk/en-gb/school-trips/secondary-schools/centres/loch-ranza

Arran Active Outdoor Shop
Shore Road
Brodick
KA27 8AJ

Cladach
KA27 8DE
tel 01770 302416
www.arranactive.co.uk

Isle of Arran Mountain Festival
Takes place in mid-May, offering guided walks and activities
www.arranmountainfestival.co.uk

Arran Wild Walks
Guided walking, wildlife and skills courses with Lucy and Wally Wallace
tel 07825 644161
www.arranwildwalks.co.uk

Arran food and drink
Most of the food and drink producers on the Isle of Arran sell direct from their premises, but are also stocked in the Co-op stores at Brodick and Lamlash, as well as in a variety of small shops, cafés and visitor attractions around the island. Most producers are part of Taste of Arran, www.taste-of-arran.co.uk

Brodick
Arran Dairies
Market Road
Brodick
KA27 8AU
tel 01770 302374

Wooleys of Arran Bakery
Invercloy
Brodick
KA27 8AJ
tel 01770 302280

Arran Chocolate Factory
Invercloy
Brodick
KA27 8AJ
tel 01770 302 873

Home Farm
Creelers Smokehouse Shop
Home Farm
Brodick
KA27 8DD
tel 01770 302797

Island Cheese Company
Home Farm
Brodick
KA27 8DD
tel 01770 302788

Cladach
Arran Brewery
Cladach
Brodick
KA11 4AB
tel 01294 216888

Lochranza
Isle of Arran Distillery
Lochranza
KA27 8HJ
tel 01770 830 334

Blackwaterfoot
Bellvue Creamery
Bellevue
Blackwaterfoot
tel 01770 302374

Kilmory
Real Arran Cheese
Torrylinn Creamery
Kilmory
tel 01770 870 240

Whiting Bay
Robin's Herbs
Whiting Bay
tel 01770 700586

Lamlash
Arran Fine Foods
Old Mill
Lamlash
KA27 8LE
tel 01770 600606

Arran Tablet Company
St Molios Park
Lamlash
KA27 8JQ
tel 01770 600125

APPENDIX D

Gaelic/English glossary

The oldest place-names on the Isle of Arran are Gaelic, since the language of earlier settlers is unknown. However, while the Gaelic culture was strong, it was also heavily influenced by Norse culture, and the most obvious place-name legacies of that time are in the 'fell', 'gill' and 'dale' names. Norse and Gaelic place-names are often highly descriptive of landscape features, so a knowledge of the basic elements is useful, although centuries of change may mean that some of the features referred to are now redundant.

abhainn	river
allt	stream
ard	high
ath	ford
auch	field
bal/bally	township
ban/bhan	white
bealach	pass/col
beag/bheag	small
ben/beinn/bheinn	mountain
breac/bhreac	speckled
biorach	pointed
buidhe	yellow
caillich	old woman/ witch
caisteal	castle
caorach	rowanberries
carn	cairn
ceum	step
cioch/ciche	breast
cir/chir	comb/crest
clachan	farm/hamlet
cliabhain/chliabhain	cradle
cnoc	small hill
coire/choire	corrie
coille	wood
creag	crag
dale (Norse)	valley
dearg	red
donn	brown
dubh	black
dun	fort
eas	waterfall
eilean	island
fada/fhada	long
fell (Norse)	mountain
fionn	fair
gaoithe	wind
garbh	rough
gearr	sharp
gill (Norse)	ravine
glais	stream
glas/ghlas	grey
gleann	glen/valley
guala	shoulder
iolaire	eagle
lagan	hollow
leac	flat rock
leathan	broad
loch	lake

lochan	small lake	*reamhar*	fat
maol/mhaoile	bald	*righ*	king
meall	rounded hill	*ruadh*	russet
mòr/mhòr	big	*suidhe*	seat
mullach	summit	*torr*	small hill
odhar	dappled	*uaine*	green
oighe	youth	*uisge*	water

NOTES

NOTES

NOTES

LISTING OF CICERONE GUIDES

BRITISH ISLES CHALLENGES, COLLECTIONS AND ACTIVITIES

The Book of the Bivvy
The Book of the Bothy
The End to End Trail
The Mountains of England and Wales: 1&2
The National Trails
The Relative Hills of Britain
The Ridges of England, Wales and Ireland
The UK Trailwalker's Handbook
The UK's County Tops
Three Peaks, Ten Tors

UK CYCLING

20 Classic Sportive Rides
South West England
South East England
Border Country Cycle Routes
Cycling in the Cotswolds
Cycling in the Hebrides
Cycling in the Peak District
Cycling in the Yorkshire Dales
Cycling the Pennine Bridleway
Mountain Biking in the Lake District
Mountain Biking in the Yorkshire Dales
Mountain Biking on the North Downs
Mountain Biking on the South Downs
The C2C Cycle Route
The End to End Cycle Route
The Lancashire Cycleway

UK BACKPACKING

Backpacker's Britain
Northern Scotland

SCOTLAND

Ben Nevis and Glen Coe
Great Mountain Days in Scotland
Not the West Highland Way
Scotland's Best Small Mountains
Scotland's Far West
Scotland's Mountain Ridges
Scrambles in Lochaber
The Ayrshire and Arran Coastal Paths
The Border Country
The Cape Wrath Trail
The Great Glen Way
The Hebrides
The Isle of Mull
The Isle of Skye
The Pentland Hills
The Skye Trail
The Southern Upland Way
The Speyside Way
The West Highland Way
Walking Highland Perthshire
Walking in Scotland's Far North
Walking in the Angus Glens
Walking in the Cairngorms
Walking in the Ochils, Campsie Fells and Lomond Hills
Walking in the Southern Uplands
Walking in Torridon
Walking Loch Lomond and the Trossachs
Walking on Arran
Walking on Harris and Lewis
Walking on Jura, Islay and Colonsay
Walking on Rum and the Small Isles
Walking on the Isle of Arran
Walking on the Orkney and Shetland Isles
Walking on Uist and Barra
Walking the Corbetts
1 South of the Great Glen
2 North of the Great Glen
Walking the Galloway Hills
Walking the Munros
1 Southern, Central and Western Highlands
2 Northern Highlands and the Cairngorms
Winter Climbs Ben Nevis and Glen Coe
Winter Climbs in the Cairngorms
World Mountain Ranges: Scotland

NORTHERN ENGLAND TRAILS

A Northern Coast to Coast Walk
Hadrian's Wall Path
The Dales Way
The Pennine Way

NORTH EAST ENGLAND, YORKSHIRE DALES AND PENNINES

Great Mountain Days in the Pennines
Historic Walks in North Yorkshire
South Pennine Walks
St Oswald's Way and St Cuthbert's Way
The North York Moors
The Reivers Way
The Teesdale Way
The Yorkshire Dales
North and East
South and West
Walking in County Durham
Walking in Northumberland
Walking in the North Pennines
Walks in Dales Country
Walks in the Yorkshire Dales

NORTH WEST ENGLAND AND THE ISLE OF MAN

Historic Walks in Cheshire
Isle of Man Coastal Path
The Lune Valley and Howgills
The Ribble Way
Walking in Cumbria's Eden Valley
Walking in Lancashire
Walking in the Forest of Bowland and Pendle
Walking on the Isle of Man
Walking on the West Pennine Moors
Walks in Lancashire Witch Country
Walks in Ribble Country
Walks in Silverdale and Arnside
Walks in the Forest of Bowland

LAKE DISTRICT

Coniston Copper Mines
Great Mountain Days in the Lake District
Lake District Winter Climbs
Lake District: High Level and Fell Walks
Lake District: Low Level and Lake Walks
Lakeland Fellranger
The Central Fells
The Far-Eastern Fells
The Mid-Western Fells
The Near Eastern Fells

The Northern Fells
The North-Western Fells
The Southern Fells
The Western Fells
Rocky Rambler's Wild Walks
Scrambles in the Lake District
North & South
Short Walks in Lakeland
1 South Lakeland
2 North Lakeland
3 West Lakeland
The Cumbria Way

DERBYSHIRE, PEAK DISTRICT AND MIDLANDS

High Peak Walks
Scrambles in the Dark Peak
The Star Family Walks
Walking in Derbyshire
White Peak Walks
The Northern Dales
The Southern Dales

SOUTHERN ENGLAND

Suffolk Coast & Heaths Walks
The Great Stones Way
The Lea Valley Walk
The North Downs Way
The Peddars Way and Norfolk Coast Path
The Ridgeway National Trail
The South Downs Way
The South West Coast Path
The Thames Path
The Two Moors Way
Walking in Cornwall
Walking in Essex
Walking in Kent
Walking in Norfolk
Walking in Sussex
Walking in the Chilterns
Walking in the Cotswolds
Walking in the Isles of Scilly
Walking in the New Forest
Walking in the North Wessex Downs
Walking in the Thames Valley
Walking on Dartmoor
Walking on Guernsey
Walking on Jersey
Walking on the Isle of Wight
Walking the Jurassic Coast
Walks in the South Downs National Park

WALES AND WELSH BORDERS

Glyndwr's Way
Great Mountain Days in Snowdonia
Hillwalking in Snowdonia
Hillwalking in Wales: 1&2
Offa's Dyke Path
Ridges of Snowdonia
Scrambles in Snowdonia
The Ascent of Snowdon
The Ceredigion and Snowdonia Coast Paths
Lleyn Peninsula Coastal Path
Pembrokeshire Coastal Path
The Severn Way
The Shropshire Hills
The Wales Coast Path
The Wye Valley Walk
Walking in Carmarthenshire
Walking in Pembrokeshire
Walking in the Forest of Dean
Walking in the South Wales Valleys
Walking in the Wye Valley
Walking on the Brecon Beacons
Walking on the Gower
Welsh Winter Climbs

INTERNATIONAL CHALLENGES, COLLECTIONS AND ACTIVITIES

Canyoning
Canyoning in the Alps
Europe's High Points
The Via Francigena: 1&2

EUROPEAN CYCLING

Cycle Touring in France
Cycle Touring in Ireland
Cycle Touring in Spain
Cycle Touring in Switzerland
Cycling in the French Alps
Cycling the Canal du Midi
Cycling the River Loire
The Danube Cycleway: 1&2
The Grand Traverse of the Massif Central
The Moselle Cycle Route
The Rhine Cycle Route
The Way of St James

AFRICA

Climbing in the Moroccan Anti-Atlas
Kilimanjaro
Mountaineering in the Moroccan High Atlas
The High Atlas
Trekking in the Atlas Mountains
Walking in the Drakensberg

ALPS – CROSS-BORDER ROUTES

100 Hut Walks in the Alps
Across the Eastern Alps: E5
Alpine Points of View
Alpine Ski Mountaineering
1 Western Alps
2 Central and Eastern Alps
Chamonix to Zermatt
The Tour of the Bernina
Tour of Mont Blanc
Tour of Monte Rosa
Tour of the Matterhorn
Trekking in the Alps
Trekking in the Silvretta and Rätikon Alps
Walking in the Alps
Walks and Treks in the Maritime Alps

PYRENEES AND FRANCE/SPAIN CROSS-BORDER ROUTES

The GR10 Trail
The GR11 Trail – La Senda
The Mountains of Andorra
The Pyrenean Haute Route
The Pyrenees
The Way of St James: France & Spain
Walks and Climbs in the Pyrenees

AUSTRIA

The Adlerweg
Trekking in Austria's Hohe Tauern
Trekking in the Stubai Alps
Trekking in the Zillertal Alps
Walking in Austria

BELGIUM AND LUXEMBOURG

Walking in the Ardennes

EASTERN EUROPE

The High Tatras
The Mountains of Romania
Walking in Bulgaria's National Parks
Walking in Hungary

FRANCE

Chamonix Mountain Adventures
Ecrins National Park
Mont Blanc Walks
Mountain Adventures in the Maurienne

The Cathar Way
The GR20 Corsica
The GR5 Trail
The Robert Louis Stevenson Trail
Tour of the Oisans: The GR54
Tour of the Queyras
Tour of the Vanoise
Vanoise Ski Touring
Via Ferratas of the French Alps
Walking in Corsica
Walking in Provence – East
Walking in Provence – West
Walking in the Auvergne
Walking in the Cevennes
Walking in the Dordogne
Walking in the Haute Savoie – North & South
Walks in the Cathar Region

GERMANY

Hiking and Biking in the Black Forest
Walking in the Bavarian Alps

HIMALAYA

Annapurna
Bhutan
Everest
The Mount Kailash Trek
Trekking in Ladakh
Trekking in the Himalaya

ICELAND & GREENLAND

Trekking in Greenland
Walking and Trekking in Iceland

IRELAND

The Irish Coast to Coast Walk
The Mountains of Ireland

ITALY

Gran Paradiso
Sibillini National Park
Shorter Walks in the Dolomites
The Way of St Francis
Through the Italian Alps
Trekking in the Apennines
Trekking in the Dolomites
Via Ferratas of the Italian Dolomites: 1&2
Walking in Abruzzo
Walking in Italy's Stelvio National Park
Walking in Sardinia
Walking in Sicily
Walking in the Central Italian Alps
Walking in the Dolomites
Walking in Tuscany
Walking in Umbria
Walking on the Amalfi Coast
Walking the Italian Lakes

MEDITERRANEAN

Jordan – Walks, Treks, Caves, Climbs and Canyons
The High Mountains of Crete
The Mountains of Greece
Treks and Climbs in Wadi Rum
Walking and Trekking on Corfu
Walking on Malta
Western Crete

NORTH AMERICA

British Columbia
The Grand Canyon
The John Muir Trail
The Pacific Crest Trail

SOUTH AMERICA

Aconcagua and the Southern Andes
Hiking and Biking Peru's Inca Trails
Torres del Paine

SCANDINAVIA

Walking in Norway

SLOVENIA, CROATIA AND MONTENEGRO

The Islands of Croatia
The Julian Alps of Slovenia
The Mountains of Montenegro
Trekking in Slovenia
Walking in Croatia
Walking in Slovenia: The Karavanke

SPAIN AND PORTUGAL

Mountain Walking in Southern Catalunya
Spain's Sendero Histórico: The GR1
The Mountains of Nerja
The Northern Caminos
Trekking through Mallorca
Walking in Andalucia
Walking in Madeira
Walking in Mallorca
Walking in Menorca
Walking in the Algarve
Walking in the Cordillera Cantabrica
Walking in the Sierra Nevada
Walking on Gran Canaria
Walking on La Gomera and El Hierro
Walking on La Palma
Walking on Lanzarote and Fuerteventura
Walking on Tenerife
Walking the GR7 in Andalucia
Walks and Climbs in the Picos de Europa

SWITZERLAND

Alpine Pass Route
The Swiss Alps
Tour of the Jungfrau Region
Walking in the Bernese Oberland
Walking in the Valais
Walks in the Engadine

TECHNIQUES

Geocaching in the UK
Indoor Climbing
Lightweight Camping
Map and Compass
Mountain Weather
Outdoor Photography
Polar Exploration
Rock Climbing
Sport Climbing
The Hillwalker's Manual

MINI GUIDES

Alpine Flowers
Avalanche!
Navigating with a GPS
Navigation
Pocket First Aid and Wilderness Medicine
Snow

MOUNTAIN LITERATURE

8000 metres
A Walk in the Clouds
Abode of the Gods
Unjustifiable Risk?

For full information on all our guides, books and eBooks, visit our website: **www.cicerone.co.uk**.

Walking – Trekking – Mountaineering – Climbing – Cycling

Over 40 years, Cicerone have built up an outstanding collection of over 300 guides, inspiring all sorts of amazing adventures.

Every guide comes from extensive exploration and research by our expert authors, all with a passion for their subjects. They are frequently praised, endorsed and used by clubs, instructors and outdoor organisations.

All our titles can now be bought as **e-books**, **ePubs** and **Kindle** files and we also have an online magazine – **Cicerone Extra** – with features to help cyclists, climbers, walkers and trekkers choose their next adventure, at home or abroad.

Our website shows any **new information** we've had in since a book was published. Please do let us know if you find anything has changed, so that we can publish the latest details. On our **website** you'll also find great ideas and lots of detailed information about what's inside every guide and you can buy **individual routes** from many of them online.

It's easy to keep in touch with what's going on at Cicerone by getting our monthly **free e-newsletter**, which is full of offers, competitions, up-to-date information and topical articles. You can subscribe on our home page and also follow us on **Facebook** and **Twitter** or dip into our **blog**.

Cicerone – the very best guides for exploring the world.

CICERONE

2 Police Square Milnthorpe Cumbria LA7 7PY
Tel: 015395 62069 info@cicerone.co.uk
www.cicerone.co.uk and **www.cicerone-extra.com**